THE INTERCONNECTED JEWISH FAMILES OF OTTAWA, CANADA

Author: Jerrold Landau

JewishGen
מרכז עולמי לגנאלוגיה יהודית
The Global Home for Jewish Genealogy

A Publication of JewishGen, Inc.
Edmond J. Safra Plaza, 36 Battery Place, New York, NY 10280
646.494.5972 | info@JewishGen.org | www.jewishgen.org

An affiliate of New York's Museum of Jewish Heritage – A Living Memorial to the Holocaust

MUSEUM OF JEWISH HERITAGE
A LIVING MEMORIAL TO THE HOLOCAUST

THE INTERCONNECTED JEWISH FAMILES OF OTTAWA, CANADA

Author: Jerrold Landau

Cover Design: Irv Osterer
Formatting: Jonathan Wind

Library of Congress Control Number (LCCN): 2023946216

ISBN: 978-1-954176-86-7 (hard cover: 266 pages, alk. paper)

About JewishGen.org

JewishGen, an affiliate of the Museum of Jewish Heritage - A Living Memorial to the Holocaust, serves as the global home for Jewish genealogy.

Featuring unparalleled access to 30+ million records, it offers unique search tools, along with opportunities for researchers to connect with others who share similar interests. Award winning resources such as the Family Finder, Discussion Groups, and ViewMate, are relied upon by thousands each day.

In addition, JewishGen's extensive informational, educational and historical offerings, such as the Jewish Communities Database, Yizkor Book translations, InfoFiles, Family Tree of the Jewish People, and KehilaLinks, provide critical insights, first-hand accounts, and context about Jewish communal and familial life throughout the world.

Offered as a free resource, JewishGen.org has facilitated thousands of family connections and success stories, and is currently engaged in an intensive expansion effort that will bring many more records, tools, and resources to its collections.

Please visit https://www.jewishgen.org/ to learn more.

Executive Director: Avraham Groll

About JewishGen Press

JewishGen Press (formerly the Yizkor Books-in-Print Project) is the publishing division of JewishGen.org, and provides a venue for the publication of non-fiction books pertaining to Jewish genealogy, history, culture, and heritage.

In addition to the Yizkor Book category, publications in the Other Non-Fiction category include Shoah memoirs and research, genealogical research, collections of genealogical and historical materials, biographies, diaries and letters, studies of Jewish experience and cultural life in the past, academic theses, and other books of interest to the Jewish community.

Please visit https://www.jewishgen.org/Yizkor/ybip.html to learn more.

Director of JewishGen Press: Joel Alpert
Managing Editor - Jessica Feinstein
Publications Manager - Susan Rosin

THE INTERCONNECTED JEWISH FAMILES OF OTTAWA, CANADA

By Jerrold Landau
Toronto, Canada

TABLE OF CONTENTS

Introduction	1
Preface from Ottawa Jewish Archives	8
Acknowledgements and Revisions	9
108 Family Entries	10
List of Cross References of Ottawa Jewish Families	186
Index of Entries with Links to Other Entries and List of Surnames Mentioned	187
Index of Surnames Linked to Entries	201
Group Photos from Ottawa Jewish Archives	225
A Visit to the Ottawa Jewish Cemetery	256

INTRODUCTION

It gives me great pleasure to present the results of my research on the connectedness of Jewish families in Ottawa.

Ever since my childhood, I have known that my family, relative latecomers to Ottawa, had some connections to other Ottawa families, and I was intrigued by these connections. I was fascinated by my "cousins of cousins" relationships to numerous people. My own genealogical interests blossomed during the 1980s as I started producing family trees for all branches of my family, the vast majority of which are not centered in Ottawa. I then became involved professionally in genealogical and historical translations, focusing my interests on the shtetls of Eastern Europe. Throughout these genealogical meanderings, my mindset moved far beyond my hometown of Ottawa. Recently, a homecoming instinct must have overcome me, as I decided to direct my genealogical interests back to my hometown.

Like most Jewish communities in North America, the Jewish community of Ottawa evolved with the various waves of Eastern European immigration. As a close-knit and somewhat insular community, interested in preserving its Jewish heritage and traditions, it was inevitable that the Jewish families of Ottawa would begin to marry into each other. As this trend accelerated, a vast network of connections ensued.

Around 2010, I started entering my family trees into a web-based family-tree repository known as Geni. (http://geni.com). The stated purpose of Geni is to forge interlinkages among disparate family trees, resulting in a single unified worldwide tree. This ambitious goal is unattainable in full, yet the concept of interlinked trees brought my thinking back to my hometown and my early knowledge of interlinkages on the local Jewish scale. I started to notice other Ottawa-based trees on Geni. A colleague of mine with an interest in Jewish genealogy of the Maritimes, and whose tree intersects with mine in no less than six ways, began an effort to unify the Jewish family trees of the Maritimes. Frequently I noticed that she was merging her tree with families that I recognized from Ottawa. At this point I realized that I could likely undertake a similar effort for Ottawa. I began to actively search out Ottawa-based trees on Geni, and I used my own knowledge, as well as various online searches of obituaries and other historical sources, to merge these Geni trees.

I then identified about 75 main family "roots" and formed a Geni group called *Interlinked Jewish Families of Ottawa, Canada*. Starting at any of these roots, one can scan through the trees and navigate from family to family through the connections. Anyone with a Geni membership, even a free basic membership, can join that Geni group. At this point, I realized that it might be useful to the community to capture the linkages in a book form. I was faced with a challenge though. The connectedness of trees is a multi-dimensional concept best illustrated by in graphical form. Capturing this information in writing would flatten the concept to a two-dimensional model. I spent many months pondering the idea, creating models in my mind, before I started to write up the information on the families. The result is this book, which describes over one hundred families in separate entries. Many other surnames are mentioned within the individual entries. The approximately 950 surnames that are mentioned in the entries are listed in the cross-reference tables at the end of the book. The book demonstrates that all 108 families form a single cluster of connections.

This book is timely. Due to the population growth of the Ottawa Jewish community in recent decades, increased mobility, as well as greater trends toward assimilation, the original tight-knit web of the Ottawa Jewish community has loosened significantly. Furthermore, as the previous generations pass on, the repository of information held by earlier generations becomes increasingly unavailable. The purpose of this book is not to overview the history of the Jewish community of Ottawa, but rather to illustrate the close-knit web of interconnected families. Several books have already been written on the history of the Ottawa Jewish community – some about individual families, and others focusing on the history of the community as a whole. I note in particular "A Common Thread: A History of the Jews in Ottawa" by Anna Bilsky, published in 2009. It is my hope that my work will be a valuable addition to the existing set of books documenting the Jewish community of Ottawa.

Format

Each entry focuses on a single family, but may also describe other related families that do not have their own entry. A family may not have its own entry for any of the following reasons: it had very few connections; it was entirely or almost entirely encompassed by a different entry; the description of a specific entry flowed better by incorporating the descriptions of the other family. In many cases, especially with prominent Ottawa families who do not have their own entry, I included a reference to non-entry families within the body of the text itself. In all cases, the extensive cross-reference tables at the end of the book will enable the reader to look up any surname mentioned in any entry, and find the entries in which it is mentioned.

The entries resemble family trees, but are not intended to complete family trees for the families they describe. Rather, they are meant to be skeletal trees that highlight the connections with other families. A complete family tree for each family would be far beyond the scope of a book such as this. I did endeavor to include town of origin where known, as well as death dates of deceased individuals where known. For privacy reasons, I did not include birth dates. I generally included death dates only when the individual is mentioned as a main member of the family that is dealt with in the entry. This reduced the duplication of death dates when the individual is mentioned as a link point in other entries. Although the presence of a death date is a sure indication that the individual is deceased, the absence of a death date does not necessarily imply that the individual is alive. It means either that the individual is alive or that a death date was not available. Lists of siblings may not necessarily follow a chronological order. I generally do not include biographical information of the individuals noted (once again, this is beyond the scope of this book), although a brief biographical statement is made in many cases. I bold highlighted names used as connections. Furthermore, at the bottom of each entry, the reader will find a list of connections to other entries.

Connections are forged by individuals marrying into other families that are represented by entries in the book. In those cases, I mention the parents' name, including the maiden name of the mother. Thus, a connection will be formed based on the surname of either the mother or father of the spouse. With few exceptions, I did not highlight connections based on surnames of grandparents, nor on connections based on brother-in-law and sister-in-law relations. (Exceptions to the latter will occur when the surname of the brother-in-law or sister-in-law does not have its own entry). Had I forged these additional connections, the description of many entries would bog down, much duplication would ensue across entries, and readability would be hampered. On the other hand, had I called out these additional connections, a much tighter web of connectedness would result. As the reader will see, even with my defined style of connectedness, the web between all entries is reasonably tight.

A note must be made on how I presented connections between families that were severed by divorce. In most cases, I included such connections. Due to obvious sensitivities, I never mention the divorce specifically, although I may mention more than one spouse of an individual. I did endeavor to use the past tense when describing a marriage that ended in divorce – as I did when describing a marriage where one or more spouses was known to be deceased. In cases where progeny exist from the marriage, as is indeed the case in the majority of such situations, the connection between the families is cemented through the progeny and remains valid even if I did not specifically mention the children. I trust that my sensitivity to this issue is sufficient, and apologize for any insult or slights that may have been caused.

Two cross-reference tables appear following the individual entries. The first lists all 108 entries, showing other entries to which that entry is linked as well as other surnames mentioned within that entry. The second lists the 900-plus surnames mentioned in the book, with a reference to the entries in which the surname is mentioned. Anyone who does not find their surname among the entries in the first table should begin their research by consulting the second cross-reference table.

Sources

I did not footnote each fact mentioned in the book, as such would have engendered many thousands of individual footnotes. The key sources for the book are as follows:

a. Family trees entered on Geni (http://geni.com). It is important to note that Geni is crowdsourced, and therefore its data is only as accurate as the data that has been entered into it.

b. Photos of tombstones from the Ottawa Jewish Cemeteries, now online at http://jewishmemorialgardens.org. In many cases, I was able to confirm connections from the name of the father mentioned on the Hebrew inscription of the tombstone. Of course, the tombstones also provided death dates.

c. Information on families posted at Canadian Jewish Heritage Link (http://cjhn.ca), online obituaries, and other online sources. I did not take out a subscription to old online newspapers, but rather restricted my searches to information accessible by a regular non-subscription web search. This may have limited the information sources available, but also ensured that all information gleaned was publicly accessible, as I was sensitive to privacy issues in constructing this book.

d. My own knowledge and information – although in almost all cases, I corroborated my own knowledge with the sources above. I also consulted with other individuals who provided me information regarding their families. (See Acknowledgements below).

e. In a few cases, individual families gave me access to their own family trees. Clearly, I used this source for my own family. I was also given trees by the Bodnoff and Glustein families. An online family tree was available for the Swedlove family.

Limitations

A work of this nature cannot be complete. I make no claim that it covers all Jewish families that have passed through Ottawa at some point. It is likely that even families with significant presence in Ottawa for many generations have been omitted. I hereby apologize for any such omissions. Furthermore, my sources were quite error prone. I take responsibility for all errors, and hereby apologize for any unintended misinformation. Some general notes on limitations are as follows:

a. My primary source of information was Geni. Thus, families whose trees are included in Geni will have much more detail than those that are not.
b. Families that were part of my parents' social circles in Ottawa, as well as those that were active in the Beth Shalom and Machzikei Hadas synagogues, which I frequented during the years I lived in Ottawa (I moved to Toronto in 1980 as a 19-year-old University student, although make visits to my Ottawa family up to this day), will be better represented than families that I did not know personally.
c. I am a member of the Hillel Academy graduating class of 1975. I used the members of that class, both from the Central Branch which I attended throughout my elementary school years, and the West-End branch which merged in to our class in grade 7, as initial test cases to prove connectedness. That being said, there are a few individuals from that class whose families I could not fit into the web.
d. The entries are heavily biased toward families that lived in Ottawa during the earlier days (1980 or prior). Given my sources of information, the connections are also heavily biased to those from previous decades rather than those forged during the current years.
e. I generally tried to avoid obscure, distant connections. (Those familiar with Geni will recognize the concept of obscure connections – for example, I am able to prove that I am related to both Queen Elizabeth and Donald Trump through a complex set of connections that can be found on Geni, but are relatively meaningless in real life.) In a few cases, though, most especially with my family and my wife's family, I allowed myself the luxury of delving a bit farther than basic connections. For example, I was able to prove that Rabbi Reuven Bulka connects to my wife's family (described under the Cohen entry) through a series of 2-3 jumps that would normally be considered somewhat obscure.

Proof of Connectedness

As noted above, this book consists of 108 entries, each describing a family, each linking to other entries, as well as non-entry surnames, and some encompassing more than one family within the entry. How do we know that these 108 entries consist of a unified cluster, in which every entry is connect to every other entry? And if the 108 entries form a unified cluster, how tight is the cluster?

(I offer a warning at this point, those uncomfortable with statistics, data analysis, and graph theory may wish to skip the remainder of this section of the introduction.)

To answer these questions, I selected five families which have a large number of connections. For each of the 108 entries, I then calculated the number of "jumps' (i.e., hops from one entry to another) needed to get to each of these five families. I found that the maximum number of jumps needed to get from any family to one of these families was four. Furthermore, four jumps were needed in fewer than 2% of the cases. Given that every one of the 950 surnames in all the entries is mentioned in at least one entry, one would add only one jump to get from any of the 950 surnames to one of the five selected families.

This methodology is not perfect. In cases where multiple families are dealt with in a single entry, the number of jumps might be underestimated. However, as noted above, as I generally did not include brother-in-law or sister-in-law connections in the entries, the number of jumps might be overestimated, as listing such relationships would have tightened the web significantly. These two factors balance each other out, and the methodology does provide a relatively good indication of connectedness.

The five highly connected families selected for this exercise were Glustein, Kardish, Shaffer, Shinder, and Torontow. Each had many connections with other entries. Furthermore, with one exception, none was within one jump of the other, so they themselves do not form a tight cluster. I deliberately did not select my own family entry or my wife's family entry, where some of the connections are admittedly more obscure. I also avoided the Greenberg and Saslove entries, each of which contains two distinct families with the same surname. Although I did not select any of these families as one of the five base families, I did use them when counting connections (and it should be noted that in both those families the two disparate branches are no more than two jumps away from each other).

A summary of findings is as follows (all numbers in columns 2, 3, and 4 are percentages):

	Jumps needed to get to the five selected families	Maximum number of jumps needed to get to all five families	Minimum number of jumps needed to get to any of the five families
1	16.75	0	52
2	57.25	32	47
3	25.75	66	1
4	.25	2	0

The columns can be interpreted as follows:

a. Jumps needed to get to the five selected families: I considered all 108 entries, multiplied across the 5 selected families, yielding a grand total of 108x5=540 total connections. I subtracted out 5, as each of the five selected families obviously connects to itself with 0 jumps. The numbers in this column represent the percentage of cases where 1, 2, 3, or 4 jumps were needed to get from an entry to one of the five families. One can readily see that the 2- and 3-jump cases heavily predominate, with a significant number of cases where only one jump was needed (these five selected families did have many connections each), and a very small number where a fourth jump was needed.

b. Maximum number of jumps needed to get to all the five families: These numbers represent the percentage across the 108 entries. The 0% in the 1 row means that there were no cases where an entry could get to all the five families in one jump. This is not unexpected. However, there were 32% of cases where an entry could get to all the five families with 1 or 2 jumps, and 66% of cases (the majority), where a 3 was needed to get to all the five families. There were only 2 entries (2% out of the 108 entries), where a fourth jump was needed.

c. Minimum number of jumps to get to any of the five families. These numbers also represent the percentage across the 108 entries. The 52% in the first row means that in over half the entries, at least one of the five families could be reached with just one jump. In 47% of cases, at least one entry could be reached with two jumps. In only 1% of cases did it take three jumps to get to at least one of the five families. There were no cases where four jumps were required to get to at least one of the five families – this is also not an unexpected result.

It is interesting to compare the b) and c) statistic. Considering the second case in b), there are 31% of entries where the 'jump map' to all the five families consisted solely of 1s and 2s. In other words, 31% of entries were relatively close to all five families. Let us compare this with the third case in c), which indicates that there were only 1% of cases where the 'jump map' to all the five families consisted solely of 3s and 4s. These are the outlying cases, somewhat distant from any of the five families.

A few more interesting facts were noted. In all the entries which had at least one 4 (2%) there was also at least one 2. This means that for any entry that was distant from at least one of the five families, there was another one of the five families to which it was relatively close. A corollary of this is that for the 1% of entries that could not reach any of the family with less than 3 jumps, there were no 4s.

I did not run a full analysis to determine the longest path from any entry to any other entry. In theory, the largest path would be no more than eight (four jumps to get to one of the five families, and four jumps to get back to another entry). However, since there were no cases where four jumps were needed to get to all the five families, the theoretical maximum can be reduced to seven jumps. I then studied the eight outlying entries (six where four jumps were needed to get to one of the five families, and two where one could not get to any of the families with less than three jumps). I calculated the maximum distance of any of these eight families to any other of them – and I found that it was four jumps. Obviously, these paths did not go through any of the five selected families -- they generally would have gone through other highly connected entries such as Dover, Feller, Greenberg, Lithwick, Saslove, or Viner. This does not offer definitive proof, but it does offer a strong indication that four is also the maximum number of jumps needed to get from any entry to any other entry (perhaps there are a few outlying cases were five jumps may be needed were a full analysis to be done).

In conclusion, this analysis of the connectedness of the 108 entries does paint a strong picture of a tightly connected web of Ottawa Jewish families.

Dedication

I hope that my readers, people connected to the Jewish community of Ottawa, and genealogists in general, find my research meaningful. Perhaps it will help some individuals discover long-lost cousins and relatives. I conducted this research with a strong sense of love and appreciation to my forebears and to the community into which I was born, raised, and nurtured. I dedicate this research to the memories of all members of the Ottawa Jewish community who have passed on to their eternal rest, whether they left their mark on the community, or simply lived out their lives as members of the community.

I would be interested in any feedback, comments, and corrections; as noted, a work like this will have numerous omissions. This is the first edition, and it is anticipated that a second edition will eventually be produced, incorporating any feedback. I repeat my sincere apologies to any individual or family who feels left out and neglected. I can be contacted at jerrold@jerroldlandau.com.

Jerrold Landau
Toronto, Canada
24 Kislev 5780   /   December 22, 2019

PREFACE FROM TEIGAN GOLDSMITH, OTTAWA JEWISH ARCHIVES

One of the most common questions I hear is:

"What can you tell me about my family history?"

Despite the short length of the sentence, it's quite a big question. Discovering your family history isn't always easy. Answering that question can take you down a long and winding road full of surprises and unexpected answers. In the last couple decades, with the help of websites like Ancestry.ca, My Heritage, and Geni.com it has become easier to access our history and people have become fascinated with finding out where they come from.

When Jerrold first approached me about writing an introduction I wasn't sure what to write. This project has seen three different archivists over the past couple years and, being the newest, I hadn't been as involved. However, my attitude changed once I read Jerrold's work. He talks a lot about connectedness, the concept of "cousins of cousins," and people you're related to through others. This resonated with me. When I moved to Ottawa a couple of years I was amazed at how connected it was. I was suddenly meeting "cousins of cousins" everywhere and realized, despite the size of the city, just how close Ottawa and its Jewish community are.

He also touches on a dwindling repository of information as older generations pass on. As an archivist, this is something I understand. As previously mentioned, the question of family history can be a big one. Our knowledge of our past is only as strong as the information saved. This means that keeping family records isn't just helpful, it's necessary! How many stories get lost in the generations? It's our job to make sure that our family history stays alive. Jerrold's book helps bridge that gap. His years of research into the families of Ottawa Jewish community have created a strong foundation for further research to be done. He has given us the branches, it's now our job to find the stories.

The Ottawa Jewish Archives is proud to be a part of this collection. We hope it bridges gaps, answers questions, and sparks the interest of researchers everywhere.

Teigan Goldsmith, Archivist
Ottawa Jewish Archives

ACKNOWLEDGEMENTS

I wish to acknowledge the following individuals who provided information on their families, and/or reviewed entries relevant to their families: Carolyn Appotive, Sharlene Cantor Bagola, Sheila Baslaw, Ross Baylin, Robert Bodnoff, Sharon Cohen, John Diener, Barbara Erlandson, Bernie Farber, Randy Fisher, Israel Gencher obm, Michael Gennis, Samuel Glass, Ada Glustein, Josh Gordon, Phillip Gosewich, Harry Greenblatt, Elliot Greenberg, David Kimmel, Elissa Krupski, Jonathan Landis, Cayla Lichtenstein, Barry Lithwick , Douglas Macy, Daniel Mann, Michael Moskovic, Michael Polowin, Connie Putterman, Hymie Reichstein, Barbara Samuel, Rabbi Idan Scher, Rhoda Shabinsky, Randi Goldstein Sherman, Paula Smith, Valerie Taller, Brent Taylor, Jeffrey Taylor, Ingrid Thompson, Lisa Vexler, Jacquie Rivers Vital, Vicky Weiss, Norman Zagerman obm. Several others were asked to review entries relevant to their families, but did not get back to me.

I acknowledge the support and encouragement of the Ottawa Jewish Archives, and the archivists Saara Mortensen, Zoe Thrumston, and Teigan Goldsmith. The vast majority of the photos which supplement my otherwise dry genealogical charts were culled from the Facebook Page of the Ottawa Jewish Archives. In many cases, I have used the photo captions directly from the Facebook Page of the Ottawa Jewish Archives.

Photos not from the Ottawa Jewish Archives were culled from publicly available websites. I have done my best to annotate sources of photos.

I express my gratitude to JewishGen volunteer Irv Osterer for the cover design. By coincidence, or perhaps providence, Irv is a fellow Ottawan, and several branches of his family are profiled in this book.

REVISIONS

1. Second revision, October 27, 2020
2. Third revision, December 14, 2021
3. Fourth revision, August 17, 2023

108 FAMILY ENTRIES

AARON

The Aaron family is descended from David (d. 1967) and Sarah (nee Steinman, d. 1977) Aaron. Sarah is a first cousin of Nat Steinman (d. 1988), married to Thelma (nee **Rivers**, d. 2004). The children of David and Sarah are:

- Hilda **Gennis** (d. 1991), married to Max (d. 1977). Their son Richard is married to Sharron (nee Strolovitch), daughter of Louis and Florence (nee Marcus, see **Marcovitch**) Strolovitch.
- Jack (d. 1991), married to Emily. Jack and Irving Aaron were land developers who donated the land for Congregation Beth Tikvah, formerly known as Beth Shalom West. There is a street called Jack Aaron Drive in the Craig Henry area of Ottawa.
- Irving (d. 2023), married to Ruth (nee **Feinstein**), daughter of Benjamin and Freda **Feinstein**. Their son Leslie is married to Lisa (nee Wolfe), who is the niece of Ab and Phyllis Flatt of Toronto. Ab and Phyllis Flatt are cousins of Marvin Flatt and Debbie (nee Breatross) Flatt (see **Murray**).

For connections to other entries, see Feinstein, Gennis, Marcovitch, Murray, Rivers.

AGES

The Ages family descends from Uri Ages, the son of Zalman Ages. The original family name was Eiges. His children included:

- Zalman (Sam), married successively to Ida (nee **Bodnoff**, d. 1918), and her sister Esther (nee **Bodnoff**, d. 1975). Zalman and Ida had three children:
  o Mary Dembe, married to Harry.
  o Isadore (Izzy, d. 1961), married to Gertrude (nee Meirovich, d. 2000). Gertrude's second husband was Aaron Morris Kushin (d. 1996).
  o Mitchell (d. 1964), married to Denise (nee Gross, d. 1977).

Zalman adopted Esther's two children, Joseph (d. 2008), married to Rose (nee Appel); and Saul (d. 1968), who were born from Esther's first marriage with Sam Dubrofsky (d. 1918). Rose (Appel) Ages is a sister of Minnie **Gershon**, married to Erwin **Gershon**, and Rhea Victor, married to Samuel (see **Rivers** entry).

Zalman and Esther had one child together:
  o Zelda (d. 1994) , married to Moe Berezin (d. 1975). Moe Berezin is the son of Samuel Berezin (d. 1932) and brother of Robert Berezin (see **Pollock**). The daughter of Zelda and Moe Berezin is Sheryl (nee Berezin) **Kardish**, married to Harvey, son of Israel (Yippy) and Eva (nee Feldberg) **Kardish**. Samuel's sister was Ida Cohen (nee Berezin, d. 1957) married to Samuel (d. 1959).

Samuel Cohen was the founder of the Ottawa Kosher Meat Market. Children of Samuel and Ida were: Sara; Hanna (Lillian) Fried (nee Cohen, d. 1970), married first to Frank Fried, and then to Maurice Tarantour (d. 1975). Frank and Lillian's daughter was Phyllis Rackow (nee Fried, d. 2015), married to Alan Rackow (d. 2016); Doris, married to Saul **Torontow**, son of Ralph and Ethel (nee Solomon) **Torontow**; Arthur, married to Miriam (nee Pearl); Irving; Rose Abramowitz, married to Louis (d. 1975). Rose and Lou's son Michael Abramowitz was married to Laya (nee Held, d. 2016), daughter of Benjamin and Freda Held (see **Pollock**).

Sam was killed in an accident before Zelda was born. Mary and Izzy were given to Jacob and Margaret Ages to raise, and Mitchell was given to Millie (nee **Bodnoff**) Shiller, to raise.

- Jacob (Jack, d. 1972) was married to Margaret (nee **Halpern**, d. 1973), daughter of Herman and Dina (nee Fox) **Halpern**. Their children are:
  o Samuel (d. 2015), married to Hilda (nee Bahar, d. 1981). Hilda is the sister of Eric Bahar (d. 2009), married to Sheila; and Thelma (d. 2006).
  o Miriam Ben-Shalom of Israel.
  o Matt Ages (d. 1994), married to Esther (nee Rafal, d. 2013).
  o Professor Arnold Ages of Toronto (d. 2020), married to Shoshana. Their daughter Sharon (d. 2013) was married to David Goldberg, the son of Eric and Edith (nee **Kardish**) Goldberg.

Uri's sister was Reiza (nee Ages) Ginsberg, married to Yosef. Their daughter Annie (d. 1947) married Abraham David **Bodnoff** (d. 1951). (See **Bodnoff** for connections to **Baylin**, **Coplan**, **Gandall**, **Kronick**, **Waserman**, **Weiner** families.). Their son Morris (d. 1963) married Sarah (nee **Bodnoff**, d. 1971). Thus a Ginsberg brother and sister married a **Bodnoff** brother and sister, thereby creating multiple connections between the Ages, **Bodnoff**, and Ginsberg families.

For connections to other entries, see Baylin, Bodnoff, Coplan, Gandall, Gershon, Kardish, Kronick, Pollock, Rivers, Torontow, Waserman, Weiner.

AGULNIK

The Agulnik family descends from Aharon and Hinda (d. 1920) Agulnik. Some branches of this family remained in the Soviet Union. The family is complex, as there are many relative marriages, as well as siblings with the same secular name, albeit different Jewish names. Children of Aharon and Hinda included:

- Shlomo, married to Lea. Their granddaughter Doris (nee Agulnik), daughter of Aharon Harry (d. 2001), and Sonia (nee Rawicka) Agulnik, is married to David **Torontow**, son of Harry and Sarah (nee **Gottdank**) **Torontow**. Aharon Harry and Sonia's son Manny is married to Paula.
- Hyman (d. 1934), married to Ida (his niece, daughter of Beryl, d. 1955). Their children were:

- o Morris (d. 1991), married to Sarah (nee Mendelson d. 1965). Their son Barry is married to Ethlyn (nee Brozovsky), daughter of Sam and Anne (nee **Kardish**) Brozovsky.
  - o Aaron Harry (d. 2003), married to his first cousin Bess (nee Lome, d. 1998).
  - o Louis (d. 1981), married to Libby (d. 1993).
  - o Bessie Frisch, married to Harry.
- Beryl (d. 1952), married to Leibe. Their children included:
  - o Morris (d. 1943).
  - o Samuel (Sholom, d. 1962), married to Mary (nee Ostroff, d. 1974)
  - o Shmuel(d. 1970), married to Fruma Malka (nee Reznitzky, d. 1958). Their son Dr. Maurice Agulnik (d. 1987) was married to Lea (nee Luterman, d. 2002), an aunt of Reba Diener (nee Luterman).
  - o Israel (d. 1970), married to Ida (nee Agulnik, d. 1970), daughter of Moshe and Esther Riva Agulnik (thus Israel and Ida were cousins). Their children are:
    - ▪ Ruth Rischall, married to Maurice.
    - ▪ Morris (d. 2019), was married to Janet (nee Glass), a first cousin of Irving Glass.
    - ▪ Lucy Glass, married to Irving (d. 1975).
  - o Ida (Esther, d. 1955), married to her uncle Hyman Agulnik.
  - o Ida (Yache, d. 1981) Lome, married to Harry Lome (d 1955). Their daughter Bess was married to her first cousin Aaron Harry Agulnik.
- Moshe, married to Esther Riva. Their daughter Beila was married to Cantor Kusiel Kronick (Chwojnik, d. 1964), who served as cantor of Beth Ora Synagogue in Montreal. Their daughter Ida was married to her first cousin Israel Agulnik.

For connections to other entries, see Diener, Gottdank, Kardish, Torontow.

APPEL

See Ages, Gershon, and Molot. The Appels in the Molot family are not connected to those in the Ages / Gershon family.

APPOTIVE

The Appotive family stems from Avraham Appotive (d. 1962), and Sarah (nee **Viner**, d. 1972), daughter of Joseph and Gittel (nee Silverman) **Viner**. The family originates from Zhitomir, Ukraine. Their children were:

- Benjamin (d. 1961), married to Sally (nee Brottman). Sally was the brother of Saul Brottman (d. 2016), married to Harriette.
- Joseph (d. 1985), married to Bas Sheva (nee Parnass, d. 1989). Their son David is married to Sharon (nee **Slack**), daughter of Samuel and Sylvia **Slack**.
- David (d. 2009), married to Edith (nee Feldblum, d. 2011).
- Rudy (d. 2003), married to Fruma (nee Parnass, d. 2017). Rudy's wife Fruma and Joseph's wife Sheva were sisters, daughters of Abraham and Shifra Parnass of Montreal. Another sister is Esther Katz (d. 2016), married to Joseph, whose daughter Myrna Beckenstein was originally married to Murry **Macy**, and is currently married to Hy Beckenstein. Rudy Appotive served as president of

Machzikei Hadas Synagogue when Rabbi Bulka was hired in 1967 and his son Stephen, married to Carolyn, also served as president of Machzikei Hadas.

My son Yisrael **Landau** is married to Menucha (nee Tuchman), who is a descendant of the Parnass family, and thus a third cousin thrice removed of Fruma and Bas Sheva Appotive, as well as Esther Katz.

For connections to other entries, see Landau, Macy, Slack, Viner.

David Appotive, Karl Waserman and other servicemen with a captured Nazi flag, 1945. (OJA 1-663-05)

ARRON

See Weinstein.

BALLON

See Saslove.

BASLAW

The Baslaw family descends from Morris Boslow (original Boguslovski, d. 1923), who immigrated to the United States from Russia. The children of Morris and Ida (nee Yarofsky, d. 1909) include:

- Mary **Shaffer** (d. 1979), married to Abraham **Shaffer**. They are the ancestors of the extended **Shaffer** clan.
- Murray Baslaw (d. 1968), married to Libbie (nee Finn). Murray's second wife was Pearl **Goldfield**. Children of Murray and Libbie were:
  - Irene Harris (d. 2000), married to Benjamin (d. 1971).
  - Morton (d. 2016), a well-known artist, who was married to Sheila (nee **Saslove**), daughter of Samuel and Lillian **Saslove**.

For connections to other entries, see Goldfield, Saslove, Shaffer.

R.C.A.F. officer Morton Baslaw in England, 1946.
(OJA 246-03)

BAYLIN

The Baylin family is descended from Max (d. 1962), and Rose (nee Satlin, d. 1973) Baylin. Max Baylin started the family business of Ottawa Iron Works . Their children include:

- Sam Baylin (d. 1972), married to Carolyn (nee Progosh), the daughter of Louis (d. 1972) and Sarah (d. 1974) Progosh. Their children are:
  - Michael (d. 2015), married to Cayla, nee **Mirsky**, the daughter of Lazarus and Gertrude (nee **Tradburks**) Mirsky.
  - Lita, married to Seymour Alper.
  - Jack

- Henry Baylin (d. 1975), married to Esther (nee Soltanoff, d. 2017). There children are
  - Julia, married to Jeffery Royer.
  - Lois, married to Brian Demone.
- Jack Baylin (d. 2012), married to Doris (nee Silverman, d. 1990), daughter of Benjamin (d. 1962) and Rose (nee Steinberg, d. 1943) Silverman. Doris' siblings were Bessie (d. 2007); Max (d. 2014) married to Ruth (known as Sunny, d. 2008); and James, married to Francis. Jack Baylin's second wife, Anne (d. 2019), is connected to the **Kardish** family. Children of Jack and Doris are:
  - Ross, married to Suzan (nee Smyth).
  - Shelly, was married to Yossi Amor. Yossi is the brother of Dina Aranov, the wife of Rabbi Saul Aranov, who served as rabbi of Beth Shalom Congregation for two periods during the mid to late 1970s and into the 1990s.
- Sylvia **Bodnoff** (d. 2012), married to Joseph Isadore (Izzie, d. 1969). Sylvia's second husband was Joseph Reiter (d. 1999). Children of Sylvia and Joseph Isadore **Bodnoff** are:
  - Robert, married to Pauline (nee **Gandall**), daughter of Hyman and Celia (nee Schnider) Gandall.
  - Frances Cogan, married to Jules.
  - Myra Allice, married to Gordon.
- Eve **Torontow** (d. 2006), married to Saul. After the death of Saul, Eve married Izzie **Flesher**. Children of Eve and Saul are:
  - Shirley Mires, married to Andre
  - Ellen Moreland, married to Greg

Max Baylin's brother Meyer (d 1936) laid the cornerstone of the Murray Street Shul.

Morris and Jennie Baylin were unrelated to this Baylin family. That family took on the name Baylin when they arrived in Ottawa (source, Bob Bodnoff). Morris and Jennie's son Ben Baylin (d. 2000) was married to Debbie, the daughter of Izzie and Shirley **Kardish**.

For connections to other entries, see Bodnoff, Flesher, Gandall, Kardish, Mirsky, Torontow, Tradburks.

Sam and Caroline Baylin & Jack and Doris Baylin out for an evening with Esther and Matt Ages, Ida and Sid Lithwick, Saul and Eve Torontow and others, ca. 1956.
(OJA 1-823-12)

BEREZIN

See Ages.

BESSIN

Moses (d. 1923) and Rachel (nee Wolinsky d. 1988) were pioneers of the Orthodox community of Ottawa. Their children who lived in Ottawa include:

- Hyman (d. 1978), married to Marion (d. 1981).
- Tessie (d. 2000), married to Dr. Nathan **Schecter** (d. 2007), son of Lazarus and Minnie Schecter.
- Ethyle (d. 2000), married to Lawrence (Lazer) Kapeller (d. 1979). Their daughter is Hannah Sibeth, married to Paul.
- Lil (d. 2002) married to Morris Lang (d. 2013). Morris Lang was the brother of Marjorie **Goldmaker**, married to Lou. Morris and Lil's daughter Elaine Kurtz (d. 2018) was married to Leon Kurtz, a member of the large Kurtz clan based in Toronto. Elaine and Leon's son, Yosef Kurtz is married to Gila (nee Diena),

the daughter of Joel and Rachel Diena. Joel Diena and his brother Baruch, married to Sarah, natives of Italy, were prominent members of the Orthodox community of Ottawa for many decades before moving to Toronto. Other Ottawa families connected to that Kurtz clan include Debbie Tenenbaum, daughter of Norman and Judy Tenenbaum (see **Diener**), and Ari Sacher, grandson of Rev. Nachman and Mollie Bornestein (see **Schreiber**).

Other children of Moses and Rachel Bessin are: Bella, married successively to Gershon Guttman, Chaim Yosef Zeifman (d. 1962), and Meyer Handelsman; Nettie Salomon (d. 2005) married to Irwin Salomon; Adele Davis (d. 2005), married to Dr. Benjamin Davis (d. 1993); Joseph (d. 1915); Bertha Sokol (d. 2011), whose first husband was Joseph Lang (d. 1955), and second husband was Nachman Sokol (d. 1992). Joseph Lang was the brother of Morris Lang, married to Betha's sister Lil as noted above (i.e. two Lang brothers married two Bessin sisters).

Rachel was the daughter of Benjamin (d. 1918), and Sarah (d. 1953) Wolinsky. She was the sister was Beckie **Petegorsky** (d. 1991), who was married to Leon **Petegorsky** (d. 1966). Their daughter is Beverley, who was married to Marvin Chodikoff (d. 1965), son of Israel and Anne (nee **Freedman**) Chodikoff. Rachel's brother was Joseph Wolinsky (d. 1980), was married to Minnie (nee **Shaffer**, d. 1952), the daughter of Samuel and Mary (nee **Baslaw**) **Shaffer**.

Moses Bessin had an uncle Yisrael Levinoff, whose wife's sister (Anna Zelcovin) was the father of Charles **Goldfield**. Thus, the Bessins and **Goldfields** share a set of common cousins.

For connections to other entries, see Baslaw, Diener, Freedman, Goldfield, Goldmaker, Petigorsky, Schecter. Schreiber, Shaffer.

Here we are
to say to you
לשנה טובה תכתבו ותחתמו
The Bessins

438 DALY AVE. OTTAWA ONT.

A New Year's card from 1961 from the Bessin Family of Ottawa:
L-R: Hy, Marion, Moshe, Leya, Berl and Herschel. (OJA 1-1037-01)

BETCHERMAN

The Betcherman family descends from Zeev Wolf Betcherman. Zeev Wolf had two sons who are ancestors of Ottawa families: Fishel and Leib. Fishel (d. 1947) and his wife Brocha (nee Addelman, d. 1955), are buried in Ottawa. Leib is not buried in Ottawa. According to Fishel's grandson David **Shore**, brothers of Fishel came to Ottawa, and later returned to Europe.

Fishel's children were:

- William Betcherman (d. 1976).
- Minnie, married to Jacob Kaplan.
- Anna **Shore** (d. 1980), married to Charles **Shore** (d. 1953). Their children are:

- o David (d. 2020), married to Debbie (nee Wisebord). Their son mark was married to Andrea (nee **Saslove**).
  - o Mendel (d. 2017), married to Anita (nee Steinberg), who is a member of the **Glustein** extended family.
  - o Evelyn Rotenberg (d. 2016).
  - o Faye Fogel (d. 1986), married to Harold (d. 1993).
- Abraham Betcherman (d. 1976), married to Fannie (d. 1993), daughter of Bernard (d. 1953) and Rebecca (nee Rhinestein, d. 1940) Smith . Bernard and Rebecca's other children were Kalman, married to Sylvia (nee **Gould**); Essie, married to Carl Fein; Jules, married to Freda (nee **Florence**). Fannie Betcherman was a cousin of Saul Sonken, married to Edith (nee **Molot**).
- Alexander Betcherman (d. 1977), married to Mollie (nee **Florence**), daughter of Abraham Lazarus and Lena (nee **Pullan**) **Florence**. Their children are Phillip, Lena Michelson, and Joy Rosenstein.
- Myer (d. 1954) married to Rose (d. 1996). Their children are:
  - o Irving (d. 1992) married to Lita-Rose.
  - o Enid (d. 1978), who was married to Dr. Edward Abrahams (d. 2021).

Leib's son was Isaac (d. 1941), married to Yetta (d. 1963). Yetta was Isaac's second wife.

The son of Leib and his first wife was:

- Samuel (d. 1984), married to Ann (nee **Torontow**), daughter of Louis and Miriam **Torontow**.

The children of Isaac and Yetta are:
- Blanche Osterer, married to Joey Osterer (d. 2016), (see **Glustein**). Their son Howard Osterer (d. 2014) was married to Ellen **Rivers**, daughter of Irving and Ethel (nee Sandler) **Rivers**. Howard and Ellen's daughter Erin **Smith** is married to Aaron **Smith**, son of Leslie and Maureen **Smith** and grandson of Jack and Inez **Smith**.
- Esther, married to Harry **Froman**. Their children are:
  - o Risa **Taylor**, married to Brent, son of Irving and Ethel (nee **Greenberg**) **Taylor**.
  - o Adam, married to Sharin.
  - o Ian, married to Jaclyn.

For connections to other entries, see Florence, Froman, Glustein, Gould, Greenberg, Molot, Pullan, Rivers, Saslove, Smith, Shore, Taylor, Torontow.

BILSKY

Moses Bilsky (December 10, 1829-January 4, 1923) is believed to be the first Jewish resident of Ottawa. Moses was married to Pauline (nee Reich, d. Dec 3, 1928). The family originates from Kovno (Kaunas), Lithuania. Children of Moses and Pauline were:

- Alexander
- Samuel (d. 1941).

- Rebecca Jacobs (d. 1941), married to Abraham. Abraham Jacobs served for a period as a member of parliament.
- Lillian Freiman (d. 1940), married to Archibald Jacob Freiman (d. 1944), well known as the founder of the Freiman's department store on George Street. Their children include:
  - Lawrence (d. 1986, married to Audrey (nee Steinkopf, d. 2006). Their children are:
    - Archibald Jacob Freiman.
    - Margo Roston married to Gordon (d. 2020).
    - Moshe Freiman (d. 1934).
  - Dorothy Alexandor (d. 1999) married to Bernard Alexandor (d. 1995), the first president of the Beth Shalom synagogue.
  - Queenie Luxenberg.
  - Mosha Freiman (died in infancy).
  - Mildred Freiman (died in infancy).
- Tillie (d. 1936).
- Nathan married to Minnie (nee Markson, d. 1923). Their son is Lawrence (d. 1969), married to Esther (nee Rabin d. 1977). Esther was the daughter of Cantor Joseph Rabin (d. 1968), and Sonia (nee Ivry, d. 1987). Cantor Rabin served as the Cantor of Beth Shalom as well as a mohel for many years. Esther's brother Eli also lived in Ottawa for many years. Lawrence and Esther's daughter is Millie **Mirsky**, married to Stephan **Mirsky**. Stephan is the son of Norman (d. 1986), and Anne (nee Fine, d. 2003), daughter of Leon Fine and Rae (nee **Feller**).
- Etta Schragge (d. 1972).
- Jacob (d. 1969).
- Lucy Bronfman (d. 1983) married to Allan Bronfman (d. 1966). Allan was a brother of Sam Bronfman, the well-known Canadian industrialist and founder of Seagram's.
- Eva (d. 1952).
- Harry (d. 1895).

Archibald Jacob Frieman had a cousin, Miriam (nee London) Goldstein Rosenfeld (d. 1995), married first to Sam Goldstein (d. 1960) and then to Murray Rosenfeld (d. 1983). Their son Morris Goldstein was married to Shirley (nee **Halpern**), daughter of Sidney and Frieda (nee Hirschhorn) **Halpern**. Their son Franklin (Frank) Goldstein is married to Elaine (nee Pearlman), daughter of Dr. Lyon and Naomi Pearlman (see **Mirsky**).

For connections to other entries, see Feller, Halpern, Mirsky.

Moses Bilsky (1829-1923) as a young man (1860).
(OJA 1-167)

Portrait of Pauline Bilsky, 1904
(OJA 1-556-01)

BODNOFF

The Bodnoff family descends from Yitzchak Yosef Bodnoff (Joseph, d. 1899). The surname is unique, and anyone with that surname likely connects to this family. A member of the family informed me that the original surname was likely Bodnief or some variant. Yitzchak Yosef had children from two wives – his second wife was Mary (nee Midlin).

Yitzchak Yosef's children from his first wife were:

- Peretz, married to Peshe.
- Eli.
- Abraham David (d. 1951), married to Annie (nee Ginsberg, d. 1947), daughter of Yosef and Reiza (nee **Ages**) Ginsberg. (note multiple connections to Ginsberg and **Ages** families within the Bodnoff family). Their children are:
  - Sadie Shapero (d. 1988), married to Irving Shapero (d. 1989). Sadie and Irving's daughter is Julia, married to Howie **Waserman**, the son of Ernie and Sadie **Waserman**.
  - Jack (d. 1931).
  - Joseph Isadore (d. 1969), married to Sylvia (nee **Baylin**, d. 2012). After Joseph's passing, Sylvia married Joseph Reiter (d. 1999). Joseph and Sylvia Bodnoff's children are:
    - Robert, married to Pauline (nee **Gandall**), daughter of Hyman and Celia (nee Schnider) **Gandall**.
    - Frances, married to Jules Cogan.
    - Myra, married to Gordon Allice, son of Israel (Al, d. 1977), and Mary Allice (d. 2000). Al and Mary Allice's other children are Murray; and Beverly, married to Irving Swedko. Irving is the brother of Norman Swedko, married to Elsa (nee **Craft**), daughter of John and Sadie (nee Richman), **Craft**.
  - Lily (d. 1980), married to Joseph Zbar.
  - Rachel, married to Victor **Gould** (d. 1990). Their children are:
    - Joan, married to Russel **Kronick**, son of Wally and Irene (nee **Coplan**) **Kronick**.
    - Jeffrey, married to Enid (nee **Taller**), the daughter of Sam and Anne **Taller**.
  - Toby (d. 1990) married to Harry **Weiner** (d. 1950). Their children were:
    - Luella (d. 1987).
    - Dorothy (d. 2014).
    - Sheila Schinman (d. 2010), married to Saul Schinman. Sheila and Saul moved from Ottawa to New Jersey in the early 1970s.

Yitzchak Yosef and Mary's children were:

- Sam (d. 1929), married to Sarah (nee Dimentstein, d. 1972). Sam and Sarah lived in Toronto. Their great-grandson Randy Fisher, grandson of Isadore and Anne (nee Bodnoff) Hercy, lived in Ottawa.
- Benjamin (d. 1960), married first to Rebecca (nee Rosenberg, d. 1918), and then to Francis (nee Aronovitch, d. 1975). Benjamin and Rebecca's daughter was Marion Mintz (d. 1992), married to Morris (d. 1985). Francis had two children from a previous marriage: Ida, and Mary Benwick (d. 1995), married to Ralph (d. 1985, see Epstein branch of **Cohen**).
- Ida (d. 1918), married to Zalman **Ages**, who then married Ida's sister Esther. Children of Zalman and Ida were:
  - Mary Dembe, married to Harry.

- o Isadore (Izzy, d. 1961), married to Gertrude (nee Meirovich).
- o Mitchell (d. 1964), married to Denise (nee Gross, d. 1977).
- Sarah (d. 1971), married to Morris Ginsberg (d. 1963), son of Yosef and Reiza (nee **Ages**) Ginsberg, and brother of Annie Bodnoff (married to Abraham David – thus a Bodnoff brother and sister married a Ginsberg brother and sister). Their children include:
  - o Anne Ginsberg Mayberger Blair (d. 2014), married to Hyman Mayberger (d. 1970). Their children are:
    - Shelley Schachnow, married to Morris.
    - Ruth Eliesen Leckman.
    - Arni (d. 2011), married to Anne.
    - Charlotte Kuttas (d. 1962).
  - o Joseph (d. 2010) married to Ruth (nee Simon), and then to Muriel (nee Marcus). Joe Ginsberg was a founding partner of the Ginsberg, Gluzman, Fage, and Levitz accounting firm.
  - o Mary (d. 1967).
  - o Raye Sheft (d. 2000 in Wisconsin), married to Alex.
  - o Ida Winestock of Los Angeles, married to Micky.
  - o Abraham (d. 1976), married to Belle (nee Teitelbaum).
  - o Bernie, married to Rochelle (nee Steinberg),
  - o Dorothy (Dolly) Blacher (d. 1990), married to Boris (Bo, d. 2012).
- Sadie (d. 1959), married to Samuel Bodnoff (d. 1936). Samuel Bodnoff and Sadie were evidently cousins. Their children are:
  - o Gerald (d. 1986), married to Doreen (nee Chezin). Doreen married Ariel Arnoni (d. 2022) after Gerald's death.
  - o Mildred Mintz married to Alexander.
  - o Gertude (d. 1980).
  - o Bernice **Feller** (d. 1979), married to Edward, son of William and Eva (nee Rosen) **Feller**.
- Esther **Ages** (d. 1975), married to Sam Dubrofsky (d. 1918), and then to Zalman **Ages**. The children of Esther and Sam Dubrofsky were Joe (d. 2008), and Saul (d. 1968). After their mother's remarriage, Joe and Saul were adopted by her second husband Zalman **Ages**, who originally had been married to Esther's sister. The child of Esther and Zalman **Ages** was Zelda (d. 1994), married to Moe Berezin (d. 1975), the son of Samuel Berezin (d. 1932) and brother of Robert Berezin (see **Pollock**). The daughter of Zelda and Moe Berezin is Sheryl (nee Berezin) **Kardish**, married to Harvey, son of Israel (Yippy) and Eva (nee Feldberg) **Kardish**. Due to the early death of Zalman **Ages**, various of his children from both Esther and Ida were given to other family members to raise (see **Ages** for full details).
- Irving Benjamin (d. 1970), married to Ann (nee Rastovsky, d. 1972). Irving and Ann's children were:
  - o Muriel (d. 2016), married to Bernie Putterman (d. 1982), son of Menachem Mendel (d. 1933), and Feiga (nee Spielberg, d. 1944). Muriel and Bernie Putterman lived in Windsor. Their daughter Connie is married to my wife's second cousin David Golden (see Epstein branch of **Cohen**).
  - o Ronald (d. 1981), married to Rhoda (nee **Torontow,** d. 2020).
  - o Morley (d. 1990), married to Sonia (nee Sinder, d. 2010), daughter of David and Mary (nee **Shore**) Sinder.

- o Phillip (d. 1965), married to Gladys (nee **Greenberg**, d. 2017), daughter of Morris and Bertha (nee **Gennis**) **Greenberg**.
- o Joseph. Sergeant Joe Bodnoff was shot down by a U boat while serving in the Canadian air force during the Second World War, and was rescued at sea. He married Sara (nee Teitelbaum).
- Millie Shiller (d. 1975). She married three times. One husband was Saul Shiller. She had no children of her own, but raised her nephew Mitchell **Ages**, son of Ida and Zalman **Ages**, whose parents died very early.

For connections to other entries, see Ages, Baylin, Coplan, Craft, Feller, Gandall, Gennis, Gould, Greenberg, Kardish, Pollock, Kronick , Shore, Taller, Torontow, Waserman, Weiner.

Wedding picture of Irving Benjamin [Bennie] and Ann [nee Rastovsky] Bodnoff.
(From Connie Putterman)

Bodnoff family (Irving Benjamin and Ann branch) gathered at the Bar Mitzvah of Mark Putterman in Windsor. (From Connie Puterman)

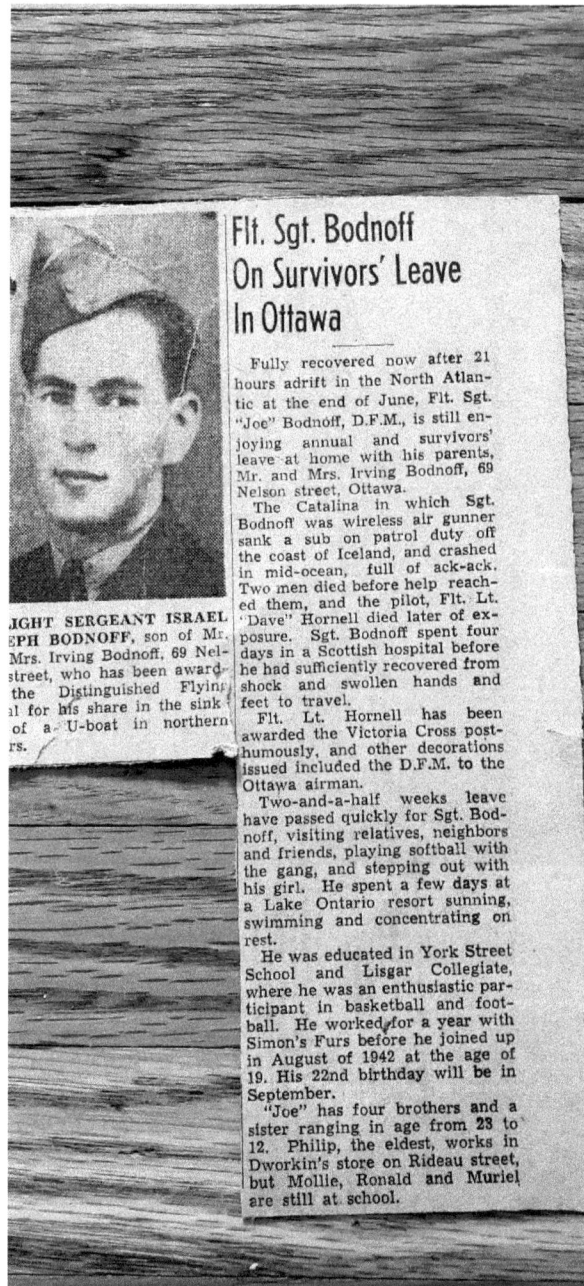

Flt. Sgt. Bodnoff On Survivors' Leave In Ottawa

Fully recovered now after 21 hours adrift in the North Atlantic at the end of June, Flt. Sgt. "Joe" Bodnoff, D.F.M., is still enjoying annual and survivors' leave at home with his parents, Mr. and Mrs. Irving Bodnoff, 69 Nelson street, Ottawa.

The Catalina in which Sgt. Bodnoff was wireless air gunner sank a sub on patrol duty off the coast of Iceland, and crashed in mid-ocean, full of ack-ack. Two men died before help reached them, and the pilot, Flt. Lt. "Dave" Hornell died later of exposure. Sgt. Bodnoff spent four days in a Scottish hospital before he had sufficiently recovered from shock and swollen hands and feet to travel.

Flt. Lt. Hornell has been awarded the Victoria Cross posthumously, and other decorations issued included the D.F.M. to the Ottawa airman.

Two-and-a-half weeks leave have passed quickly for Sgt. Bodnoff, visiting relatives, neighbors and friends, playing softball with the gang, and stepping out with his girl. He spent a few days at a Lake Ontario resort sunning, swimming and concentrating on rest.

He was educated in York Street School and Lisgar Collegiate, where he was an enthusiastic participant in basketball and football. He worked for a year with Simon's Furs before he joined up in August of 1942 at the age of 19. His 22nd birthday will be in September.

"Joe" has four brothers and a sister ranging in age from 23 to 12. Philip, the eldest, works in Dworkin's store on Rideau street, but Mollie, Ronald and Muriel are still at school.

FLIGHT SERGEANT ISRAEL JOSEPH BODNOFF, son of Mr. and Mrs. Irving Bodnoff, 69 Nelson street, who has been awarded the Distinguished Flying Medal for his share in the sinking of a U-boat in northern waters.

(From Connie Putterman)

BORDELAY

The Bordelay family stems from Avraham and Devorah Bordelay. Their children were:

- Marsha **Gorelick** (d. 1985), married to Max (d. 1980). Their son Ron was married to Debbie (nee Levine), daughter of Abe (d. 1994), and Tillie (nee Greenberg, d. 2012) Levine.

- Tom (known as Tevye, d. 1970), married to Miriam (nee Steinberg, d. 1978). Their children were:
  - Betty (d. **1983**).
  - Shirley **Kardish** (d. 2003), married to Louis (d.1991), son of David **Kardish**.
- Meyer (d. 1975), married to Jennie (Zelda, d 1948). Their daughter Beatrice Koffman was married to Milton (see **Gennis**). Zena, the daughter of Milton and Beatrice Koffman, is married to David **Lieff**, son of Samuel and Libby (nee **Kardish**) **Lieff**. It is interesting to note that the children of Louis and Shirley **Kardish** are cousins to both Zena and David – i.e. both have Bordelay connections.
- Jacob (d. 1915).

For connections to other entries, see Gennis, Gorelick, Kardish, Lieff.

CANTOR

The Cantor family is descended from Hyman (d. 1949), and Ida (d. 1963) Cantor, originally from Rokisek, Lithuania. Their children were:

- Bessie **Taller** (d. 2010) married to Sam, son of Hyman (d. 1960), and Eva (d. 1953) **Taller**. Their children are:
  - Mendy, married to Ruth (nee **Kerzner**, d. 1996), daughter of Sydney and Ethel (nee Kott) **Kerzner**.
  - Herbie married to Vivian (nee Gelman), daughter of Ben and Rebecca (nee **Schecter**) Gelman.
  - Carolyn Katz, married to Sid.
- Benes (d. 1997) married to Sarah (nee Cohen, d. 2001). Sarah was the daughter of Jacob (d. 1950) and Bessie (nee Butovsky, d. 1977) Cohen, and the sister of Pearl (nee Cohen) **Taller**, wife of Jack; and Maxwell Cohen.
- Morris (d. 2002) married to Goldie (nee **Rivers**), daughter of Jacob and Leah (nee Keller) **Rivers**. Their daughter Lynn is married to Mordechai Ben-Dat, who served as editor of the Canadian Jewish News for many years.
- Wolfe (d. 1980) married to Miriam (nee Cohen, d. 1998). Their children are:
  - Ron, married to Anna (nee Cohen), the daughter of Israel (d. 1992) and Polly (nee Landsman, d. 2010). Israel Cohen is the brother of Al Cohen (d. 2010), who was married to Shirley (nee Zagerman), daughter of Morris and Mildred Zagerman (see **Krantzberg**). Al and Shirley's children include Joan Brodie; Joel Brodie; Alice, married to Richard **Kronick**; Elizabeth **Mosion**, married to Max, the son of Rudy and Joan **Mosion**; and Robert Brodie. Ron and Anna's son Adam Cantor is married to Sari, daughter of Izzy and Katie (nee Pivnick, d. 1986) Farber. Izzy later married Mary. Izzy's parents were Richard (d. 1984) and Cilla (d. 2018), and his brothers are Barry, married to Zahava (nee Feig), daughter of Shmuel (d. 2008), and Malka (d. 2018) Feig (see **Cohen** entry for connection to Shmuel's brother Moshe); and Leonard, married to Barbara (nee Katz) daughter of Stan and Libby (nee **Leikin**) Katz.
  - Danny married to Bev (nee Segal). Their son Mark is married to Stacey (nee Levencrown), daughter of Richard and Ann (nee **Max**) Levencrown.

- o Charlotte.
- Leizer, married to Gertie. They lived in South Africa.
- Bunim (d. 1974), married to Esther (nee **Viner**, d. 2000), the daughter of Melech (Milton, d. 1918), and Eva (d. 1957) **Viner**.
- Pauline Zellick, married to Harry.
- Harry.

For connections to other entries, see Kerzner, Krantzberg, Kronick, Leikin, Max, Mosion, Rivers, Schecter, Taller, Viner.

Sergeant Morris Cantor (fourth from the left) poses with his Royal Canadian Air Force broom hockey team. This was taken some time during WWII while he was stationed in the Yukon. (OJA-1-782-06)

Family portrait of the Cantor Family, 1927. L-R standing: Wolf Cantor, Bessie (Cantor) Taller, Bunem Cantor, Pauline Cantor. Seated: Mrs. Chaya Cantor, Bainesh Cantor, Morris Cantor, Mr. Chaim Cantor. Photograph taken in Rokisek, Lithuania.
(OJA 1-040)

CAPLAN

See Feller.

CHERM

The Cherm family descends from Harry (d. 1969), from Minsk, Belarus, and Tillie (Tibel, nee Viner, d. 1975), daughter of Joseph and Gittel **Viner**. Their children are:

- Donald.
- Sylvia Kaiman (d. 2015), married to Sol (d. 2011). Their children are:
  - Gaye, married to Joel **Taller** (d. 2017), daughter of Archie and Lillian **Taller**.
  - Stephen, married to Janet (nee Kimmel), daughter of Morris Kimmel (d. 2014) and Lillian (nee Spector, d. 2006). Morris Kimmel is not related to the larger Kimmel family of Ottawa. Lillian is the sister of Estelle Huniu (d. 2020), married to Larry (known as Lazar, see **Reichstein**). Lillian Kimmel and Estelle Huniu are the daughters of Jack (d. 2001) and Ettie (Molly, d. 2001) Spector.

- Dora **Waserman** (d. 2013) married to Hyman (d. 1972). Their daughter Arlene Schwey was married to Melvyn (d. 2020).
- Mollie **Fine** (d. 2012) married to Natal (d. 1974). Their son Jeffrey is married to Julie, the daughter of Kurt (d. 1994) and Joan (nee Rodgers, d. 1993) Orlik.

For connections to other entries, see Fine, Reichstein, Taller, Viner, Waserman.

Tillie and Harry Cherm celebrating their 40th Wedding Anniversary in 1954.
(OJA 1-541)

CHERUN

See Feller, Krantzberg, Viner.

COHEN

The Cohen surname is quite common within any Jewish community. For a community the size of Ottawa, it is bound to occur in many families, and will not always point to an interconnection. This entry relates to one particular Cohen family with widespread connections within the Ottawa Jewish community. This family originates from Osveya, at the northernmost tip of Belarus.

This family stems from two brothers, Shmuel and Yosef. Yosef, my wife's great-great-grandfather, was married to Ita (nee Dobkin, d. 1925, buried in Ottawa). Shmuel and Yosef died in Europe.

A. **Shmuel Cohen Branch**

Shmuel Cohen had a son, Charles (Yechezkel) Cohen (d. 1941). His wife was apparently Sheina (nee Margolies). Their children were:

- Sam (Zelig, d. 1943), married to Fanny (Feige, nee Hoichberg). Members of this Cohen family owned the R&A Cohen Furniture Company. Their children were:
  - Alexander (known as Andy, d. 1988), married to Edyce (nee Freedman, d. 2004).
  - Wolfred (d. 1991), married to Rose (nee Karon, d. 1987). Their daughter is Brenda Caplan, married to Thomas, who lived in Ottawa prior to moving to Israel.
  - Reuben (d. 1991).
  - Mona **Slover** (d. 2004), married to Lawrence (d. 2005), son of Abraham Chaim and Malca **Slover**.
- Gabriel (d. 1950) married to Rebecca (d. 1993). Their children were:
  - Ruth.
  - Morris (d. 1981), married to Mina (nee **Dover**, d. 2010), daughter of Harry and Calla (nee Lecker) **Dover**. Morris and Mina's son Eric (d. 2020) was married to Janet (nee Ginsburg), daughter of Martin and Theadora Ginsburg (see **Smolkin**).
- Dora Fagin (d. 1966), married to Isaac Fagin (d. 1967). Children were:
  - Becky Bauer (d. 2004) married to Werner Bauer (d. 1992). Werner Bauer was a beloved elementary school teacher who taught for decades at Hillel Academy.
  - Rose Fagin (d. 1992)
  - Bessie Davy (d. 1990), married to Rabbi Dr. Gabriel Davy (Dawidowicz d. 1974)
  - Freda **Halpern** (d. 1971) married to Sidney (d. 1982), son of Herman and Rachel **Halpern**. Their daughter Shirley Abtan was married to Morris Goldstein, and then married Nessim Abtan.
  - Alec Fagin (d. 1955) married to Frances (nee Cohen d. 2002)
- Max Cohen (d. 1944), married to Grete (d. 1992). Their children are:
  - Sidney (d. 2017), who was married to Ruth (d. 1977), and then married Barbara (nee Smith), daughter of Kalman and Sylvia (nee **Gould**) Smith.
  - Edward (d. 2005), married to Fern.
  - Erica (d. 2016) Cherney, married to Harry.
  - Ben, married to Rhona.
- Fanny **Swedlove** (d. 1949), married to Samuel (d. 1973), son of Herschel and Rebecca (nee Weiss) **Swedlove**. Their children were:
  - Joseph (d. 1989), married to Irene (nee Aisenberg, d. 2009), daughter of Harry and Ente (nee **Lithwick**) Aisenberg..
  - Tillie Paulin, married to Arthur.
  - Philip (d. 1993), married to Deborah (nee **Polowin**, d. 1993), daughter of Jacob and Dina (nee Gordon) **Polowin**.

B. **Yosef Cohen Branch**

Yosef Cohen and Ita (nee Dobkin) had 4 children:

- Solomon (Shneur Zalman) Epstein (d. 1943), married to Sadie (nee Rosenfeld d. 1954). Sadie is the daughter of Louis Abbey Rosenfield (d. 1904), married Fruma Esther Rosenfield (d. 1944), who was the first Jewish midwife in Ottawa. Solomon changed his name from Cohen to Epstein to avoid the Russian draft. Solomon and Sadie were my wife's great-grandparents. See below for full details of all Epstein connections.
- Kasriel Cohen (d. 1957) married to Reva (nee Speyer). Kasriel and Reva had one son, Saul, married to Minnie (nee **Dover**), the daughter of David and Libbie **Dover**.
- Samuel Cohen (d. 1952) married to Mesha Pia. Their daughter Sarah **Zelikovitz** (d. 1966) was married to Morris (d. 1968). Their great-grandson Evan **Zelikovitz** is married to Lenora (nee **Levitan**).
- Ada Segalowitz (d. 1971), married to Hershel (d. 1929). Their son Hy Harris (d. 1997), was married to Pearl (Pat) (nee **Pollock**, d. 1982). Hy and Pearl were the aunt and uncle of Barbara **Fine** (nee Goldenberg), married to Louis **Fine**. Other children of Ada and Hershel were Norman Segalowitz married to Sylvia (nee Riven), and then to Bess (nee Zinman), Reva Ferrucci married to Baruchi, Kalman married to Pessa, Sarah Morell married to Isadore, Molly Silverman married to Arthur. Norm Segalowitz played for the Montreal Alouettes Canadian Football League team in 1946-1947. Bess (nee Zinman, d. 2015) Segalowitz was a cousin of Edward Zinman (d. 1989), married to Phyllis (Fuzzy, nee Gursky, later Teitelbaum, d. 2009), a veteran teacher of Hillel Academy. Bess' brother, Peter Zinman (d. 2003) was married to my mother-in-law's first cousin Nancy Aberback (d. 2009). Bess' sister Nellye Aber (d. 2010), was married to my mother'in-law's first cousin Irving Aber (d. 1974) – thus forging a triple connection between my wife's family and the Zinman family (one on my father-in-law's side and twice on my mother-in-laws's side).

Solomon and Sadie Epstein had 9 children: Goldie Sacksner, Fanny Rachlin, Joseph Emerson, Sam Epstein, Gabriel Epstein, Mike Emerson, Harry Epstein, Bertha (Bunnie) Fink, Hynda Weihl. Of the nine children, five have connections to Ottawa families.

- David Sacksner, the son of Goldie and Moses Sacksner, was married to Joan (nee Eisenstadt). Joan was the daughter Joseph Eisenstadt (d. 1954), and Esther (nee Benwick, d. 1989). Esther was the daughter of Bernard (d. 1930), and Elizabeth (Betsy, d. 1978) Benwick, and the sister of Ernest (Sonny, d. 1999), and Ralph (d. 1985), married to Mary (d. 1985, see **Bodnoff**).
- Fanny Rachlin (d. 1967), was married to Louis (d. 1956). Louis Rachlin was the son of Joseph (d. 1960), and Annie (nee **Leikin**, d. 1957). The children of Fanny and Louis are Sybil (d. 1992) married to Phillip Wigdor (d. 2011); Bernard married to Sara (nee Aberback); and Faith (d. 2001). Tzipora, the daughter of Bernard and Sara Rachlin is married to Jerrold **Landau**. Sarah's brother Abe Aberback and his wife Shanie lived in Ottawa for many years before moving to Toronto.

- Joseph Emerson (d. 1998), and Helen (d. 2003) lived in Toronto. Note that two of the Epstein brothers changed their surnames from Epstein to Emerson. Their daughter Roslyn (Reizel) was married to Sidney Golden. Roslyn died very young, and Sidney then married Nancy (Rosen). Nancy's aunt was Rose **Betcherman**, married to Myer. Their grandson David Golden, son of their daughter Roslyn, is married to Connie Putterman, of the Ottawa based **Bodnoff** family. Their son Stanley Emerson is married to Ilana, whose first cousin Esty and Rabbi Moshe Yeres of Toronto are the in-laws of Eliezer Bulka, the son of Rabbi Reuven and the late Naomi Bulka. Rabbi Bulka served as rabbi of Machzikei Hadas of Ottawa for close to 50 years, and is currently the Rabbi Emeritus. Although a distant relation (through this connection, Rabbi Bulka and Naomi are the in-laws of my wife's second cousin's second cousin), this does bring them into the Ottawa Jewish family web.
- Sam (d. 1996) and Eva (nee Cornblat d. 2000) lived all their lives in Ottawa and had no children. Eva is the daughter of Max (d. 1944) and Bella (d. 1962) Cornblat. Eva's brother Isaac Cornblat (d. 1973), married to Cecilia (nee Freedman d. 2004), daughter of William and Fanny (nee Addelman) Freedman (see **Krantzberg**). Other sisters are Edith Cornblat (d. 1989), Esther Cornblat (d. 1967), and Rose Montagnes (d. 1963) married to James Montagnes (d. 1993). James is the brother of Mariette Woolfson (nee Montagnes, d. 2006) married to Morris (d. 1996) a well-known architect in Ottawa. Morris and Mariette Woolfson are the parents of Roslyn Snyder, married to Gerald Snyder. Gerald Synder's uncle and aunt were Samuel (d. 1994), and Ida (d. 1996) Morin, whose daughter Lily Feig was married to Moshe Feig (d. 2005, see **Cantor** for connection to Moshe's brother Shmuel).
- Mike Emerson (d. 1979) married to Elaine (nee Plaskow). Their son Donny is married to Laurie (nee Cooper), who is a sister to Cindy, married to Bart Ehrenkranz. The large Ehrenkranz is a US based family, but with connections to both the **Diener** and **Landau** families of Ottawa.

From the Rachlin branch (my wife's grandparents' family), there are two interesting connections to wide-branched families outside of Ottawa, which loop back into Ottawa in numerous ways.

My mother-in-law's mother was Etka Aberback (nee Wolpin). She was a member of the very large Wolpin family, which has many large branches of rabbinical families. Three connect back to Ottawa families, albeit in a distant fashion.
- My mother-in-law's fourth cousin Avraham Wolpin is married to Rivka (nee Jakobovitz), who is Naomi Bulka's first cousin. Thus, Rabbi Reuven and Naomi Bulka connect once more into the large Ottawa web, albeit quite distantly. While discussing the Bulka connection to Ottawa, I have found that another of Naomi Bulka's cousins, through the Jakobovitz family (Silbinger and Rapaport branches) is a cousin through marriage of Rabbi Abraham Eckstein, the brother of Rabbi Simon Eckstein (d. 2016), married to Belle. Rabbi Simon Eckstein was the long-time rabbi of Beth Shalom and its precursor synagogues.
- My mother-in-law's third cousin once removed Sara Chana (nee Wolpin) is married to Nosson Fasman, the grandson of Rabbi Oscar (d. 2003) and Jeanette Fasman. Rabbi Fasman served the Ottawa community during the 1940s, and

later went on to become the president of the Hebrew Theological College of Chicago.

- My mother-in-law's third cousin Nisson Wolpin is married to Necha Devora (Dorothy) Cohen, a member of the Ottawa **Silver** family, she is the daughter of Laibel **Silver's** first cousin Mayer Cohen. Nisson Wolpin was the long-time editor of the Jewish Observer magazine.
- From a different branch of my mother-in-law's family, her cousin's daughter Shari (nee Ontell) Lemonik has a connection to the Schapira family (see **Florence**).

My wife's uncle Phillip Wigdor was a member of the extensive Montreal-based Richler family, which spreads out in many directions and has numerous connections. Incidentally, the well-known writer Mordecai Richler was Phil Wigdor's second cousin. Upon studying the Richler tree, connections that I have found include the following, (I am not mentioning full details of the connections – in most cases it is through cousins of cousins – and I did not include the distant relations mentioned here on the list of interconnections):

- Moses **Bilsky**, via the Bronfman family.
- Leon and Doris Bronstein, via the Godel and Cape families. Their son Allen is married to Andrea (nee Grafstein), daughter of Murray and Diane Grafstein of Peterborough, and granddaughter of Louis Slavin (d. 1978) and Ida (d. 1998) who lived in Ottawa.
- David and Edith Friendly (see **Gosewich**) via their nephew Harold who is married to Lilly (nee Richler).
- Diana (nee Keeb) Malomet, married to Alvin (d. 2018), via the Bordan and Petrushka families. Alvin Malomet is also connected to the Richler's via the Deckelbaum family.
- Ricky Saslove (nee Hart), married to Martin, via the Hart family.
- Harvey and Karen Slipacoff (see **Saslove**), via the Brownstein family.
- Zipporah Rabinovitch / Dunsky / Shnay (see Goldmaker) via the Steinberg and Liverant families.
- The Drazin family via the Deitcher family (multiple connections). Myer Drazin (d. 1970), married to Mildred (d. 1999) served in many important communal positions, including parnas at Beth Shalom. Max Drazin (d. 1933) married to Michla (d. 1980), served as the president of Machzikei Hadas during his last years. The large Drazin family originated in Ottawa, but largely relocated to Montreal.
- Louis Rasminsky, via the Moldaver family. Louis Rasminsky (d. 1998), married to Lyla (nee Rotenberg, d. 1976), served as the 3rd governor of the Bank of Canada (see **Freedman**).

For connections to other entries from the Shmuel Cohen branch, see Dover, Gould, Halpern, Lithwick, Polowin, Slover, Smolkin, Swedlove.

For connections to other entries from the Yosef Cohen branch, see Betcherman, Bilsky, Bodnoff, Cantor, Diener, Dover, Fine, Florence, Krantzberg, Landau Leikin, Levitan, Pollock, Silver, Zelikovitz.

For mentions of other Cohen families, seemingly not related to this Cohen family, see Ages (Berezin branch), Cantor, Gershon (Tanner branch), and Kardish.

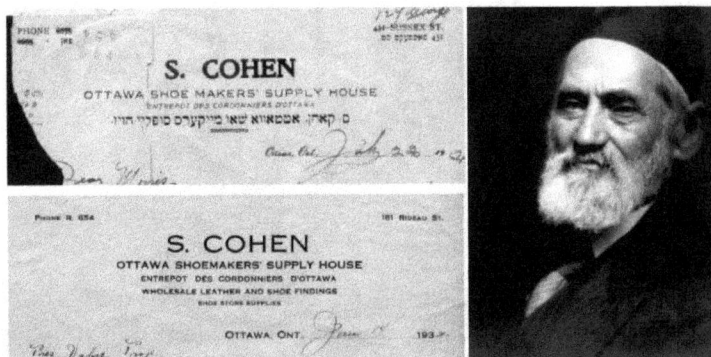

Samuel Cohen, 1945 (OJA 1-907-03)

Grete Cohen, the 1971 JNF Ottawa Negev Dinner honouree, surrounded by members of her family. Grete was the first woman to be honoured at a JNF Ottawa Negev Dinner. In 1988, she also became the first woman to receive the Gilbert Greenberg Distinguished Service Award – the highest honour bestowed by the Jewish community of Ottawa. (Ottawa Jewish Bulletin, May 22, 2018)

A different Cohen family. Cohen family portrait, ca. 1912. L-R: Doris Cohen (Torontow), Ida (nee Berezin) Cohen, Arthur Cohen (Fried), Lillian Cohen, Sarah Cohen, Samuel Cohen and baby Irving Cohen. This Cohen family is described under the Ages entry. Samuel Cohen was the founder of the Ottawa Kosher Meat Market. (OJA 1-573-0)

COPLAN

The Coplan family is descended from Hyman and Estelle Lillian (nee Pameth, d. 1914). Their children were:

- Naomi Ruben (d. 1958), married to David (d. 1944). Their daughter Sarah **Kizell** (d. 1973) was married to Archie (d. 1969) son of Moses Tuvia and Rachel Leah **Kizell**. Greta, daughter of Archie and Sarah **Kizell**, was married to Earl **Florence** (d. 1996).
- Solomon (d. 1932) married to Rebecca (nee Blachov, d. 1944). Their children were:
    - Irene **Kronick** (d. 2009) was married to Abraham Samuel (known as Wally, d. 1980). Their son Russel is married to Joan (nee Gould), daughter of Victor and Rachel (nee **Bodnoff**) **Gould**.
    - Louis (d. 1995) was married to Anne (nee Slonemsky, d. 1990) daughter of Israel (d. 1922) and Ethel (nee Horwitz, d. 1937) Slonemsky. Israel was the son of Solomon (d. 1916), and Sarah Slonemsky. Eli Slonemsky (d. 1946), a teacher at the Ottawa Hebrew school was a cousin of Israel. Eli was married to Reba (d. 1960). Their children were Dr. Abram Slone (d. 1971), known as the first Jewish dentist in Ottawa, married to Jean (nee Goldstick, d. 1984); Nathan Slone (d. 1963) married to Bessie (d. 1975); Leo Slone (d. 1991) married to Molly (nee **Gorelick**, d. 2001); David; Moses Slone (d. 1998); Rose Cooper (d. 1970) married to Sam (d. 1969); Esther Levin (d. 1996) married to Moe.

- Estelle Slone (d. 2001) was married to Sydney. Note that the Slone family is part of the Slonemsky family.
- Archibald d. 1937) married to Lena (nee **Pullan**, d. 1953), daughter of Henry Mayer **Pullan**. Their daughter Lillian (d. 2007) was married to Sol Gertsman (d. 1977).
- Zishcha Rubin (d. 1949), married to Jacob Moses (d. 1957). See **Rubin** for full details of this family, with connections to the Abelson, **Kardish**, **Kizell**, **Levitan**, **Mosion**, and Slover families.

For connections to other entries, see Bodnoff, Florence, Gould, Kardish, Kizell, Kronick, Levitan, Mosion, Pullan, Rubin, Slover.

CRAFT

The children of Hyman (d. 1947), and Anne (nee Michelin, d. 1967) are:

- Bess Freed (d. 1984), married to George (d. 1987), son of Michael and Rachel Freedlander. Their son Howard was married to Sandy, son of Samuel and Bertha (nee Wail) **Victor**.
- John (d. 2005), married to Sadie (nee Richman, d. 2010). Their children are:
  - Hinda Ritter (d. 2016), married to Sidney.
  - Elsa Swedko, married to Norman (d. 2016). Norman was the brother of Irving Swedko, married to Beverly (nee Allice, see **Bodnoff**); and Clair Berkovitch, married to Irving.
- Molly **Sadinsky** (d. 2004), married to Joseph (d. 1973), son of Hyman (d. 1923), and Rachel **Sadinsky** (d. 1977).
- Sadie (known as Stish, d. 1974), married to Herb Mason (d. 1971), son of Max and Fannie **Mosion**. Their son Morley Mason was married to Marcia **Kardish**, son of Louis and Mary (nee Udashkin) **Kardish**, and was then married to Cathy.

For connections to other entries see Bodnoff, Kardish, Sadinsky, Mosion, Victor.

CRATZBARG

See Kardish, Murray.

DIENER

The Diener family stems from Nathan Diener (d. 1995) of Grzymalow, Ukraine, and Reba (nee Luterman). Nathan was a Holocaust survivor who arrived in Ottawa after the war. Connections to Ottawa families are as follows:

- Two of Nathan and Reba's sons, Seymour and Joel, are married to two sisters, Aviva and Barbara (nee Singerman), the children of Sidney and Raye (nee Friberg) Singerman (both d. 2004). Jeff **Pleet** is married to Felice, another daughter of the Singermans. Raye Singerman is the sister of Molly Mintz, married to Jim Mintz, a first cousin of my father Issie **Landau**.

- Reba's brother Arnold Luterman (d. 1969) was married to Debbie (nee **Greenberg**), the daughter of Max and Fritzie **Greenberg**. Debbie later married Norm Ferkin.
- Nathan's mother, Freida (nee Diener) was a first cousin of Breina Tenenbaum (nee Diener, d. 1965). Max and Breina's son is Dr. Norman Tenenbaum, married to Judy (nee Friedberg). Nathan's mother was a first cousin of Goldie Silbert (nee Diener, d. 1996) married to Sam Silbert (d. 1999). Goldie Silbert was a sister to Breina (nee Diener) Tenenbaum. Debbie, daughter of Norman and Judy Tenenbaum, was married to Isaac Kurtz (d. 2015), of the large Toronto Kurtz family. Other families married into the Kurtz family include Elaine Kurtz (nee Lang, see **Bessin**), and Ari Sacher, grandson of Rev. Nachman and Molly Borenstein (see **Shreiber**).
- The extended Diener family is also cousins of the Ehrenkranz family. Although a US based family, my mother Edith **Landau**'s second cousin Eleanor Ehrenkranz is married into a branch of that family. The Ehrenkranz family also has a connection to the Epstein branch of the **Cohen** family.
- Reba Diener's second cousin is Maxine Lauterman Padolsky. Maxine's mother was Frieda Greenberg (d. 2006), a sister of Arnold Greenberg (d. 2017, see **Weiner**).
- Reba Diener's aunt Leah (nee Luterman, d. 2002) Agulnik was married to Dr. Maurice Agulnik (d. 1987).

For connections to other entries, see Agulnik, Bessin, Cohen, Greenberg, Landau, Pleet, Schreiber, Weiner.

DOCTOR

See Florence.

DOVER

The Dover family is descended from William (Zeev) Dover (d. 1909), and Sarah (nee Joseph). They originate from Yourbrick, Lithuania. Their children were Henry, John, David, and Emma.

Henry Dover branch

Henry Dover (d. 1933), was married to Edith (nee Feinberg, d. 1903), and then to Nettie (nee Feinberg, a sister of Edith, d. 1963). Children of Henry and Edith were:

- Esther **Kizell** (d. 1978) married to Jacob (d. 1960). Their son Bobby **Kizell** (d. 1969), married his first cousin Edith (nee Dover) **Kizell** (d. 2009). Their daughter Frances Waiser (nee **Kizell**, d. 2000), was married to William Waiser (d. 1984), whose children married into the **Flesher** and Dolansky families.
- Archibald Dover.
- Fanny Herman (d. 1961), married to Joseph (d. 1949).
- Jacob (d. 1970), married to Bertha (nee Saipe, d. 1978). Their daughter Edith married her first cousin Bobby **Kizell**. Their son Mark Dover (d. 2019) married

Nina (nee **Saslove**). Bertha is the sister of Roy Saipe (d. 1987), married to Helen (nee **Dworkin**, d. 2021 at the age of 106), the parents of Marcia and Geraldine. Geraldine was married to Sidney Goldstein. Bertha is also the sister of Sylvia (nee Sapie) **Molot**, married to Reuben.

Children of Henry and Nettie were:

- Thelma Ritt (d. 1975) married to Simon Ritt (d. 1945). Their children are Kenneth (d. 1985), and David (d. 2012).
- Rachel, married to Paul Horowitz.
- Dorothy **Koffman** (d. 1969), married to Moe (d. 1975).
- Ida Hollander (d. 1991), married to Hyman (d. 1951).
- Robert (d. 1970) married to Sasa (nee **Max**, d. 1987). Sasa's sister is Rose Goldberg (d. 1996), married to Samuel Goldberg (d. 1965). Samuel and Rose Goldberg are the parent of Evelyn (nee Goldberg) **Tradburks – Rivers**, first married to Irwin **Tradburks**, and then to Irving **Rivers**. Children of Robert and Sasa are:
    - Helen **Polowin**, married to Gerald, son of Benjamin and Bessie **Polowin**.
    - Mark, married to Anne (nee Abrahamson), daughter of Arnold and Bella Flora (nee **Veschsler**) Abrahamson.
- William (d. 1991), married to Nelly.
- Edythe Sourkes, married to Joseph
- Kenneth (d. 1920).

John Dover Branch

John Dover (d. 1942), married to Minnie (nee Cohen, d. 1914). Their children are:

- Dr. Harry (d. 1960), married to Calla (nee Lecker, d. 1930). Calla is a first cousin twice removed of Naomi (nee Ulpian) Levinson, the husband of Yitz Levinson. Yitz Levinson is the son of Cantor Pinchas and Sarah Levinson. Pinchas Levinson served as the long-time chazzan of Machzikei Hadas. Children of Harry and Calla Dover are:
    - Mina Dover **Cohen** (d. 2010), married to Morris **Cohen** (d. 1981). Their son Eric (d. 2020) was married to Janet (nee Ginsburg, see **Smolkin**).
    - Martin (d. 2007), married to Eleanor (nee Zabitsky). Their niece Sharon Zabitsky is married to Martin Goldberg, a nephew of my mother Edith **Landau** (nee Goldberg), and Issie.
    - Joy Fireman (d. 2003).
- Harriet (Hattie) Nathanson (d. 1984), married to Joseph. Joseph Nathanson was the son of Benjamin Nathanson and Fanny (nee Bach, d. 1943). Benjamin died very young, and Fanny married Reverend Jacob **Mirsky** (d. 1942).
- David Dover (d. 1986), married to Anne (nee **Torontow**, d. 1999). Their children are:
    - Myra Evans.

- Jay (d. 2017), married to Betty (d. 2018). Their son John is married to Cheryl (nee Zides) son of Milton and Lorraine (nee Levine) Zides (see **Glustein**).
- Joseph Dover (d. 1983).
- Sylvia Loeb Rosenthal married to Charles.
- Myer Dover (d. 1985) married to Pauline.
- John C. Dover.

David Dover Branch

David Dover (d. 1924), was married to Libbie (nee Herman, d. 1949). There children are:

- Cornelius Conn Dover (d. 1973), married to Irene.
- Harry Dover (d. 1939), married to Pearl (nee Lerner).
- William Dover.
- P. Dover.
- Sarah Dover (d. 1948).
- Gertrude Steinberg (d. 2009), married to Jack (d. 1985).
- Ruth Levine (d. 2010), married to Harry (d. 2012).
- Rae Goodman, married to Robert Goodman.
- Minnie Cohen, married to Saul. Saul was the son of Kasriel and Reva **Cohen**.

Emma Spector branch

Emma Spector was married to Abraham (d. 1918). Their children were Sarah Michael, married to Solomon, Annie, Rosa, Dora, Leah, Bess, Mortimer, William.

For connections to other entries, see Cohen, Dworkin, Flesher, Glustein, Kizell, Koffman, Landau, Mirsky, Molot, Polowin, Rivers, Saslove, Smolkin, Torontow, Tradburks, Vechsler.

Ottawa's First Jewish Baby, Doctor, and Canada's First Jewish Coroner –
Dr. Harry Dover (photo from 1914). (OJA 1-695)

DWORKIN

The Dworkin family descends from Jacob (d. 1908) the son of Zalmon, and Esther (nee Minkoff, d. 1939). Their children were:

- Hyman (d. 1952), married to Annie (nee Progosh, d. 1963), daughter of Samuel and Sarah (nee Freedman, d. 1943) Progosh. Annie's siblings were: Rose **Vechsler** married to Richard, and Louis (d. 1972), married to Sarah (d. 1974). (See **Ellenberg** and **Baylin** for further connections).
- Samuel (d. 1915), married to Rebecca Reva (nee **Smolkin**, d. 1976), daughter of Abraham and Sima (nee Levine) **Smolkin**. Rebecca Reva later married Jack Boro (d. 1948).
- Max (d. 1979), married to Minnie (nee **Petegorsky**, d. 1973), daughter of Mordechai Eliezer and Esther (nee Fertig) **Petegorsky**. Children of Max and Minnie were:
  - o Ann Silver (d. 1984), married to Max.
  - o Zelda **Roodman** (d. 1999), married to Herman (d. 2001), son of Louis and Frieda **Roodman**. Their daughter Joy **Karp** is married to Richard, son of Ben and Etta (nee **Shulman**) Karp.
  - o David, married to Bonnie.
- Samuel Benjamin (d. 1994), married to Ethyl (nee Goldman, d. 1973).
- Ida Fonberg (d. 1973), married to Alex (d. 1976).
- Tzipa Hinda.
- Joseph (d. 1959), married to Rae (nee Banks, d. 1984).

Jacob's brother was Abraham Dworkin (d. 1951), married to Deborah (nee Azmier, d. 1922). Their children were:

- Ben (d. 1994).
- Fay Brill (d. 2008), married to Harry (d. 2002).
- Alex (d. 2004).
- Helen Saipe (d. 1921 at the age of 106), married to Roy (d. 1987), son of Mark and Fanny (nee Sogman), and brother of Bertha **Dover**, married to Jacob.
- Clara Schwartz (d. 2007), married to Maurice.
- Neil
- Sarah

For connections to other entries, see Baylin, Dover, Ellenberg, Karp, Petegorsky, Roodman, Shulman, Smolkin, Vexler.

EDELSON

See Ballon branch of Saslove.

ELLENBERG

The Ellenberg family descends from Moses (d. 1950), and Rachel Leah (d. 1927). Their son was Israel (d. 1975), married to Dora (nee Dutnoff (d. 1975). Dora's siblings were Gus Dutnoff and Samuel Danoff (see **Glustein**). Children of Israel and Dora are:

- Harry (d. 1996), married to Seyre (nee Segall, d. 2003).
- Joseph (d. 2013).
- Marion **Vexler**, married to Myer (d. 2008), son of Richard (d. 1969), and Rose (nee Progosh) **Vexler**.
- Leah Chodikoff (known as Lee, d. 2023), married to Donald (d. 2007), son of Anne (nee **Freedman**) and Israel Chodikoff.
- Abraham, married to Ida.
- Faye Davis, married to Lou.
- Sadie Labovitch (d. 1981), married to Frank (d. 1994), son of Motel and Sirca (nee **Flesher**) Labovitch.
- Ann Yankoo (d. 1998), married to Joseph (d. 1992). Their son Melvyn is married to Tziona, daughter of Harry and Sarah (nee Engel, d. 2014) Greenberg. Harry Greenberg's brother is Fred, married to Gertrude (nee Marcus, see **Marcovitch**).

For connections to other entries, see Flesher, Freedman, Glustein, Marcovitch, Vechsler.

Portrait of Mr. & Mrs. Ellenberg & Family in Ottawa, 1940s. (OJA 1-299)

EPSTEIN

See Cohen.

Solomon and Sadie Epstein (my wife Tzippy's great-grandparents).
(My own private collection, and OJA 1-209)

The Epstein clan gathered at the wedding of Jerrold Landau and Tzipora Rachlin, July 1, 1992. Five of the nine Epstein siblings, children of Solomon and Sadie Epstein, all Ottawa natives, are present.

On extreme left: Harry and Fay Epstein. Fifth from left, standing: Gabe Epstein. On extreme right, standing: Sam and Eva Epstein. Third from right, Hynda Weihl (her husband Willy Weihl is sitting on extreme left). Third from left, seated: Joe and Helen Emerson. No longer alive at the time: Mike Emerson, and Tzippy's grandmother Fanny Rachlin. Alive at the time but not present at our wedding: Goldie Sacksner and Bunny Fink. (from my wedding album)

FEINSTEIN

The Feinstein family stems from Benjamin (d.2001), and Freda (nee Dickstein, d. 1986). Their four children are:

- Miriam Levitin, married to Nathan (Nat, d. 1995). Nat was the son of Meyer (d. 1944), and Bertha (d. 1948). His brothers include Joseph (d. 1995) and Morris (d. 1982).

- Ruth **Aaron**, married to Irving (d. 2023), son of David and Sarah (nee Steinman) **Aaron**. Their son Leslie is connected by marriage to the Flatt family (see **Murray**).
- Pearl Moskovic (d. 2010), married to David.
- Abraham (d.2021), married to Beverly (nee Kavanat), the daughter of Esau (d. 1998), and Rose (nee Gossack, d. 2001).

For connections to other entries, see Aaron, Murray.

Nathan (Nat) Levitin [son-in-law of Benjamin and Freda Feinstein] enlisted in the air force on July 1, 1940. Eventually he became a navigator, and later a Squadron Leader, and was assigned patrol duty over the Atlantic Coast. Nathan Levitin received the Distinguished Flying Cross for exemplary service on May 23, 1945. The photo of him feeding pigeons in the streets is most likely taken in Trafalgar in the 1940s.
(OJA 1-391-06)

At his 90th birthday celebration, David Moskovic [son-in-law of Benjamin and Freda Feinstein] is surrounded by his children Michael, Bev Alberga, and Lawrence. Born in Czechoslovakia, David is a survivor of Auschwitz (photo from Ottawa Citizen, Stephen Thorne)

FELLER

The Feller family is descended from Joseph Feller (b. 1850), and his two wives, Chana (nee Berkovici, d. approx. 1890) and Anna (nee Salzburg, d. 1921)

Children of Joseph and Chana are:

- Simon (d. 1936) married to Rosa (nee Nathanson).
- Sophie Handel (d. 1947), married to Samuel. Their son Jack (d. 1993) was married to Beatrice (d. 2002).
- Sol (d. 1973) married to Bertha (nee Haimovitch, d. 1955).
- Rosa Kominker (did not immigrate to Canada).
- Max (d. 1956), married to Rebecca (nee Kaufman, d. 1960).
- Rae Fine (d. 1979) married to Leon (d. 1982). Leon Fine is not related to the large Fine clan of Ottawa. Leon Fine had a cousin Paul Fript in Connecticut, whose daughters are Annice (d. 1995), married to Dr. Sydney **Kronick**; and Ruth **Leikin** (d. 1999), married to Julius (d. 1985), the son of Louis **Leikin**. Rae and Leon' children were:
  - Anne **Mirsky** (d. 2003) married to Norman (d. 1986). Their son Stephan is married to Millie (nee **Bilsky**).
  - Sarah **Shaffer** (d. 2012), married to Milton (d. 2015). Their daughter Marilyn is married to Dan **Kimmel**.
- William (d. 1942) married to Eva (nee Rosen, d. 1958). Their children are:
  - Joseph (d. 2015), married to Betty (nee Goldman, d. 2010). Joe Feller was a leader in the fashion industry in Ottawa and beyond. Betty was the daughter of Walter Goldman (d. 1921), and Malka (nee Finerman, d. 1949). Betty's sisters who lived in Ottawa were Sonia **Viner** (d. 2003) married to Arthur (d. 1997); Edith Cherun (d. 1989), married to Alexander (d. 1988).

Alexander and Edith's son Walter is married to Carole (nee Caplan), daughter of Samuel (d. 1983) and Marcia (nee Singer, d. 2003), and granddaughter of Ottawa pioneer Caspar Caplan (d. 1943) and Dora (nee Roston, d. 1969). The Caplan family were the founders and owners of Caplan's department store.

o Henry (Hank, d. 2001), married to Gertrude (nee **Victor**, d. 1999), their son Robert is married to Bernice (nee **Lieff**), daughter of Samuel (d. 1969), and Libby (nee **Kardish**). Bernice Feller married to Bobbie is to be differentiated from their aunt Bernice Feller, mentioned below.

o Sally (d. 1957).

o Edward (d. 1991), married to Bernice (nee **Bodnoff**, d. 1979), daughter of Sadie and Samuel **Bodnoff**.

Children of Joseph and Anna are:

- Moe (d. 1982), married to Germaine (nee Zittrer). Their daughter Annette was first married to Lou Lesonsky (d. 1976), and then to Val **Lithwick** (d. 2004).
- Gertrude (d. 1974).
- Frances (d. 1995).

For connections to other entries, see Bilsky, Bodnoff, Kardish, Kimmel, Kronick, Leikin, Lieff, Lithwick, Mirsky, Shaffer, Victor, Viner.

Joe and Betty Feller (Ottawa Citizen:
https://ottawacitizen.com/news/local-news/egan-joe-feller-a-top-clothier-when-clothes-mattered)

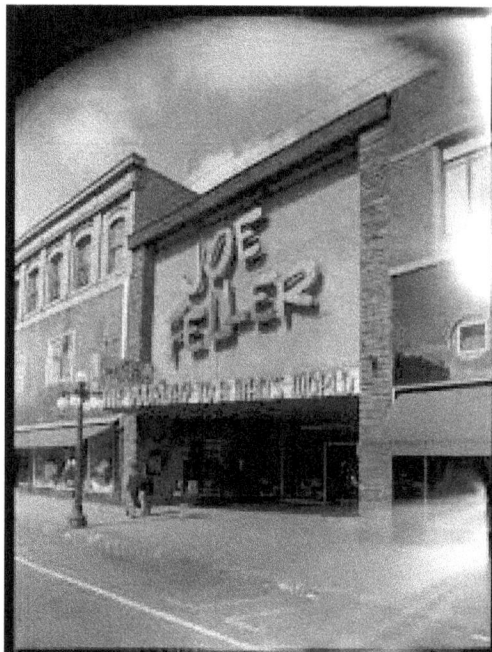

Joe Feller's clothing store, 139 Rideau St.
(Ottawa Jewish Archives via City of Ottawa Archives CA032944)

FINE

The Fine family is descended from Abraham Israel Joseph Fine (d. 1951), and Ada Tseepa (d. 1959). They are known as the proprietors of Fine's Flowers. Their children who lived in Ottawa were:

- Sidney (d. 1967) married to Rose (nee **Levitan** d. 2006), daughter of Maurice and Rachel **Levitan**.
- Natal (d. 1974), married to Mollie (nee **Cherm**, d. 2012), daughter of Harry and Tillie (nee **Viner**) Cherm. Their son Jeffrey is married to Julie, daughter of Kurt and Joan Orlik.
- Hyman (Harry, d. 1988), married in turn to: a) Rachel Lesha (nee **Polowin**, d. 1936) daughter of Oscar and Sonia **Polowin**; b) Eva (nee **Slover**, d. 1977), daughter of Abraham Chaim and Malca **Slover**; c) Anna Gertler Berger Fine (d. 1983).   Harry and Rachel Lesha's children are:
  - Reuben (d. 2014). Reuben's former wife was Phyllis (nee Ross), who later married Laz Newman (d. 2022), son of Pinkas (d. 1987) and Yehudit (nee Altman, d. 1970) Newman, and sister of Helene Zaret (see **Gorelick**). Phyllis is the daughter of Jack Ross (d. 1983), and Esther (nee Kooperstock, d. 2001). Phyllis' sister is Hennie Ross **Palmer**, who was originally married to Philip **Gosewich**, and later married to Morris **Palmer**. Reuben and Phyllis' daughter Lori was first married to Arthur **Loeb**, son of David and Joyce **Loeb**, and then to Mendy **Taller**, son of Samuel and Bessie (nee **Cantor**) **Taller**.
  - David (d, 1992), married to Rose (nee Smurlick, d. 1993). Their children are:

- Raymond, was married to Maxine (nee Brown, d. 2003).
- Paula Smith, married to Robert, son of Kalman and Sylvia (nee **Gould**) Smith.
- Peter, was married to Barbara (nee Hymes), daughter of Hyman (d. 2012) and Dorothy Hymes. Barbara is currently married to Steven **Levinson**, son of Jacie and Sandra **Levinson**.
- Joan, married to David, son of Charles and Mary (nee **Saslove**) Slipacoff.
  - Louis (d. 2013), married to Barbara (nee Goldenberg), daughter of Harry and Annie (nee **Pollock**) Goldenberg.
  - Charles.
  - Sara married to Hugh Shabsove (d. 2009).

Leon Fine (see Feller), is not connected to this Fine family.

For connections to other entries, see Cantor, Cherm, Gorelick, Gosewich, Gould, Levinson, Levitan, Loeb, Palmer, Pollock, Polowin, Saslove, Slover, Taller, Viner.

FLESHER

The Flesher family is descended from Fattal and Chia Zelda (d. 1912, buried in Ottawa) Flesher. Their children were:

- Isaac Berl, married to Gita. Their children were:
  - Mary **Lesh** (d. 1982), married to Samuel (d. 1961), son of Yehuda and Frieda **Lesh**. Their children were:
    - Frieda **Levitan** (d. 2009), married to Harry, son of Maurice and Rachel **Levitan**.
    - Norman (d. 2015) was married to Isabel (nee **Kimmel**), daughter of Arthur and Sarah (nee **Hanser**) **Kimmel**.
  - David (d. 1974).
  - Frank (d. 1980) married to Leah (d. 1981).
  - Hymie married to Becky (nee Rosenberg, d. 1991).
- Joseph (d. 1955), married to Rachel (nee Pont, d. 1973). Children were:
  - Moses (d. 1976), married to Anne (nee Carlofsky, d. 1999), daughter of David (d. 1939) and Hannah (d. 1950) Carlofsky. Other children of David and Hannah Carlofsky were: Abe (d. 2004), Freda (d. 1984), Sol (d. 2002), Rose Breakstone (d. 1970) – a poet and short story writer. The Carlofsky family were cousins of Jennie (nee Morris d. 2003), married to Harry Hecht (d. 1990). Harry Hecht served as Gabbai of Machzikei Hadas for many years.
  - Ben (d. 1987) married to Rose (nee Sinclair, d. 2008), daughter of Frank (d. 1945) and Annie (d. 1956) Sinclair, and the sister of Marjorie (d. 2022), married to Ben Achbar (d. 2018), son of Morris Mendelson and Rose (nee **Swedlove**) Achbar. Ben and Rose's son Stanley is married to Cynthia, daughter of Bill and Frances (nee **Kizell**) Waiser.
  - Belle **Slover** (d. 1991), married to Dave (d. 1977).
  - Ida.
  - Gordon (d. 1993).

- Meyer (d. 1960), married to Kayla (d. 1948). Children were:
  - Bessie Frumkin (d. 1991) married to Moe (d. 1995).
  - Hilda **Sadinsky** (d. 1939), married to Nathan (d. 1985), son of Nesanel **Sadinsky** (d. 1937). Their daughter is Eileen Tanner, who was married to Lionel (d. 2002 see **Gershon**).
  - Frank married to Anne.
  - Israel Bernard (d. 1986) married to Jessi Ruth (nee LaBreton).
- Sirca (Sarah) Labovitch (d. 1941), married to Motel Labovitch. Their children were:
  - Ida Flesher (d. 1974) was married to her first cousin Izzy Flesher.
  - Clara Hassan (d. 1991).
  - Frank Labovitch (d. 1994) married to Sadie (nee **Ellenberg**, d. 1981), daughter of Israel and Dora **Ellenberg**.
  - Edith Lorwill.
- Dora Cantor (d. 1974), married to Abe. Children are:
  - Hymie (d. 1912).
  - Eva Weiner (d. 1990), married to Irwin.
  - Helen Lavitt, married to Jack.
- Gershon married to Manya. Children are:
  - Moishe.
  - Freda Pont, married to Sam.
- Israel (d. 1960), married to Eta (d. 1944). Their children were:
  - Isadore (known as Izzy, d. 1996) was married to his first cousin Ida (nee Labovitch, d. 1974). Izzy's Hebrew name was Yitzchak, and his father was Yisrael. Izzy and Eta's son Jack (d. 2004) was the father of Ian Flesher, who is married to Beth (nee **Kerzner**), daughter of Eddie and Judie (d. 2014) **Kerzner**. Izzy married Eve (nee **Baylin**, d. 2006), after Eta died. Eve's first marriage was to Saul **Torontow** (d. 1974).
  - Frank (d. 1989), married to Muriel (nee **Petigorsky**, d. 1989), daughter of Tevya and Elizabeth **Petigorsky**.
  - Ida (d. 1979).
  - Faye Smith (d. 2002), married to Morris **Smith** (d. 1987), son of Louis and Annie **Smith**, and brother of the famed Ottawa caterer and restaurateur Jack **Smith**.

For connections to other entries, see Baylin, Ellenberg, Gershon, Hanser, Kerzner, Kimmel, Kizell, Lesh, Levitan, Petigorsky, Sadinsky, Slover, Smith, Swedlove, Torontow.

FLORENCE

Abraham Lazarus Florence (d. 1936) and Lena (nee **Pullan**, d. 1925), daughter of Bernard and Malka **Pullan**, were the parents of:

- Frank (d. 1995).
- Harold (d. 1952).
- Jack.
- Esther Smith (d. 1987).
- Rose Doctor (d. 1987), married to Moses (d. 1934), son of Rabbi Louis Doctor (d. 1934) and Dena Chaya Doctor (d. 1925), natives of Vilna. Other children of Rabbi

Louis and Dena Chaya Doctor were David (d. 1976), married to Betty (d. 1989); Mindel, married to Leon **Lieff**, son of Avraham Chayim Lifschitz; Benjamin; Abraham; Samuel; Philip; Hyman.

- Molly **Betcherman** (d. 1982), married to Alexander (d. 1977), son of Fishel and Brocha (nee Addelman) **Betcherman**.
- Freda (d. 1979), married to Jules, son of Bernard and Rebecca (nee Rhinestein) Smith.

Another branch of the Florence family with Ottawa connections, cousins of the aforementioned branch, descends from Louis and Jennie Florence of Peterborough. Their children include:

- Earl (d. 1996), married to Greta (nee **Kizell**, d. 2016), daughter of Archie and Sarah (nee Ruben, of the **Coplan** family) **Kizell**.
- Max, married to Rochelle (nee Schapira), the daughter of Solomon (d. 1958), and Regina (nee Fliegelman, d. 1992) Schapira. Solomon and Regina were also the parents of Rosalie (d. 2016), who was married to her first cousin Dr. Edward Shapiro (d. 2001). Edward was the son of Rabbi Hersh Leib Shapiro (d. 1966), a brother of Solomon Schapira. Another brother of Rochelle and Rosalie was Henry Schapira (d. 1995), married to Judy (nee Schoen). Max Florence was a dentist in Ottawa where he founded the fluoridation program. He left for Israel in 1969. He and his family subsequently settled in Toronto in the late 1970s.

A sister of Solomon Schapira and Rabbi Hersh Leib Shapira was Pesil Kroch, married to Motke Kroch. Their son Jack Kroch worked for Turpin Pontiac Buick for any years. Another brother was Victor Nathanson, who took on the maiden name of his mother. He was married to Rebecca Nathanson (nee Lemonik), who is a second cousin twice removed of Zack Lemonik of Teaneck, NJ, married to my wife's second cousin Shari (nee Ontell, see **Cohen**).

For connections to other entries, see Betcherman, Cohen, Coplan, Kizell, Lieff, Pullan.

Lena Florence (Photo from the 1890s). (OJA 1-604-01)

FREEDMAN

The Freedman family descends from Jacob (d. 1957), and Leah (nee Phillips, d. 1973) Freedman of Zhitomir, Ukraine. Jacob Freedman was a nephew of Naphtali Hertz and Esther Baila (nee Lerner) **Lithwick**. Children of Jacob and Leah were:

- Michael (d. 1978), married to Anna (nee Smith, d. 1943). Their children were:
  - Jarvis (d. 1985) married to Riva (nee **Schreiber**) daughter of Rev. Samuel and Leah (nee Schiff) **Schreiber**. After Jarvis' death, Riva married David Rotenberg, who served as member of provincial parliament in North York from 1977-1985. David Rotenberg is a first cousin of Lyla Rasminsky (d. 1976), married to Louis Rasminsky (d. 1988), who served as the third governor of the Bank of Canada. Children of Riva and Jarvis are:
    - Jacob, married to Esther (nee Koreen), daughter of Dr. Joseph and Esther (nee **Greenberg**) Koreen.
    - Jonathan Ben-Choreen, married to Aviva. Jonathan is very active in many Jewish organizations in Ottawa, and recipient of the Gilbert Greenberg Community Service Award.
    - Roseann, originally married to Harry Prizant, and then married to Sydney Goldstein.
  - Lawrence (d. 2006), married to Zelda (nee Achbar), daughter of Arie Louis and Rose (nee **Swedlove**) Achbar.
- Anne Chodikoff (d. 1931), married to Israel Chodikoff (d. 1963. Their children were:
  - Marvin (d. 1965), married to Beverly (nee **Petigorsky**), daughter of Leon and Beckie (nee Wolinsky) **Petigorsky**.
  - Donald (d. 2007), married to Leah (nee **Ellenberg**), daughter of Israel and Dora **Ellenberg**. Donald Chodikoff was the founder of Toy World.
- Jennie Glickman (d. 1939), married to Dr. Abraham (d. 1951). Their children were:
  - Frances (d. 1922).
  - Joyce **Loeb** (d. 1995), married to David (d. 2016), son of Moses and Rose **Loeb**.
  - Elsa (d. 2013).

For connections to other entries, see Ellenberg, Greenberg, Lithwick, Loeb, Petigorsky, Schreiber, Swedlove.

Leah, Jacob and Anne Freedman, circa 1910.
(OJA 73-103)

FREIMAN

See Bilsky.

Archibald Jacob Freiman and Lillian Freiman with their granddaughter Betsy
Alexandor, 1940.
Photographer: Hugo Levendel (OJA 1-131)

Portrait of Lillian Freiman, 1923 (OJA 1-005)

Freiman's Department Store (from Ottawa Jewish Archives)

FROMAN

The Froman family stems from Simeon (d. 1922), and Tobya Froman. Their children were:

- Samuel (d. 1968), married to Sadie (nee Weiss, d. 1973).   Their children are:
  - Gordon (d. 2004), married to Helen.
  - Harry (d. 2018), married to Esther (nee **Betcherman**), daughter of Isaac and Yetta **Betcherman**. Their children are:
    - Risa **Taylor**, married to Brent, son of Irving and Ethel (nee **Greenberg**) **Taylor**.
    - Adam, married to Sharin.
    - Ian, married to Jaclyn.
  - Sidney.
  - Benjamin, married to Ida.
  - Lillian Reiter, married to Samuel.
  - Edith Drazen, married to Larry.
- Sarah Marcus (d. 1986), married to Nathan Marcus (d. 1982), son of Abraham and Freida (nee Haimovici) **Marcovitch**. Their children are:
  - Lillian
  - Gertrude Greenberg, married to Fred. Their daughter Andrea Zagerman is married to John, son of Herbert and Corinne (nee Ross), Zagerman (see **Krantzberg**).
- Esther Cowan (d. 1964), married to Abraham (d. 1951). Their children are:
  - Lawrence (d. 2000), married to Adelaide (nee **Sadinsky**, d. 2014), daughter of Louis and Rose **Sadinsky**.
  - Lillian Cobrin, married to Saul.
  - Marjorie.
  - Gertrude.
  - Henrietta (d. 1938).

For connections to other entries, see Betcherman, Greenberg, Krantzberg, Marcovitch, Sadinsky, Taylor.

GANDALL / GANDELMAN

Hyman (d. 1974), and Celia (nee Schneider d. 1966) Gandall are the parents of Pauline Bodnoff, and Stella **Torontow** (d. 2020). Celia was the sister of Hyman Schnider (d. 1994, married to Sally, d. 2009), and Ettie Landau (d. 1997). Parents of Celia, Hyman, and Ettie were William (d. 1953), and Anna (d. 1954) Schnider.

Ettie (nee Schnider) **Landau** was married to Issie **Landau** (d. 1984). Ettie and Issie were my great aunt and uncle (distinct from my father, Issie **Landau**). They lived in Ottawa for much of their lives, and moved to Montreal in their old age. Their children are Jessie Goldstein and Rose Manis.

Hyman Gandall's brother was Avrom (Abe) Gandelman, married to Molka. Their daughter was Libby **Steinberg** (d. 1997), who was married to Jack **Steinberg** (d. 1996). Molka Gandelman (nee Lerner) had a sister Rachel Gutteit (d. 1967), who was married to Isaac Gutteit. Rachel and Isaac Gutteit lived in Argentina. Their daughter was Betty **Mosion**.

Through this family, we can see a string of cousins of cousins – all of whom resided in Ottawa. Jim Mintz is a first cousin of my father Issie **Landau**, who was a first cousin of Jessie Goldstein, who is a first cousin of Pauline **Bodnoff**, who is a first cousin of Libby **Steinberg**, who was a first cousin of Betty **Mosion**. This string of cousins is a prime example of the interconnectedness of Ottawa based Jewish families.

For connections to other entries, see Bodnoff, Gandall, Landau, Mosion, Steinberg, Torontow.

GENCHER

The Gencher family is descended from Mayer Dov and Tsipora Gencher. Their children were:

- Shaindel (Sarah) **Greenberg**, married to Isaac (d. 1927). They are the ancestors of the larger branch of one of the two major **Greenberg** clans in Ottawa. See full details under **Greenberg** for connections to the Soloway, **Levitan**, **Shabinsky**, **Shinder**, and **Schreiber** families. Their son Lazar **Greenberg** is married to his first cousin Esther (nee Gencher, d. 1954).
- Binyomin (d. 1931), married to Aidel Bryna (d. 1912). Their children were:
  - Esther (d. 1954), married to her first cousin Lazar **Greenberg** (d. 1933);
  - Coleman (d. 1952).
- Jacob Joseph Gencher (d. 1937), married to Pessie (nee Soloway, d. 1951). Pessie is a sister of Louis Soloway, and the aunt of Harry Soloway, whose wife Rachel was the daughter of the aforementioned Lazar **Greenberg** and Esther (Gencher) **Greenberg**. Thus, there are multiple connections between the Gencher, **Greenberg**, and Soloway families. The children of Jacob Joseph and Pessie were:
  - Aaron (Harry d. 1976), married to Anne (nee Weiner, d. 1982). Anne is not related to the Ottawa Weiner family. Their children are
    - Irving (d. 2011), married to Merle.
    - Robert (d. 2014), married to Leah (nee Engel), sister of Abraham (d. 2002) and Cynthia (d.20120 Engel.
    - Dr. Moses Gencher (d. 2006).
    - Rita Mortimer, married to Sydney.
    - Abe, married to Anne.
    - Jean.
  - Eva **Pollock** Gertler (d. 2006), married to Gordon **Pollock** (d. 1954), son of Pinchas and Rivka **Pollock**. After Gordon's death, Eva married Cantor Hyman Gertler (d. 1975), who served as the cantor of Beth Shalom Synagogue. Their children were:
    - Thelma (Tami) Berezin (d. 2011), married to Robert (d. 2002).
    - Bernard Pollock, married to Anita.
  - Rivka **Pollock**, married to Pinchas Polyak (d. 1906). This family also connects to the **Taylor** family, and has a double connection to the Gencher family, as their son Gordon married his first cousin Eva (nee Gencher).

Nathan **Greenberg**, married to Sarah, was also a **Pollock**. He was adopted by his aunt and uncle Isaac and Sarah (Shaindel) **Greenberg**, and took on the **Greenberg** name. See the **Pollock** for full details.

For connections to other entries, see Greenberg, Levitan, Pollock, Shabinsky, Shinder, Schreiber, Soloway, Taylor.

GENNIS

The Gennis family is descended from Elimelech Yitzchak and Leah (nee Dragushan) Gennis. Their children were:

- Bertha **Greenberg** (d. 1965), married to Morris (d. 1981). See the **Greenberg** for a full description of their family, including their connections to the **Bodnoff**, **Levinson**, Rose, **Saslove** and **Shinder** families.
- Isaac (d. 1981), married to Fanny (d. 1947). Their children are:
  - Rose Rosen (d. 2011), married to Louis (d. 1985).
  - Gertrude, married to Joe Jacobson.
  - Max (d. 1977) married to Hilda (nee **Aaron**, d. 1991), the daughter of David and Sarah (nee Steinman) **Aaron**. Their children are:
    - Richard, married to Sharron (nee Strolovitch), daughter of Louis and Florence (nee Marcus, see **Marcovitch**) Strolovitch.
    - Philip, married to Sandy.
    - Michael.
- Joseph (d. 1968), married to Fanny (d. 1982).
- Pearl (d. 1966), married to Sam **Koffman**. Their children were:
  - Doris (d. 2008).
  - Barry (d. 2006) married to Fay (nee Yanover, d. 2022). Their daughter Sandra was married to Jimmy Zagon (d. 2002), the son of Bertram and Beatrice (nee **Shaffer**) Zagon. Their daughter Sharon (d. 1993) was married to Jeff Arron, son of Larry and Yetta (nee **Weinstein**) Arron.
  - Sammy (d. 1985), married to Clara (nee **Pleet**, d. 1973). Sammy's second wife was Mulya Rosen. Sammy was indeed the son of Sam, in Hebrew: Shmuel ben Shlomo.
  - Harry (d. 2006), married to Edith (nee **Torontow**, d. 2006), daughter of Samuel and Annie **Torontow**.
  - Jack (d. 1981) married to Beck (nee **Tradburks**, d. 1999), daughter of Osias and Minnie **Tradburks**.
  - Milton (d. 1992), married to Beatrice (nee **Bordelay**, d. 2001), daughter of Meyer and Zelda **Bordelay**. Their daughter Zena is married to David **Lieff**, son of Samuel and Libby (nee **Kardish**) **Lieff**.
  - Moses (Moe, d. 1975), married to Dorothy (nee **Dover**, d. 1969) daughter of Henry and Nettie **Dover**.
  - Max (Musty, d. 1975), married to Jessie (d. 1992).
  - Anne Bloom (d. 2002), married to Alfred (d. 2002).
  - Joseph (d. 1999), married to Margaret (nee Peddlar, d. 2017).

For connections to other entries, see Aaron, Bodnoff, Bordelay, Dover, Greenberg, Kardish, Levinson, Lieff, Marcovitch, Pleet, Saslove, Shaffer, Shinder, Torontow, Tradburks, Weinstein.

Gennis, Greenberg, Koffman family reunion, 1988. (From Philip Gennis)

GERSHON

The Gershon family is descended from Yaakov, of Kobryn, Ukraine. The original family name was Gerszengauz. His children were:

- David (d. 1972), married to Tilly (nee Herszman, d. 1994). Their children were:
  - Maureen Newton (d. 2005), married to Dennis (d. 1992), brother of Jean **Lichtenstein**, and then to Israel **Shinder** (d. 2014).
  - Sam (d. 2009), married to Roslyn (nee Wilko), daughter of Elias and Clara (nee Baker, see **Glustein**).
  - Sydney.
- Erwin (d. 1991), married to Minnie (nee Appel, d. 1974). Minnie was the sister of Rose **Ages**, married to Joseph; and Rhea Victor, married to Samuel (see **Rivers**).
- Fanny Tanner (d. 1981), married to Saul (d. 1976) Tanner (originally Tenenbaum), son of Shlomo Gershon Tenenbaum. Saul Tanner's brothers were Samuel (d. 1987), married to Claire (d. 1987); and Charles (d. 1979), married to Lillian (d. 1974). Charles and Lillian's son Lionel Tanner (d. 2002) was married to Eileen (nee **Sadinsky**), daughter of Nathan and Hilda (nee **Flesher**) **Sadinsky**. Shlomo Gershon Tenenbaum is the brother of the grandfather of Hyman **Reichstein**. Children of Saul and Fanny Tanner were:
  - Minerva Cohen (d. 2015), married to Louis (d. 1986), son of Moses and Sophie (nee Weinberg, d. 1958) Cohen. Moses and Sophie's other children were Dr. Goodman (d. 1990), married to Rita (d. 1985); David (d. 2000), married to Queenie (d. 1989); Ethel Goodman, married to Eddie; Sam, married to Sylvia; Rose (d. 1989). Children of Louis and Minerva Cohen are: Stephen married to Gina; Linda Weiner married to Stephen.
  - Morton (d. 2005), married to Sheila (nee Goodman, d. 2006).

For connections to other entries, see Ages, Flesher, Glustein, Lichtenstein, Reichstein, Rivers, Sadinsky, Shinder.

GLUBE

See Lithwick.

GLUSTEIN

The Glustein family descends from Yaakov Glustein, son of Moishe Glustein of Uman, Ukraine. Yaakov died in a pogrom.

Yaakov's son Avrum and his wife Chaya (nee Warshavsky) Glustein, are the parents of a Montreal based Glustein family. Their son Jacob (d. 1988), was married to Rachel (Baron Brissman). Children of Jacob and Rachel are:
- Shirley Cement (d. 2021), married to Rabbi Jacob (Yechiel) Cement (d. 1988), who served as Chazzan Sheini, Torah Reader, and Ritual Director of Beth Shalom Synagogue for many decades. Rabbi Cement was a Romanian Holocaust survivor. After Rabbi Cement's death, Shirley married Meshullam Dear (d. 2018).
- Sophie Pernikoff, married to Rabbi Mayer Pernikoff (d. 1997), a rabbi in Pennsylvania, whose brother Aaron Pernikoff was married to Frieda (nee Schecter), a great-niece of Rochel Bluma (nee Szeroszewsky) and Benjamin **Silver**. The Pernikoff family is also connected through a mutual cousin to Eliyahu Haber, married to Hava (nee Gross), daughter of Tzvi and the late Pearl Gross, and granddaughter of Cantor David (D. 2022) and Mrs. Gita (d. 2017) Aptowitzer. Cantor Aptowitzer served as the longtime chazzan of Agudath Israel as well as a community mohel for many decades. Cantor Aptowitzer's great-niece Aviva (nee Aptowitzer) Rotenberg is married to David, son of Chuck Rotenberg. Aviva's brother is Adam, married to Elana (nee Setton).
- Rabbi Moshe Glustein, married to Sistie. Rabbi Glustein is the retired head of Yeshiva Gedola of Montreal.
- Yechiel Glustein (d. 2007), married to Mena.

The Ottawa based Glustein family is descended from Yaakov's son Hershel (known also as Tzvi Hersh or Harris, d. 1942), married to Sarah (nee Belinke, d. 1933). Hershel served as a Baal Tefillah [prayer leader] at the original Agudath Israel Synagogue, before their first rabbi was hired. Hershel and Sarah's children were:

- Moses (d. 1916).
- Jack Gladstone (d. 1994), married to Pearl (nee Brill, d. 1973).
- Israel (d. 1988), married to Rebecca (nee Perlman, d. 1999). Rebecca and Israel were first cousins, as Rebecca was the daughter of Froim (Ephraim or Frank) and Aidyeh (nee Glustein) Perlman. Aidyeh was a daughter of the common ancestor Yaakov, and a sister of Avrum and Hershel. Their daughter Shirley Kline (later Kriger) was married to Phillip Kline (originally **Wexler**, d. 1969), the son of Charles **Wexler** (d. 1933) and Pearl (nee **Goldfield**, d. 1963), daughter of Meyer and Chana **Goldfield**. After her husband died, Pearl Hymie Kline (d. 1941). After her second husband died, Pearl married Murray **Baslaw**. After the death of Phillip,

Shirley married Akiva Kriger (d. 2011), whose first wife was Shirley (nee Movshovitz, d. 1972). Akiva was the son of Jacob (d. 1965) and Dora (d. 1986) Kriger, and brother of Maynard Kriger (d. 2016). Shirley and Phillip's daughter Cheryl is married to Richard **Kizell**, son of Raymond and Joan (nee Cowan) **Kizell**. Other children of Israel and Rebecca are Ada of Vancouver, and Marilyn of Barrie, Ontario.

- Dora Litwack (d. 1953), married to Jack (d. 1984). Jack was the son of Mordechai David Litwack (d. 1942), and brother of Gordon (d. 1987), and Yudel (d. 1980). Children of Jack and Dora Litwack were:
  - Israel (Izzie, d. 2007), married to Pauline (nee **Kizell**, d. 2007), daughter of Max and Bella **Kizell**.
  - Michael (killed in action in 1944).
  - Gertrude Brown (d. 2014), married to Herbert (d. 2015). They lived in North Bay.
  - Samuel (d. 2018), married to Dora (nee Ehrenreich, d. 2019). Sam and his brother Moe owned Commercial Tire. Note: Dora Litwack the wife of Sam is to be distinguished from her mother-in-law Dora Litwack the wife of Jack. Dora's uncle was Morris Berliner (d. 2001), married to Molly (nee Dubrofsky) Berliner (d. 2014). Molly was the brother of Reuben Dubrofsky (see **Kardish**).
  - Moses (Moe, d. 2016), married to Rose (nee Simon. d. 2008). Their son Alan's second marriage is to Resa (nee Lax), who was first married to Aryeh Glustein, a third cousin of Alan, son of Yechiel and Mena Glustein, and nephew of Rabbi Yechiel and Shirley Cement. Moe and Rose's son Gary was married to Rhonda (nee Silverman), the daughter of William (d. 2015), and Flora (nee Wolman) Silverman. Moe and Rose's daughter Debbie is married to Jerry Solomon, who was formerly married to Joyce, and worked as an employee of the Jewish Community of Ottawa for a period of time.
- Fanny Osterer (d. 1994), married to Leo (d. 1982). Their children are Betty Finkelman (d. 2017) married to Sid; and Joseph (d. 2016), married to Blanche (nee **Betcherman**), daughter of Isaac **Betcherman**. Joey and Blanche's son Howard (d. 2014) was married to Ellen (nee **Rivers**), daughter of Irving **Rivers** and Ethel (nee Sandler, a descendant of the **Shinder** family). Howard and Ellen's daughter, Erin **Smith**, is married to Aaron, son of Leslie and Maureen **Smith** and grandson of Jack and Inez **Smith**.
- Mary Rosenblatt (d. 1997), married to Ben (d. 2002). Their children are:
  - Evelyn Hoffman (d. 2022), married to Issie (d. 2023).
  - Bernie, married to Ethel (d. 2017).
  - Sidney, married to Christine.
- Jenny **Skulsky** (d. 1970), married to Samuel, the son of Menachem Mendel and Chaya **Skulsky**. Their daughter Rebecca Goldberg (d. 1984), was married to Zawel (d. 1982). Zawel and Rebecca's son Samuel is married to Sheryl (nee Newman), daughter of Laz Newman (see **Fine**). Other children of Jenny and Samuel are Clara (d. 1924), Mary, Mindel.
- Esther Baker (d. 1987) married to Tevya (d. 1971). Their children were:
  - Rebecca Steinberg (d. 2004), married to Hyman (d. 1995). Their daughter Anita **Shore** was married to Mendel, son of Charles and Anna (nee **Betcherman**) **Shore**.
  - Mary (known as Babe) Dubinsky (d. 2015), married to Hyman (d. 2000).

- o Clara Wilko **Dworkin** (d. 1994), married to Elias Wilko (d. 1966). Their daughter Roslyn was married to Sam **Gershon** (d. 2009), son of David and Tilly **Gershon**.
- Hyman Glushtein (d. 1991), married to Pearl (nee Dutnoff, d. 1977). Their children were:
  - o Rachel **Petigorsky**, married to Leo (d. 1957), son of Tevya and Elizabeth (nee Nemerovsky) **Petigorsky**.
  - o Joe (d. 1953), married to Edith (nee Finkelstein).
  - o Jack (d. 1952), married to Lily (nee Fireman).
  - o Laya Lefton, married to Mel.
- Eva Dutnoff (d. 2000), married to Gus (d. 1981). Gus was a brother of his sister-in-law Pearl Glushtein, Hyman's wife. Other Dutnoff siblings were Samuel Danoff (d. 1973), married to Dora (nee **Roodman**, d. 1995), daughter of Moshe and Bethsheva **Roodman**; and Dora **Ellenberg** (d. 1975), married to Israel, son of Moses and Rachel Leah **Ellenberg**. Sons of Eva and Gus were Archie (d. 1952), Joe (d. 1989).
- Robert (d. 1978), married to Marion (nee Yosman, d. 1958). Their children are:
  - o Sarah Yanofsky.
  - o Ethel Guttman.
  - o Harold Gladstone, married to Helen (nee Monson).

Yaakov, the ancestor of the Glustein family, had a brother David whose won Kalman came to Nova Scotia. Two of Kalman's grandchildren ended up in Ottawa. The children of Kalman's daughter Katherine Levine (d. 2001), married to Simon, are Dr. Len Levine, and Lorraine Zides, married to Milton (d. 1986). Milton's daughter Cheryl is married to John **Dover**, son of Jay and Betty **Dover**.

For connections to other entries, see Baslaw, Betcherman, Dover, Dworkin, Fine, Gershon, Goldfield, Kizell, Petigorsky, Roodman, Shore, Silver, Skulsky, Smith.

Glustein family in Hillel Lodge on July 1987. Back row L-R: Chaim Glushtein, Jack Gladstone, Israel Glustein. Front row: Mary Rosenblatt, Esther Baker, Fannie Osterer, Eva Dutnoff. (OJA 1-941-02)

GOLDENBERG

See Pleet.

GOLDFIELD

The Goldfield family descends from Mayer (d. 1924), and Annie (nee Zelcovin, d. 1929), of Yelisavetgrad, Russia. Annie shares common relatives with the **Bessin** family via the Levinoff family (see details under **Bessin**). The children of Mayer and Annie were:

- Archie (d. 1981), married to Esther (nee Dorsky, d. 1975).
- Benjamin (d. 1944), married to Libby (nee Rapp). Their daughter Sybil Budd was married to Bernard Budd (Budovitch), a member of the New Brunswick based Budovitch family, connected to Gertude Budovitch (nee **Greenberg**), married to Sam Budovitch, and a sister of Irving **Greenberg** (see **Pollock**). Libby was a first cousin of Shimshon Dunsky, a well-known Yiddish educator in Montreal, and father of Zipporah Dunsky / Rabinovitch / Shnay (see **Goldmaker**).
- Charles (d. 1943), married to Eva (nee Cohen, d. 1957). Their children were Jack (d. 1991) married to Asa; Morley (d. 2016), married to Diane (nee Altschuler, d. 1997), who was a granddaughter of Cecil and Freda **Viner**; Anita Landis (d. 2014), married to Edward (d. 2011). Morley and Diane's son Gary was married to Alison (nee Saxe), a granddaughter of Edward and Pearl **Torontow**.

- Mitchell (d. 1937), married to Mary (nee Cohen).
- Pearl (d. 1968), married successively to Mr. Kline, Charles **Wexler** (d. 1933), Hyman Kline (d. 1941), and Murray **Baslaw** (d. 1968). Pearl's son Phillip Kline (d. 1969 – and originally went by the name **Wexler**) was married to Shirley (nee **Glustein**), daughter of Israel and Rebecca (nee Perlman) **Glustein**. Their daughter Cheryl is married to Richard **Kizell**. Charles Wexler's brother Frank was married to Jessie (nee Greenberg, d. 1945), the daughter of Samuel Greenberg, and Frances (nee **Taller**).

For connections to other entries, see Baslaw, Bessin, Glustein, Goldmaker, Kizell, Pollock, Taller, Torontow, Viner.

A cow tied outside Goldfield's Meat Market, at 228 Bank Street, ca. 1921. (OJA 2-100)

GOLDMAKER

The Goldmaker family is descended from Zeidel (d. 1970), and Golda (nee **Weiner** d. 1945), daughter of Labe and Sheva (nee Millstone) **Weiner**. Their children were:

- Sarah (d. 2005) married to Moe Resnick.
- Louis (d. 2012), married to Marjorie (nee Lang, d. 2017). Marjorie is the sister of Morris and Joseph Lang (see **Bessin**). Their daughter Glenda is married to David Moss. David's brother William is married to Katherine, daughter of Edward and Rosalie Shapiro (see **Florence).** David and William Moss' mother Dena (nee Gordon) was a first cousin of Zipporah Dunsky / Rabinovitch / Shnay (see

Goldfield). Zippora and Jack Rabinovitch (d. 2017) lived in Ottawa during the 1960s and early 1970s with their three daughters. Jack later married Doris Giller. After Doris' death, he founded the well-known Giller Prize (now the Scotiabank Giller) in memory of his late wife.

- Sol (d. 2013), married to Sybil (nee Zilberg). Sol was the owner of the United Fuels Company.
- Sam Goldmaker (d. 2019), married to Roberta. Roberta is the sister of Judie Ross Hendin, whose second husband was Arnell Goldberg (d. 2015), son of Morris (d. 1978) and Zena (d. 1982) Goldberg. Arnell's first was Simone (nee Bright), daughter of Maurice (d. 1981) and Phyllis (d. 1981) Bright.

For connections to other entries, see Bessin, Florence, Goldfield, Weiner.

GOLDMAN

The Goldman family originates from Krasnostav, Volyn, Russia. See Krantzberg.

Walter (Wolf) Goldman
(From Linda Brown-Kaplan)

The Goldman family in 1948.
From left standing: Wally Cherun, Gital Viner, Arthur Viner, Sonia (Goldman) Viner, Edith (Goldman) Cherun, Alex Cherun, Francis Goldman, James Goldman, Malka Goldman, Rachel (Goldman) Jewett, David Jewett, Harry Kaplan, Anne (Goldman) Kaplan, Joe Feller, Betty (Goldman) Feller. Seated: Wally Viner, Carol Cherun, Walter Kaplan. (From Linda Brown-Kaplan)

GORELICK

Abraham (d. 1959), and Dvaroh (d. 1939) are the parents of:

- Marsha **Bordelay** (d. 1985), married to Max (d. 1980), son of Avraham and Devorah **Bordelay**. Their son Ron was married to Debbie (nee Levine), daughter of Abe (d. 1994), and Tillie (nee Greenberg, d. 2012) Levine.
- Bertha Bookman (d. 1982), married to Jacob (d. 1986). Their children were:
  - o Abraham (d. 2015), married to Lila (nee **Pleet**, d. 2006), daughter of Abraham David and Rose **Pleet**. (Note: Abraham Bookman was born to a different mother, who died young before Jacob Bookman arrived in Canada).
  - o Mildred **Weinstein** (d. 2022), married to Percy (d. 2003), son of Joseph and Sonia **Weinstein**.
- Sela Zaretsky (d. 1988), married to Chaim (d. 1964). Their children were:
  - o Sam Zaret (d. 1976), married to Helene (nee Newman, d. 2004), daughter of Pinkas (d. 1987) and Yehudit (d. 1970) Newman, and sister of Laz Newman (see **Fine**). Their children are:
    - Neil, married to Debbie. Their son Josh is married to Jen (nee Levine, see **Horwitz**).
    - Mark, married to Simmy.
  - o Sarah Satov (d. 2010), married to Louis (d. 2010).
- Benny, married to Ann.

For connections to other families, see Bordelay, Fine, Horwitz, Pleet, Weinstein.

GOSEWICH

The Gosewich family descends from Zvi Hirsch (d. 1952), and Etta (d. 1952) Gosewich, of Lakhva, Belarus. Various members of the family spelled the name as Gosewich, Gosevitz, and Gosewitz. The children of Zvi Hirsch and Etta were:

- Julius Gosevitz (d. 2001) married to Fanny (d. 2012). Their granddaughter Shauna (nee Gosevitz) Pichosky, is married to Steve Pichosky, of the Toronto based Pichosky family. The brother of Arieh Rosenblum, former director of development of the Ottawa Jewish Community Foundation, is also married into the Pichosky family.
- Sam Gosewich (d. 1991) married to Rae (nee Rosen. d. 1988). Rae was a cousin of Saul **Saslove**. Their children are:
  - Herbert (d. 2015), married to Dena (nee Markson). Herb Gosewich was the owner of Ritchie's Sport Shop in Ottawa. Dena is the brother of Frank Markson (d. 2023), married to Marilyn (nee Kaplan), daughter of Max (d. 1997) and Eva (nee **Kathnelson**, d. 2003). Dena and Frank are originally from Scotland, the children of David (d. 1981, buried in Ottawa) and Rudy (nee Caplan) Markson.
  - Philip, was originally married to Hennie (nee Ross), who is the sister of Phyllis Newman (see **Fine**). Hennie later married Morris **Palmer** (d. 1991), son of Moses and Rose (nee Greenberg), **Palmer**.
  - Arnold, married to Jackee (nee Spunt). Arnold is a literary agent and book publishing consultant, and was a founder, along with Harvey Glatt, of the Treble Clef music shop.
- Joseph Gosewitz (d. 1991), married to Sarah (d. 1965). Their son was Saul (d. 2000).
- Eva Bosloy (d. 1968), married to Louis (d. 1948). Their children are:
  - Sydney, married first to Lily (nee **Smith**, d. 1969), and then to Noreen (nee Silverman). Their daughter Karyn is married to Bernie Farber, a descendant of the **Lithwick** family. Noreen is the sister of Ivan Silverman (d.2020) who was married to Anna (nee **Smith**), the daughter of Jack and Inez **Smith**; and Audrey Levy, married to Lewis Levy (d. 2013). Lew Levy is the sister of Helen Gilboa (d. 2016), married to Chaim (d. 2019).
  - Jack (d. 2010).
  - Phillip, who fell in action during World War Two in 1943.
  - Mary Brewer (d. 2010), married to Kurt (d. 2012).
- Edith Friendly (d. 1980), married to David (d. 1966).
- Jack Gosewitz (d. 1975), married to Sadie (nee Hirschel d. 1969).

For connections to other entries, see Fine, Greenberg, Kathnelson, Lithwick, Palmer, Saslove, Smith.

Gosevitz (Gosewitz), Bosloy and Friendly families at 116 York Street, Ottawa, ca. 1929.
(OJA 1-109).

Classic "Sez Herb" advertisement for Ritchie's Sport Shop, Ottawa Journal, Feb 23,
1970, (from Freeview clippings of newspapers.com:
https://www.newspapers.com/clip/19632052/the-ottawa-journal/)

GOTTDANK

David (d. 1922), and Rachel (nee Nitupski, d. 1938), were the parents of:

- Jeanne **Lieff** (d. 2003), married to Louis (d. 1993), son of Bernard and Esther Malca (nee **Palmer**) **Lieff**.
- Sarah **Torontow** (d. 1958), married to Harry (d. 2008), son of Abraham Raphael and Ethel Rhoda **Torontow**. Their son David is married to Dorothy (nee **Agulnik**), daughter of Harry and Sonia **Agulnik**.
- Esther **Mirsky** (d. 1988), married to David (d. 1983), son of Harris and Ida Cayla **Mirsky**.
- Arthur, married to Violet (d. 2014).
- Sydney.

For connections to other entries, see Agulnik, Lieff, Mirsky, Palmer, Torontow.

The Gottdank family,
L-R: Syd, David, Sarah, Arthur, Rachel , Esther, and Jeanne. (OJA)

GOULD

The Gould family is descended from Abraham (d. 1912) and Anna (nee Horowitz, d. 1955). Their children were:

- Ben (d. 1969), married to Betty.
- Alexander (d. 1981), married to Irene (nee Cohen, d. 1995).
- Pat Polly Renaud (d. 1979).
- Sylvia Smith (d. 2006) married to Kalman (d. 1969), son of Bernard and Rebecca (nee Rhinestein). Their children are:

○ Barbara was first married to Joel **Palmer**, son of Bertha and Abe, and then to Sid **Cohen**, the son of Max and Grete **Cohen**.

○ Robert, married to Paula (nee **Fine**), daughter of David and Rose (nee Smurlick) **Fine**.

- Hyman (d. 1995), married to Lillian (nee Levine, d. 1997).
- Rose (d. 1982).
- Lillian Bergsiem (d. 2008), married to Jack.
- Victor (d. 1990) married to Rachel (nee **Bodnoff**, d. 2009), daughter of Abraham David and Annie (nee Ginsberg) **Bodnoff**. Their children are:
  ○ Joan **Kronick**, married to Russell, son of Wally and Irene (nee **Coplan**).
  ○ Jeffrey, married to Enid (nee **Taller**), daughter of Sam and Anne **Taller**.

For connections to other entries, see Bodnoff, Cohen, Coplan, Fine, Kronick, Palmer, Taller.

(L-R) Victor and Hy Gould in ca. 1928 in their newly opened 83 Bank St. store, and then again in 1978 at their 50th anniversary, just a few months before closing.
(OJA 1-720-01, OJA 2-101)

GREENBERG

There are two major Greenberg families in Ottawa, which are believed to be unrelated. Given that the surname is common, there are also other Greenberg families, and individuals who may not be related to either family.

Greenberg family A.

This family is descended from Isaac (d. 1927), son of Eliezer, and Shaindel (Sarah, nee **Gencher**), daughter of Mayer Dov and Tsipora **Gencher**. The original surname was Nepomiazchy. They took on the Greenberg name upon immigration to Canada. Their children included:

- Lazar (d. 1933), married to his cousin Esther (nee **Gencher**, d. 1954), the daughter of Binyomin and Bryna **Gencher**. Their children included:
  - Rachel Soloway (d. 1979), married to Harry (d. 1985). Harry Soloway was the son of Louis (d. 1950), and Anna (d. 1960) Soloway, and the brother of Hyman Soloway (d. 2004), married to Ruth (d. 2020). Hy Soloway was a prominent lawyer and Jewish communal leader in Ottawa. The Soloway JCC is named after his family. Harry and Rachel's children were:
    - Zelda Adessky (d. 1998), married to Irving (d. 2010). Their daughter Elizabeth was married to Arnon Vered (d. 2014), son of Zeev (d.2008) and Sara Vered. Arnon's brother Gilad is married to Susan (nee **Viner**), daughter of Joseph and Ruth (nee **Macy**) **Viner**.
    - Roslyn Sanders (d. 1997) married to Ben-Ami (d. 1991).
    - Irving Soloway (d. 2017).
    - Jean Berger (d. 2016), married to Victor Levy, and later to Monty Berger.
  - Rebecca **Shore** (d. 1978), married to Israel (d. 1978).
  - Moses (d. 1947), married to Bessie (nee Schecter, d. 2006), daughter of Yakov Schecter. Yakov Schecter's second wife was Chaya Coblentz, mother of Alice Edelson (see Ballon section of **Saslove**). Children of Moses and Bessie are:
    - Laya **Shabinsky**, married to Solomon, son of Morris and Goldie (nee **Shinder**). **Shabinsky**.
    - Syrille Rosman, married to Paul.
    - Elissa Iny, married to Avraham.
  - Samuel (d. 1990), married to Beatrice (nee Cohen, d. 2011).
  - Rose (d. 1926).
  - Michael (d. 1970)
- Moses (d., 1929), married to Rachel. Their children were:
  - Mervin (d. 2014).
  - Jennie.
  - Abraham (d. 1925).
- Joseph (d. 1982).
- Roger (d. 1955), married to Rose (nee Bezumny, d. 1959). Rose had a sister Gertie, married to Morris Balsky, whose first marriage was to Sophie Wiseberg (d. 1918), a sister to Meir Wiseberg, the grandfather of Reba **Diener** (nee Luterman). The children of Roger and Rose Greenberg were:
  - George (d. 1919).
  - Louis (d. 1974), married to Helen (nee Raport, d. 1979). Helen is the daughter of Michael (d. 1949), and Elizabeth (nee **Sugarman**, d. 1923), daughter of Harry and Esther **Sugarman**. Helen is the sister of Esther Aronson, married to Harry. Esther and Harry are the parents of Lester Aronson (d. 2020), married to Myra (nee **Slack**), daughter of Louis and Stella (nee Gilbert) **Slack** (see **Silver**).
  - Jennie **Shinder** (d. 1991), married to Israel (d. 2014), son of Jack and Nellie **Shinder**. Israel's second marriage was to Maureen (nee **Gershon**) Newton (see Glustein).
  - Gilbert (d. 1980), married to Bessie (nee **Levitan**, d. 1984), daughter of Maurice and Fanny **Levitan**. Gilbert and his brothers were the founders of Minto Construction.

- Grace Koreen (d. 1989), married to Dr. Joseph Koreen. Their daughter Esther **Freedman** is married to Jacob **Freedman**, son of Jarvis and Riva (nee **Schreiber**) **Freedman**.
- Irving (d. 1991) married to Shirley (nee Schnell).
- Lawrence (known as Lorry, d. 1999), married to Carol (d. 2018). Lorry Greenberg served as Mayor of Ottawa from 1975-1978.

Nathan Greenberg (d. 1983), married to Sarah (d. 1984) was the son of Rivka (nee **Gencher**) and Pinye **Pollock** (Polyak), and a nephew of Isaac and Sheindel Greenberg. He was sponsored and then adopted by his aunt and uncle when he came over to Canada, and adopted the Greenberg name. His family will be discussed under the **Pollock**.

Bertha (nee Greenberg) **Palmer**, wife of Abraham **Palmer**, is also connected to this Greenberg family.

Another branch of the Greenberg family is descended from Avraham Abba Greenberg. The exact connection to Isaac Greenberg is unclear, but it is surmised that Avraham Abba was likely a brother of Isaac Greenberg. Avraham Abba's children included:
- Isaac (d. 1952).
- Max (d. 1938), married to Bayla. Their son Samuel (d. 1970) was married to Bessie (nee **Murray**, d. 1994), daughter of Joseph and Bertha **Murray**. Samuel and Bessie's children are:
  - Doris **Dover** (d. 1987). She was married to William.
  - Ethel **Taylor** (d. 2009), married to Irving (d. 2012), son of Samuel and Bertha (nee **Slover**) **Taylor** . Their son Brent is married to Risa (nee **Froman**), the daughter of Harry and Esther (nee **Betcherman**) **Froman**.
  - John married to Gladys (nee **Viner**), daughter of Arthur and Sonia **Viner**. Their daughter Karen is married to Ian Zunder, son of Mark (d., 2015) and Lillian Zunder. Mark's parents were Isaac (d. 1958) and Bessie (d. 1990) Zunder, and his siblings are Srul, married to Rachel (nee Kalir, d. 2009); Sam (d.2022), married to Sandra (d. 2022); Miriam Ross, married to Sydney. The Zunder family owned Zunder's Fruitland on the Byward Market. Isaac Zunder was the sister of Leika **Greenberg**, married to Menashe (see **Greenberg** Family B).
  - Alan, married to Jacqui.
  - Jack, married to MonaLee.
  - Benjamin, married to Dorothy.

Greenberg Family B

The second major Greenberg family in Ottawa is descended from two brothers, Yitzchak, and Mordechai, married to Raber. A son of Mordechai married a daughter of Yitzchak.

Yitzchak's children included:

- Menashe (d. 1990), married to Lily (known as Leika, nee Zunder, d. 1976). Leika Greenberg was the sister of Isaac Zunder (see **Greenberg** Family A). Children of Menashe and Lily are:
  - Sylvia (d. 2019), married to Morton **Pleet** (d. 2019), the son of Archie and Edith **Pleet**. Their son Jeffrey is married to Felice (nee Singerman), the daughter of Sydney (d. 2004) and Raye (nee Friberg d. 2004) Singerman. Felice's sisters Aviva and Barbara are married to Seymour and Joel **Diener**. Felice's aunt and uncle are Jim and Molly (nee Friberg) Mintz, cousins of my father Issie **Landau**.
  - Beatrice, married to Barry Muroff.
- Mollie (d. 1967), married to her first cousin Joseph Greenberg (d. 1969), son of Mordechai and Raber Greenberg. Their children were:
  - Milton (known as Murph, d. 1988), married to Laura (nee Shadlesky).
  - Frances Hodess, married to Maurie.
  - Rossie Perlman, married to David.

Mordechai and Raber's children included:
- Joseph (d. 1969), married to his first cousin Mollie Greenberg (d. 1967), daughter of Yitzchak as noted above.
- Ben (known as Berchick, d. 1998), married to Ida (nee **Kardish**, d. 1989), daughter of Moshe and Rivka **Kardish**. Their children are:
  - Lily Penso, married to Jerry. The Pensos were among the founders of the Tamir organization.
  - Bernice **Kerzner**, married to Isaac (d. 1999), son of Avrum and Gittel **Kerzner**. Their son Avrum was married to Cathy (nee Goldstein) daughter of Stanley and Norma (nee Druckman) Goldstein (see **Sherman**).
  - Max, married to Ellie (nee **Steinberg**), daughter of Jack and Joyce (nee Litwin) **Steinberg**.
- Morris (d. 1981), married to Bertha (nee **Gennis**, d. 1965) the daughter of Elimelech and Zahaie **Gennis**. This branch of the family is cousins with the Koffman family. The children of Morris and Bertha were:
  - Max (known as Chief, d. 1964), married to Freda (known as Fritzi, nee Boguslovsky, d. 2000). Their daughter Debbie Ferkin is married to Norman, and was first married to Arnold Luterman (d. 1968), the brother of Reba **Diener**.
  - Sydney (known as Snooki, d. 2013), married to Barbara (nee **Levinson**, d. 2016), daughter of Morris and Clara (nee **Schecter**) **Levinson**.
  - Rossie Rose (d. 2002) , married to Issie (d. 2009).
  - Gladys **Bodnoff** (d. 2017), married to Phillip (d. 1965), son of Irving and Ann **Bodnoff**.
  - Milton (known as Mutt, d. 1997), married to Mildred (known as Minnie, nee Sandler d. 2014), daughter of Issie and Malya Rachel (nee **Shinder**) Sandler.
  - John (d. 2007) married to Zelda (nee **Saslove**, d. 2009), daughter of Saul and Lillian **Saslove**.

A different Greenberg family, descended from Pesachya and Tillie Greenberg, is descried under Lesh. Other Greenberg families and individuals exist in Ottawa as well.

For connections to other entries for the first Greenberg family, see Betcherman, Diener, Freedman, Froman, Gencher, Glustein, Levitan, Macy, Murray, Pollock, Saslove, Schreiber, Shinder, Shore, Silver, Slack, Sugarman, Taylor, Viner.

For connections to other entries for the second Greenberg family, see Bodnoff, Diener, Gennis, Kardish, Kerzner, Landau, Levinson, Palmer, Pleet, Saslove, Sherman, Shinder, Slover, Steinberg.

Lorry Greenberg, the first Jewish mayor of Ottawa, circa 1974. (OJA 1-703)

HALPERN

The Halpern family is descended from Herman Halpern (original surname was Hirschhorn), the son of Betzalel Hirschhorn. Herman's first marriage was to Dina (nee Fox, d. 1906), and his second marriage was to his niece Rachel (known as Rae, nee

Hirschhorn, d. 1941), daughter of William (Wilmos) and Esther (nee Pilze). Betzalel and William Hirschhorn were brothers.

Children of Herman and Dina included:

- Clara **Viner** (d. 1987), married to Irving (d. 1981), son of Joseph and Gittel (nee Silverman) **Viner**. Their son Joseph (d. 2014), was married to Ruth (nee **Macy,** d. 2020).
- Margaret **Ages** (d.1973), married to Jacob (d. 1972). See the **Ages** for connections to the Bahar and **Kardish** families.
- A daughter, married to Jack Israel (d. 1942).

The children of Herman and Rachel were:

- Sidney (d. 1982), married to Frieda (nee Fagin, d. 1981), a daughter of Isaac and Dora (nee **Cohen**) Fagin. Their daughter Shirley Abtan was married to Morris Goldstein, and then married Nessim Abtan. Morris Goldstein is the son of Sam and Miriam (nee London) Goldstein (Miriam is a cousin of A. J. Freiman – see **Bilsky**).
- Donald, married to Ann (nee Naginsky).
- Lawrence, married to Bessy.
- Teresa, married to Jim.
- Alfred.
- Lily (d. 1952).
- Charles (d. 1959), married to Katie (nee **Skulsky**, d. 1999), daughter of Solomon **Skulsky**. Their children are:
  - Ray Goldstein, married to Ernest, son of Jack (d. 1988) and Gertude (nee **Shinder**, d. 2002).
  - Herman (d. 2006), married to Pauline.
  - Walter (d. 1962).
  - Sam, married to Rebecca (nee Bookman), daughter of Max and Celia (nee Sherman) Bookman (see **Sherman**).

For connections to other entries, see Ages, Bilsky, Cohen, Kardish, Macy, Sherman, Shinder, Skulsky, Viner.

Marriage of Herman and Pauline Halpern. Rabbi Simon L. Eckstein in center.
(From Charlene Halpern)

HANSER

The Hanser family is descended from Ephraim and Chaya Rivka Hontsher. Their children were Israel Faivish (d. 1947) married to Slova Bella (nee **Kronick**, d. 1924), daughter of Aaron David and Riva **Kronick**; and Daniel (d. 1926), married to Tillie (nee **Victor**, d. 1963), daughter of Aizik **Victor**.

Children of Daniel and Tillie were:

- Sarah **Kimmel** (d. 1978), married to Arthur **Kimmel** (d. 1971), son of Jacob Leib (d. 1965) and Elka (nee Guz d.1959) **Kimmel**. Their children are:
  - Isabel, married to Norman **Lesh** (d. 2015) son of Samuel and Mary (nee **Flesher**) **Lesh**.
  - Daniel, married to Marilyn (nee **Shaffer**), daughter of Milton and Sarah **Shaffer**.
  - Arnold, married to Roslyn (nee Magidson), son of Sam and Leema (nee **Lithwick**).
- Samuel (d. 1988).
- Annie Lang (d. 1971), married to Nathan (d. 1996).
- Nelly Shapiro (d. 1996), married to Abraham (d. 1989). Their children are:
  - Daniel, married to Elaine (nee Steinman), daughter of Nathan and Thelma (nee **Rivers**) Steinman.
  - Leonard.
  - Jack, married to Carol-Sue (nee **Swedlove,** d. 2020) daughter of Casey and Bess **Swedlove**. Their son Michael is married to Nicole (nee **Smolkin**), daughter of Howard and Patricia **Smolkin**.
- Jack (d. 1963).
- Moses (d. 2009) married to Jean (nee Rotman, d. 2009).

- Faye Zolov (also known as Fanny, d. 1986), married to Hyman
- Abraham (d. 1990)

For connections to other entries, see Kimmel, Kronick, Lesh, Lithwick, Rivers, Shaffer, Smolkin, Swedlove, Victor.

HELD

See Pollock.

HORWITZ

The Horwitz family stems from Max (d. 1930) and Rebecca (nee Rodkin, d. 1929) Horwitz. Their children were:

- Charles (d. 1972), married to Anne (d. 1955). Their children are:
  - Corinne Levine, married to Percy (d. 2007). Their granddaughter, Jennifer Zaret, is married to Josh, son of Neil and Debbie Zaret (see **Gorelick**).
  - Harriet Slone, married to Irving (see **Coplan** for note on Slone / Slonemsky family).
- Jacie (d. 1998), married to Jeanne (nee Rich, d. 2013). Jacie was a prominent judge, and was active in many Jewish institutions. He was one of the founders of Hillel Lodge as well as Camp B'Nai Brith. He served as president of the Ottawa Jewish Community Council in 1970-1971. Their children are:
  - Betsy Borden married to Allan.
  - Dale.
  - Jack, married to Ellen Goodman.
- Jacob (d. 1931), married to Yetta (nee Rosen, d. 1998). Yetta later married Max Fenster (d. 1974). Jack and Yetta's daughter was Anita Chernove, married to Robert.
- Sarah.
- Muriel Hertz (d. 1947), married to Harry (d. 1974)
- Joshua.
- Phillip (d. 1982), married to Audrey (nee McClelland, d. 1988). Their daughter Nina Arron is married to Elliott (see **Weinstein** for description of Arron family).

For connections to other entries, see Coplan, Gorelick, Weinstein.

KARDISH

The Kardish family stems from Moshe and Rivka (nee Plotken) Kardash, daughter of Yehuda Leib Plotken. The family originated in Kamenets-Podolsk. Various family members also use the Kardash or Cardash spellings. The Kardish family is known as the founders of Rideau Bakery, which continues to be run by descendants of the family.

The children of Moshe and Rivka were:

- David (d. 1947), married to Etta (d. 1962). Their children were:

- o Louis (d. 1981), married to Mary (nee Udashkin, d. 1983). Their children are:
  - Marcia was married to Morley Mason (d. 2017), son of Herb and Sadie Mason (see **Mosion**).
  - Kevin, married to Rose.
  - David (known as the Bear), married to Margie.
  - Ellie Greenberg, married to Gary.
- o Anne Brozovsky (d. 2021), married to Sam (d. 2007), son of Abram (d. 1961) and Ida (d. 1984) Brozovky. Sam's sister was Edith Dubrofsky (d. 1976), married to Reuben Dubrofsky (d. 2013). Children of Ann and Sam are:
  - Roslyn Wollock.
  - Rhoda, who was married to Paul Bregman.
  - Ethlyn **Agulnik**, married to Barry, son of Morris and Sarah (nee Mendelson) **Agulnik**.
- o Samuel (d. 2004), married to Tillie (nee Steinberg. d. 2004), daughter of Frank (d. 1971), and Laura (nee **Lachovitz**) Steinberg. Their children are:
  - Cheryl Levitan, is married to Brian, son of Elliott and Cecelia (nee Monson) Levitan (see **Rubin**).
  - Larry, originally married to Judith (nee **Molot**), son of Reuben and Sylvia (nee Saipe) Molot, and then to Jill (nee Slonim).
  - David, married to Joy.
- o Moses (d. 2013), married to Esther (nee Cohen d. 2013).
- o Edith Goldberg (f. 3032), married to Eric. Their son David was married to Sharon (nee Ages, d. 2013), a descendent of the **Halpern** family.
- o Jenny (d. 1991) Cohen, married to Lefty. Their children are:
  - Linda is married to Kenneth **Mirsky**, son of Lazarus and Gertude (nee **Tradburks**), **Mirsky**.
  - Rhoda Caplan, married to George.
  - Murray, married to Bryna.
- o Libby **Lieff** (d. 2002), married to Samuel (d. 1969), son of Moses **Lieff**. Their children are:
  - Murray, married to Judy (nee Copeland).
  - Bernice **Feller**, married to Robert, son of Henry (Hank), and Gertude (nee **Victor**) **Feller**.
  - David, married to Zena (nee Koffman), daughter of Milton and Beatrice (nee **Bordelay**) Koffman (see **Gennis**).
- o Isadore (Izzie, d. 1991), married to Shirley (nee **Bordelay**, d. 2003), daughter of Tom (d. 1978) and Miriam (d. 1987) **Bordelay**. Their children are:
  - David, married to Monica.
  - Debbie Baylin, married to Ben (d. 2000), son of Morris and Jennie Baylin.
  - Louis, married to Muriel.
  - Ellie Kamil, married to Ari.
- o Israel (known as Yippy, d. 1998), married to Eva (nee Feldberg, d. 2006). Their children are:
  - David, married to Margo, daughter of Max and Tessie (nee **Weiss**) **Zelikovitz**.

- Harvey, married to Sheryl (nee Berezin) daughter of Moe and Zelda (nee **Ages**) Berezin.
- Victor, married to Gale (nee Jankielewitz).
- Abraham Kardash (d. 1974) married to Tzipora (nee Rosenthal). Their daughter Rose **Taylor** (d. 2012), was married to Charles (known as Chick), son of Samuel and Bertha (nee **Slover**) **Taylor**.
- Samuel Cardash (d. 1977), married to Celia (d. 1982). Their son Martin is married to Ellen (nee Ellis), daughter of Bessie (nee **Lieff**), and Samuel Ellis.
- Percy (known as Pinney, d. 2007), married to Libby (nee Cratzbarg, d. 2000), daughter of Sam and Bessie (nee Krupnick) Cratzbarg. Libby was the sister of Esther **Murray**, married to Boruch; and Joseph Cratzbarg, married to Anne. Pinney and Libby's children are:
  - Bess **Weiner** (d. 2007), wife of Lawrence (d. 2008), son of Edward and Eva **Weiner**, and previously the wife of Hyman Kurzner, son of Louis and Bessie Kurzner (see **Kerzner**).
  - Sidney, married to Cally (nee Gluzman), daughter of Leon (d. 2012), and Ann (nee Greenberg) Gluzman. Cally is the sister of Ingrid Levitz, married to Gerald (d. 2009).
- Goldie Muster (d. 1983), married to Leon (d. 1963).
- Littman Cardash (d. 1984), married to Kayla (nee Greenberg, d. 1972). Their children are:
  - Bessie Lewis married to Phillip.
  - Lillian (d. 2015).
  - Rabbi Dr. Edward Yehuda Cardash (d. 1991), married to Esther.
  - Moses (d. 2012).
- Ida **Greenberg** (d. 1989), married to Ben (known as Berchick, d. 1998), son of Mordechai and Raber **Greenberg**. Their children are:
  - Lily Penso, married to Jerry.
  - Bernice **Kerzner**, married to Isaac (d. 1999), son of Avrum and Gittel **Kerzner**.
  - Max, married to Annie (nee Newman, d. 1980), and then to Ellie (nee **Steinberg**), daughter of Jack and Joyce Steinberg.

For connections to other entries, see Ages, Agulnik, Bordelay, Feller, Gennis, Greenberg, Halpern, Kerzner, Lachovitz, Lieff, Mirsky, Molot, Mosion, Murray, Rubin, Slover, Steinberg, Taylor, Tradburks, Victor, Weiner, Weiss, Zelikovitz.

These two photos show Rabbi Yehuda Cardash standing outside his family home on Friel Street, with the bottom photo labelled on the back as "looking North".
(OJA 1-1164, OJA 1-1165)

The iconic Rideau Bakery, founded and run for 90 years by the Kardish family.
(from Ottawa Jewish Bulletin).

KARP

The Karp family is descended from Max and Dora Kapinsky. Their original name was Kapinsky or Karpionack. Some members of the family bear the Kapinsky name. Children of Max and Dora were:

- Harry (d. 1988), married to Ruth (nee Keyfitz, d. 2013). Their daughter Deanna was married to Ian **Sadinsky**, son of Edward (d. 1976), and Esther (d. 2009) **Sadinsky**.
- Nathan (d. 1974), married to Jennie (d. 1986).
- Napoleon Kapinsky (known as Nap, d. 2000), married to Fay (nee **Torontow**, d. 1997), daughter of Joseph and Dora (nee Laitman) **Torontow**. Their children are:
    - Sheldon, married to Sandy.
    - Mina **Max** (d. 1998), married to Leonard, son of Sol and Lillian (nee Abrams) **Max**. Their daughter Melanie **Polowin** is married to Michael, son of David and Betty (nee Cowan) **Polowin**.
- Maurie (d. 2009), married to Dorothy (nee **Saslove**, d 2019), daughter of Samuel and Lillian (nee **Marcovitch**) **Saslove**.
- Charles, married to Lillian.
- Howard, married to Shirley (nee Simon).
- Ben (d. 1991), married to Etta (nee **Shulman,** d. 2020), daughter of Harry and Lily (nee Jaffe) **Shulman**. Their son Richard is married to Joy (nee **Roodman**), daughter of Herman and Zelda (nee **Dworkin**) **Roodman**.
- Allan, married to Barbara.

For connections to other entries, see Dworkin, Markovitch, Max, Polowin, Roodman, Sadinsky, Saslove, Shulman, Torontow.

Kapinsky family portrait: Mr. and Mrs. Max Kapinsky and their eight sons, circa mid-late 1920.

Standing in the back row in suits, from L-R are Charlie, Nathan, Nap, and Harry. In the front row is Ben (standing), Mr. Max Kapinsky (seated), Allan (striped shirt in front of father), Howard (between parents), and Mrs. Dora Kapinsky holding baby Maurie.

(OJA 1-298)

November 25, 1983 — The Ottawa Jewish Bulletin & Review — Page 27

The sons of Max and Dora Kapinsky, from left to right: Morrie Karp, Allan Karp (England), Ben Karp, Howard Karp (Montreal), Harry Karp, Nap Kapinsky, Charlie Karp (Florida).

Brothers together for first reunion in twenty-five years

(OJA, from Ottawa Jewish Bulletin and Review archives)

KATHNELSON

Sisman Kathnelson (d. 1958), and Sarah (d. 1970), were the parents of:

- Hiram (d. 1980) married to Lillian (nee Nadler, d. 2001). Their daughter Anita **Roodman** was married to Michael (d. 2014), son of Dr. Harry and Beatrice **Roodman**. Their son Allan was married to Diane (nee Goldstein), daughter of Jack and Gertude (nee **Shinder**) Goldstein. Diane is currently married to Allen Abramson. Allan Kathnelson served as director of Camp B'nai Brith of Ottawa from 1989-1995.
- Eva Kaplan (d. 2003), married to Max (d. 1997). Their daughter Marilyn Markson is married to Frank (d. 2023), son of David and Rudy Markson, and brother of Dena **Gosewich**.

For connections to other families, see Gosewich, Roodman, Shinder.

KERZNER

The Kerzner family descends from Sheika and Kressla (nee **Weiner**) Kerzner. Some members of the family spell the surname as Kurzner. Their children were:

- Itzik Mayer (d. 1947) married to Pessia (nee Neistein, d. 1963). Their children were:
  - Rachel Wise (d. 1995), married to William Wise (d. 1998). Their daughter Susan Dain (d. 2003), was married to Sidney (d. 2008), son of Morris (d. 1993), and Mildred (nee Smith, d. 1983) Dain. Morris's brother Irving Dain is the father of Dr. Steven Dain, who is married to Stephanie (nee Loomer), daughter of Joseph (d. 2007)and Rickie (d. 2004) Loomer. Stephanie's first husband was Donald Abelson (see **Rubin**).
  - Sara Rivka Leibov, married to Hyman (d. 1964).
  - Charlotte **Slack** (d. 2000), married to Moses (Moe) **Slack** (d. 1975), son of Naftali Hertz and Dobrish Schlak.
  - Nellie Schlessinger (d. 2004) married to Ferdinand (known as Fred, d. 2002). Their daughter Lisa Berman was married to Jeff, the son of Harold and Adele Berman. Harold's sister Ruth (nee Berman) Abramowitz, is the mother of Judith Kerzner, Nellie's Schlessinger's first cousin.
  - Sydney (d. 2004), married to Ethel (nee Kott, d. 2021). Their children are:
    - Ruth **Taller** (d. 1996), married to Mendy, son of Hyman and Bessie (nee **Cantor**) **Taller**.
    - Steven, married to Linda (nee Hochberg), daughter of Abe and Bernice Hochberg (see **Weiss**).
  - Morris (d. 2013), married to Lorraine (nee Cogan).
  - Edward (d. 2021) , married to Judith (nee Abramowitz, d. 2014). See above for the dual connection to Edward's sister Nellie Schlessinger. Their children are:
    - Mark (d. 2014), married to Arlene (nee Broitman), daughter of Abraham (d. 1986), and Sara (d. 1984) Broitman. Abraham's brother was Leon Broitman (d. 2013).
    - Beth **Flesher**, married to Ian, son of Jack **Flesher**.

- ▪ Cari Meil, married to William.
  - ○ Benjamin (d. 1910).
- Louis Kurzner (d. 1962) married to Bessie (nee Barg). Their son Hyman was married to Bess (nee **Kardash**), daughter of Pinney and Libby **Kardash**.
- Nojma Dickstein married to Szmul.
- Shlomo Kerzner.
- Temma Lisak (d. 1942) married to Simcha.
- Avrum Kerzner married to Gittel (nee Demb). Their son Isaac (d.1999) was married to Bernice (nee **Greenberg**), daughter of Ben (Berchick) and Ida (nee **Kardish**) Greenberg. Isaac and Bernice's son Avrum was married to Cathy (nee Goldstein), daughter of Stanley and Joyce (nee Druckman) Goldstein (see **Sherman**).
- Brucha Schecter married to Lazar.
- Sara Hollander (d. 1990), married to Sam.
- Shimon (d. 1972), married to Perel (nee Schecter, d. 1993).

For connections to other entries, see Cantor, Flesher, Greenberg, Kardish, Rubin, Sherman, Slack, Taller, Weiner, Weiss.

KILINOVSKY (KALIN)

See Saslove, Sherman.

KIMMEL

The Kimmel family stems from Jacob Leib Kimmel (d. 1965), and Elka (nee Guz, d. 1959). Elka's sister Hinda Leah **Lithwick** was married to Shamma **Lithwick**, son of Naphtali Hertz and Esther **Lithwick**. The children of Jacob Leib and Elka Kimmel were:

- Hannah Golda Chepovetsky (d. 1972), married to Yankel (d. 1946). This branch of the family remained in the Soviet Union.
- Arthur (d. 1971), married to Sarah (nee **Hanser**, d. 1978), daughter of David Daniel and Tillie (nee **Victor**) **Hanser**. Their children are:
  - ○ Isabel **Lesh**, married to Norman (d. 2015), son of Samuel and Mary (nee **Flesher**) **Lesh**. Their son Steven is married to Hildy (nee **Reichstein**), daughter of Hymie and Marlene Reichstein.
  - ○ Daniel, married to Marilyn (nee **Shaffer**), daughter of Milton and Sarah (nee Fine) **Shaffer**. Their daughter Linda Melamed is married to Warren, son of Morris and Leah Melamed. It is worthwhile to note that Linda Melamed and her brother David Kimmel are descended from the **Baslaw**, **Feller**, **Hanser**, **Kimmel**, **Shaffer**, and **Victor** families, and are also cousins of the **Lithwick** and **Lesh** families – all of which have entries in this book.
  - ○ Arnold, married to Roslyn (nee Magidson), daughter of Sam and Leema (nee **Lithwick**) Magidson.
- Hasia Rashevsky (d. 1978). This branch of the family remained in the Soviet Union. Hasia's daughter-in-law Nina Rashevsky was a sister of Vera Litvak, married to Emmanuel, grandson of Shamma and Hinda (nee Guz) **Lithwick**.
- Isaac (d. 1988), married to Bertha (nee Brodsky, d. 1965).

- Phillip (d. 1979), married to Ettie (nee **Shulman**, d. 1988), daughter of Max (d. 1965), and Rose (d. 1964) **Shulman**. Their children are:
  - Milton is married to Joyce (nee **Saslove**) daughter of Morris and Edythe (nee **Taller**) **Saslove**.
  - Stanley, married first to Shirley (nee **Wiseman**), and then to Carol **Sadinsky** Spiro (d. 2010), daughter of Joseph and Molly (nee **Craft**) **Sadinsky**.

Morris and Lillian (nee Spector) Kimmel (see Cherm), are not related to this Kimmel family.

For connections to other entries, see Baslaw, Craft, Feller, Hanser, Lesh, Lithwick, Reichstein, Sadinsky, Saslove, Shaffer, Taller, Victor.

KIZELL

The Kizell family stems from Moses Tuvia (d. 1942), and Rachel Leah (nee Feinberg, d. 1941). Rachel Leah is the daughter of Rafael and Sarah Feinberg, and sister of Nettie **Dover** and Edith **Dover**, successive spouses of Henry Harry **Dover**, son of William Zeev and Sarah **Dover**. Children of Moses Tuvia and Rachel Kizell were:

- Jacob (d. 1960), married to Esther (nee **Dover**, d. 1978). Esther was the daughter of Henry Harry and Edith (nee Feinberg) **Dover**, and thus a first cousin of her husband Jacob. Their children were:
  - Robert (d. 1969), married to his second cousin Edith (known as Buddy, nee **Dover**, d. 2009), daughter of Jacob and Bertha (nee Saipe) **Dover**.
  - Frances **Rubin** (d. 2000), married to Michael James **Rubin** (d. 1996), son of Jacob Moses, and Zishe (nee **Coplan**) **Rubin**. Frances' first marriage was to William (Bill) Waiser (d. 1984). Frances and William are the parents of Donna Dolansky, married to Bernard; and Cynthia, married to Stanley **Flesher**, son of Ben and Rose (nee Sinclair) **Flesher**.
- Archie (d. 1969), married to Sarah (nee Ruben, d. 1973), daughter of David and Naomi (nee **Coplan**) Ruben. Their children include:
  - Raymond (d. 2003), married to Joan (nee Cowan, d. 2010). Their son Richard is married to Cheryl (nee Kline), daughter of Phillip and Shirley (nee **Glustein**) Kline.
  - Greta **Florence** (d. 2016), married to Earl **Florence** (d. 1996), son of Louis and Jenny **Florence**.
- David (d. 1962), married to Musia (nee Litt, d. 1986).
- Robert (d. 1956).
- Tauba (d. 1989), married to Hyman Berman (d. 1927), and then to Joseph Simon (d. 1947).
- Helen Beiles (d. 2003), married to Isaac (d. 1988). Their daughter Eileen was married to David Marcus, son of Max and Reta Marcus (see **Marcovitch**).
- Norman (d. 1973), married to Sonia (nee Gitkin, d. 2003).
- Chyeneh Beiles married to Jacob Beiles.
- Max (d. 1976), married to Bella (nee Diamond, d. 1943), and then to Sarah (nee Achbar, d. 1998). Pauline Litwack (d. 2007), daughter of Max and Bella **Kizell**,

was married to Israel Litwack (d. 2007), son of Jack and Dora (nee **Glustein**) Litwack.

- Gitel Zuckerman, married to Ithak.
- Samuel (d. 1958), married to Florence (nee Horowitz).
- Isaac.
- Sybel.
- Rally.

For connections to other entries, see Coplan, Dover, Flesher, Florence, Glustein, Marcovitch, Rubin.

Seven Kizell brothers on the steps of the King Street Shul: l to r front row: Robert, Max, David. back row Jake, Norman, Archie, Sam (OJA 1-741)

Family reunion of Moshe and Rachel Kizell in Yurburg, Lithuania, 1922. Standing L-R: Samuel, Norman, David, Max (Michael), Archie, Jacob. Seated: Mrs. Gittel Zukerman, Cheina Beiles, Moshe, Rachel, Leah. Seated on ground at centre: Robert Kizell and Helen Kizell. (OJA 1-026)

KOFFMAN

See Gennis.

KRANTZBERG

The Krantzberg family is descended from Moses (d. 1936), married to Leah (nee Vineberg, d. 1960). Their children were:
- Israel (d. 1990).
- Morris (d. 2011), married to Gertrude (nee Tannenbaum).
- Jack (d. 1994), also known as Jack Krane, married to Evelyn (nee Levi, d. 2015). Evelyn's second husband was Irving Berlin. Jack and Evelyn Krane were the founders and owners of Kiddie Kobbler. Their son Sam is married to Myra (nee **Shaffer**), daughter of Sheldon and Sonia (nee Lazear) **Shaffer**.
- Julius (d. 2007), married to Clair (nee Singerman). Their son Robert was married to Leiba (nee **Smith**), daughter of the renowned Ottawa Kosher caterer Jack and Inez **Smith**.
- Anna Froimovitch (d. 2015), married to Harry (d. 2004).

Moses Krantzberg's parents were Menashe (d. 1919), and Nachama (nee Shmuter, d. 1929). Nachama's first husband was Moshe Millstein (d. 1874). Their children were:

- Wolfe (William) Freedman (name changed from Millstein, d. 1944), married to Fanny (nee Addelman, d. 1958), son of David Addelman (see **Torontow**). Their daughter Cecilia Cornblat (d. 2004), was married to Isaac, son of Max and Bella Cornblat (see Epstein branch of **Cohen**).
- Bas Sheva Zagerman, married to Gershon. Their son was Morris (d. 1967), married to Mildred (nee **Sadinsky**, d. 1971), daughter of Nesanal and Sara Feiga **Sadinsky**. Their daughter Anna was the second wife of Mildred's brother Nathan **Sadinsky**. (The children of Morris and Mildred Zagerman are:
  - Joel (d. 1944).
  - Herbert (d. 2020), married to Corinne (nee Ross, d. 2021). Corrine's sister is Gloria Krugel, married to Bert (d. 1976). John, son of Herbert and Corinne, is married to Andrea (nee Greenberg), daughter of Fred and Gert (nee Marcus, see **Marcovitch**) Greenberg.
  - Norman (d. 2018), married to Valerie (d. 1976), and then to Carole (nee Saxe), daughter of Harry and Frances (d. 2004) Saxe. Carole was formerly married to Stanley Arron (see **Weinstein**). Carole is the sister of David Saxe, married to Brenda (nee **Torontow**), daughter of Edward and Pearl (nee Tanzer) **Torontow**.
  - Shirley Cohen, married to Al Cohen (d. 2010) (see **Cantor**). Their daughter Elizabeth is married to Max, son of Rudy and Joan **Mosion**.

Nachama is the sister of Gitel (nee Shmuter, d. 1928) Goldman, married to Yelik Yoel Goldman. Their son Walter (Wolf) Goldman (d. 1921) was married to Malka (nee Finerman, d. 1949). The children of Walter and Malka were:

  - Sonia **Viner** (d. 2003), married to Arthur (d. 1997), son of Cecil and Freda (nee **Skulsky**) Viner.
  - Edith Cherun (d. 1989) , married to Alex (d. 1988).
  - Betty **Feller** (d. 2010), married to Joseph (d. 2015), son of William and Eva (nee Rosen) **Feller**.
  - Rachel Jewett (d. 1981) married to David (d. 1965).
  - Ann Kaplan (d. 2009), married to Harry (d. 2005)

For connections to other entries, see Cantor, Cohen, Feller, Marcovitch, Mosion, Sadinsky, Shaffer, Skulsky, Torontow, Viner, Weinstein.

KRONICK

The Kronick family stems from Aaron David Kronick, of Osveya, Belarus.

From his wife Sara Rifka, his son was Jacob Meyer.

From his wife Riva (nee Saverson), his children were:

- Slova Bella **Hanser** (d. 1924), married to Israel Faivish (d. 1947).
- Selig, married to Raisyl Rivka. Their children were:

- ○ Abraham Samuel (Wally) Kronick (d. 1980), married to Irene (nee **Coplan**, d. 2009) daughter of Solomon and Rebecca (nee Blachov) Coplan. Their children include:
    - ▪ Russell, married to Joan (nee **Gould**), daughter of Victor and Rachel (nee **Bodnoff**) **Gould**.
    - ▪ Stanley, married to Elizabeth (nee Rosenes), daughter of David and Sylvia (nee Fonberg d. 1990) Rosenes.
- ○ Sara **Zelikovitz** (d. 1987), married to Nathan (d. 1975), son of Joshua and Minnie **Zelikovitz**. Their daughters are Marlene Burak and Judith Schneiderman.
- ○ Tillie Leslie (d. 2009) married to Dr. Harold Leslie.
- ○ Ann Sobcov (d. 1970), married to Sam (d. 1978), son of Isaac and Rachel (nee **Taller**) Sobcov.

Aaron David's brothers were Levy Nachom and Shmuel Mordechai. Shmuel Mordechai's son was Chaim, who had a son Jacob Kronick (d. 1962), married to Toba, and then to Rae (nee Samuels), who was first married to Sol Abrahams (d. 1928). The children of Jacob and Toba Kronick were:

- Sol (d. 2007), married to Mildred.
- Dr. Sidney (d. 2019), a well-known gynecologist, married to Annice (nee Fript, d. 1995). Annice was the sister of Ruth **Leikin**, married to Julius **Leikin**. Annice's father Paul Fript was a cousin of Leon and Rae (nee **Feller**) Fine.
- David (d. 2004), married to Daphne (nee Newton, d. 1989). Daphne Kronick was a cousin of Jean (nee Newton) **Lichtenstein** and Dennis Newton. Children of David and Daphne are:
    - ○ Tracey, married to Bob Horlick, son of Hyman (d. 1984), and Frances (d. 1999) Horlick.
    - ○ Lynne **Shulman**, married to Barry, son of Joseph and Faye **Shulman** (see **Kimmel**).
- Ben.
- Anne **Taller** (d. 2001), married to Morris (d. 1964), son of Maier and Anna Clara **Taller**. Their son Myles was married to Roslyn (nee Weidman, d. 2022), daughter of Harry and Rae Weidman.

For connections to other entries, see Bodnoff, Coplan, Feller, Gould, Hanser, Kimmel, Leikin, Lichtenstein, Shulman, Taller, Zelikovitz.

LACHOVITZ

Chaim Jacob Lachovitz was the father of:

- Abraham (d. 1954), married to Mindel (nee Shentok).
- Max (d. 1950) married to Gitel (nee **Weiner**, d. 1942), daughter of David and Sarah Vinerman (see **Viner**). Their children were:
    - ○ Jennie Monson (d. 1981), married to Moses (d. 1970) son of Shmuel and Rebecca Monheit. They were the parents of:

- Rabbi David Monson (d. 2008), married to Susan (nee Strashin, d.2003). Rabbi Monson was the rabbi of Beth Shalom synagogue of Toronto for many years.
- Juair (d. 2007), married to Jean (nee Vorner, d. 2019).
- Daniel, married to Edith (nee Bogomolny).
- Connie Kussner, married to Norman (d. 1979).
  - Sarah **Petegorsky**, married to Rev. Simon, son of Mordechai and Esther (nee Fertig), **Petegorsky**.
  - Laura Steinberg, married to Frank (d. 1971). Their children are:
    - Tillie **Kardish** (d. 2004), married to Samuel (d. 2004), son of David and Etta **Kardish**.
    - Mary **Potechin**, married to Len, son of Isidore and Mary (nee Bernstein) **Potechin**.
  - Beatrice Sugarman, married to Edward.
  - May Silverman, married to Irving.
  - Maurice Lach (d. 1982), married to Fay (d. 2000).
  - Florence Nelson.
  - Jack Lach, married to Tillie (nee Mendelson).
  - Sadie Stulberg.

For connections to other entries see Kardish, Petigorsky, Potechin, Viner, Weiner.

LANDAU

The Landau family is descended from Avraham Yosef (d. 1911 in Poland), and Itta (nee Pilczewicz d. 1931 in Montreal), of Zawiercie, Poland. They had seven children, one of whom was killed in the Holocaust. Three of the children are connected to the Ottawa community.

- Jacob Landau (d. 1980), married to Rose (nee Sheinfeld, d. 1970), my paternal grandparents. Jacob Landau served as the Gabbai Rishon of the Chevra Kadisha of Ottawa for many years. Their children are:
  - Sylvia Shier (d 2023), married to Irving (d. 1998).
  - Issie (d. 1996), married to Edith (nee Goldberg). Issie and Edith's children are Jerrold, married to Tzipora (nee Rachlin, a descendant of the Epstein branch of the **Cohen** family as well as the **Leikin** family); and Michael. Jerrold and Tzipora's son Yisrael Landau is married to Menucha (nee Tuchman), a descendant of the Parnass family (see **Appotive** and **Macy**).
- Issie (d. 1984), married to Ettie (nee Schnider d. 1997). My great uncle Issie Landau shares the same name has my father. Issie Landau senior was Yitzchak, and my father was Isser, named after his maternal grandfather. Ettie was a sister to Celia **Gandall**.
- Sam (known as Shea, d. 1957), married to Yetta (nee Weinman, d. 1981). Yetta was the sister of Sadie Schlossberg, who is the mother of Rebecca Liff, married to Joe Liff (see **Murray**), and Bessie Bromberg, married to Morty. Bessie and Morty's son Sheldon is married to Alyse (nee Morris), the granddaughter of Bessie Morris (nee **Rubin**), of the Ottawa based **Rubin** family. After Shea Landau died, Yetta married Sam **Shinder** (d. 1974), who was first married to Annie (nee **Weiner**, d. 1968). Sam and Yetta Landau's son Bob Landau (d. 2004) was married

to Eileen (nee Shabinsky), the daughter of Morris and Goldie (nee **Shinder**) Shabinsky. Morris Shabinsky is a member of the **Taller** family, and Goldie is a member of the **Shinder** family.

Members of Rose Landau's family who have connections to Ottawa include:

- Jim Mintz (d. 2019), married to Mollie (nee Friberg). Jim was the son of Eva (nee Sheinfeld) Mintz, a sister of Rose. Molly is the sister of Raye Singerman, married to Sidney. Their daughters Aviva and Barbara (nee Singerman) are married to Seymour and Joel **Diener** respectively, and their daughter Felice is married to Jeff **Pleet**.
- Ethel (nee Sheinfeld) and Gerald Sarwer-Foner lived in Ottawa for many years. Ethel was the daughter of Rose's brother Israel Sheinfeld, married to Sarah. Ethel's sister Roslyn was married to Monte Swartzman (d. 2021), whose mother Freda Swartzman (d. 1998) lived in Ottawa for many years. Freda's sister-in-law Pearl (nee Davidow) Perlmutter of Winnipeg, who was married to Bert, is a descendent of the **Pollock** family, which has many branches in Ottawa. Israel Sheinfeld's grandson Stephen Sheinfeld, married to Mindy (nee Cohen) lives in Ottawa.
- Steven Bindman is a descendent of the brother of Aaron Bindman. Aaron and Freda (nee Sheinfeld) Bindman were the uncle and aunt of Rose Landau.
- Sharron **Vechsler**, the daughter of Jim Mintz's brother Irving (Jim and Irving are first cousins of Issie Landau), is married to Howard, granddaughter of Harry **Vechsler**.
- Louis Leffell, a nephew of Joseph and Gittel **Viner** and Labe and Sheva **Weiner**, was married to Fanny (nee Malkus), a sister of Frank Malkus. Frank was married to Miriam (nee Mintz), sister of Jim Mintz and cousin of Issie Landau.

Irving Shier's family was based in Montreal. He had two second cousins in Ottawa: Simon Dermer (d. 1959), married to Molly (d. 1982), and Regina Menczer (nee Dermer, d. 1982), married to Mottel (d. 1952).

Edie Landau is from Winnipeg. Her paternal grandparents Shmuel Leib Goldberg (d. 1966) and Sarah (nee Rozenworcel, d. 1946) lived in Ottawa during the 1930s and 1940s, where Shmuel Leib served as a shammas, melamed, and shochet at the James Street Shul.

- Edie's second cousin, Eleanor Ehrenkranz (nee Rozenworcel), has connections to the **Cohen** and **Diener** families of Ottawa.
- Edie's great aunt and uncle, Mordechai and Rochel Goldberg (nee Garber) of Winnipeg, are also the great aunt and uncle, from the Garber side, of Hy Calof (d. 2009), married to Ruth, as well as to Alan Brass, married to Marion.
- Edie's maternal aunt and uncle, Abraham Steinberg, married to Goldie (nee Berg), were the sister and brother-in-law of Sam and Gertie Tennenhouse of Winnipeg, who were the aunt and uncle of Arnold Tennenhouse, married to Faye.
- Edie's nephew Martin Goldberg is married to Sharon (nee Zabitsky), the niece of Marty and Eleanor **Dover**.
- Edie's sister-in-law's two brothers (the brothers of my aunt Serky Goldberg, married to my mother's brother Ben), Ken Mozersky, married to Anne (nee

Linowitz, d. 2012), and Danny Mozersky (married to Joy, nee Amsel), both settled in Ottawa. Dan was the proprietor of the chain of Prospero bookstores. Ken's late wife Anne was the daughter of Sol Linowitz, a well-known American diplomat who was involved in the negotiations of the Panama Canal treaty and the Camp David accords.

- Edie's aunt Sylvia (nee Goldberg) Sosnovich is the grandmother of Shawna (nee Sosnovich) Silver, married to Mark Silver. Mark Silver is a second cousin of Heather (nee Posner) Biderman, who was the first wife of Harold Biderman, currently married to Cayla **Lichtenstein**.

Mayer and Rose Landau, parents of Sally Taller, married to Morton, are not related to this Landau family.

For connections to other entries, see Apptotive, Cohen, Diener, Dover, Gandall, Leikin, Lichtenstein, Macy, Murray, Pleet, Pollock, Rubin, Shinder, Taller, Torontow, Vechsler, Viner, Weiner.

Wedding photo of my grandparents, Jacob and Rose (nee Sheinfeld) Landau,
December 1922 (4th night of Chanukah) in Montreal.
(from my private collection, and OJA 1-934-02)

Wedding of Issie and Edith (Goldberg) Landau, November 4, 1956 in Winnipeg. Fromleft: Franceen Shier, Sylvia (Landau) Shier, Irving Shier, my mother Edith (Goldberg)Landau, my father Issie Landau, Aaron Shier, my grandparents Rose and Jack Landau. (from my private collection)

Obituary of my great-grandfather Shmuel Leib Goldberg (grandfather of Edith Landau) from a Winnipeg Jewish newspaper, 1966. Zeidy Shmuleib served as a shamash,melamed, and shochet at the James Street Shul in Ottawa during the 1930s and 1940s. The obituary neglects to mention the Ottawa period.
(from my private collection)

LANG

See Bessin.

LEIKIN

The Leikin family is descended from Shmaryahu Leikin, of Nobozybkhov, Russia. Some members of the family spell their name as Leiken. Children of Shmaryahu Leikin were:

- Joseph (d. 1914). His children were:
  - Harry (d. 1998), married to Zena (nee Yerenbourg, d. 1968). After Zena's death, Harry married Bella (nee Rosenblatt, d. 2007), whose first husband was Max Altman (d. 1960). Bella and Max were the parents of Irving Altman (d. 2001), married to Betty; and Helen Hochberg, married to Joe. Max was the sister of Yehudit Newman (d. 1970, see **Fine**). Bella was the cousin of Helen (nee Brandes) Angel (d. 2003), married to Saltiel (d. 1981). The children of Harry and Zena are:
    - Ethel Kessler (d. 2017), married to William.
    - Libby Katz, married to Stanley (d. 2004). Stan Katz served as principal of Hillel Academy of Ottawa for several years. Libby and Stan Katz' daughter is Barbara, married to Len Farber (see **Cantor**).
    - Goldie Spieler, married to Theodore (d. 1965). Theodore's sister was Blanche **Loeb**, married to Bertram.
    - Josephine Harris, married to Jules.
  - Bertha **Palmer** (d. 2016), married to Abraham (d. 1997), son of Moses and Rose (nee **Greenberg**) **Palmer**. Their daughter Sunny Tavel is married to John.
- Keila Bodovsky (d. 1973), married to William (d. 1970). Their children are:
  - Sylvia Kershman, married to Harry (d. 1997). Sylvia Bodovsky Kershman wrote a book about her family and Jewish life in Ottawa, entitled "Life Lines... and Other Lines."
  - Anne Wormann (d. 2004), married to Bert (d. 1993).
  - Goldie Applebaum (d. 1970), married to Harry (d. 1990), son of Benjamin (d. 1914), and Yetta (d. 1960) Applebaum. Other children of Benjamin and Yetta were Jacob (d. 1983), married to Rebecca Applebaum **Wexler** (d. 1973); Pinhey (d. 971); Michael (d. 1970).
- Louis (d. 1949), married to Rose (nee Merson, d. 1951). Their children were:
  - Julius (d. 1985), married to Ruth (nee Fript, d. 1999). Ruth is the sister of Annice **Kronick**, married to Dr. Sydney **Kronick**. Ruth's father Paul Fript was a cousin of Leon Fine, married to Rae (nee **Feller**) Fine. Children of Louis and Rose are:
    - Steven
    - Molly Ann
    - Teri Levine, married to Ellis. Ellis' sister Sandra **Slover** is married to Norman **Slover**.
    - Linda
  - Harold (d. 1987), married to Phyllis (nee Cohen, d. 2006).

Shmaryahu's siblings were:

- Aryeh Leib Leikin (my wife's great-great-grandfather). His daughter Annie Rachlin (d. 1957) was married to Yehuda (d. 1961). See Epstein branch of **Cohen** for further details.
- Baruch Aharon Leikin. Aryeh Leib died very young, and Baruch Aharon then adopted Annie.

For connections to other entries, see Cantor, Cohen, Feller, Fine, Greenberg, Kronick, Landau, Loeb, Palmer, Slover.

Stan and Libby [nee Leikin] Katz on their wedding day in 1947, as well as Stan after being presented with The Gilbert Greenberg Distinguished Service Award in 2001, which is the highest tribute the Ottawa Jewish Community can bestow on an individual for exceptional service over the course of many years. (OJA 1-574-016)

LESH

The Lesh family descends from Yehuda and Frieda Lesh. Their children were:

- Samuel (d. 1961), married to Mary (nee Flesher, d. 1982), daughter of Isaac Berl and Gita **Flesher**. Their children were:
    o Bernard (d. 2003) married to Ida (nee Ochas, d. 2011).
    o Frieda **Levitan** (d. 2009), married to Harry **Levitan** (d. 1994), son of Maurice and Rachel **Levitan**.
    o George (d. 2011).

- o Norman (d. 2015), married to Isabel (nee **Kimmel**), daughter of Arthur and Sarah (nee **Hanser**) **Kimmel**. Their son Steven is married to Hildy (nee **Reichstein**), daughter of Hymie and Marlene **Reichstein**.
- Esther, married to Abe Zinn.
- Lena, married to Moshe.
- Morris, married to Becky.
- Sarah Futeral (d. 1935), married to Abraham (d. 1937). Their children were:
  - o David (d. 1981), married to Lillian.
  - o Anne Cohen, married to Lewis. Their daughter was Pearl Greenberg, married to Israel (Izzy. D. 1996) Greenberg. Izzy Greenberg was the son of Pesachya (d. 1964), and Tillie (nee Dachs, d. 1973), and the brother of Rose Konick (d. 2012), married to Morrie (d. 2012); Lee Hutt, and Jay Greenberg. Izzie and Pearl's daughter was Sheila Smith Saltzberg (d. 2004), married to Walter Saltzberg, and first married to Harvey Smith.
- Rebecca Lobel (d. 1960), married to Morris (d. 1969). Their children were:
  - o Edward (d. 1991).
  - o Sid.
  - o Jack (d. 2007), married to Goldie (nee Halpern, d. 2014). Goldie is the sister of Sadie, married to Ernie **Waserman**.
  - o Maxwell (d. 2012), married to Frieda (d. 2008). Their daughter Norma Slipacoff was married to Jerry (d. 1999), son of Charles and Mary (nee **Saslove**) Slipacoff.

For connections to other entries, see Flesher, Hanser, Kimmel, Levitan, Reichstein, Saslove, Waserman.

A third year class of the Ottawa Talmud Torah afternoon class, taught by Rabbi Boruch Kravetz – 1949.The girl with ringlets and a bow; Isabel Kimmel Lesh.
(OJA 6-010)

LEVINSON

The Levinson family descends from Morris (d. 1974), and Clara (nee **Schecter**, d. 1969), daughter of Lazarus and Minnie **Schecter**. Their children are:

- Jacie (d. 2016), married to Sandra (nee **Macy**, d. 2017), daughter of Sam and Freda (nee Kishinofsky) **Macy**. Their son Steven was married to Ida, daughter of Jack (d. 1980), and Tanya (d. 2008) Firestone, and is currently married to Barbara (nee Hymes), daughter of Hyman (d. 2012) and Dorothy Hymes.
- Barbara **Greenberg** (d. 2016), married to Sydney (known as Snooki, d. 2013), son of Morris and Bertha (nee **Gennis**) **Greenberg**.
- Frances Ballon, married to Henry, son of Jack and Esther (nee **Saslove**) Ballon.

Cantor Pinchas and Sarah Levinson are from a different family with no intrinsic roots to Ottawa, but their son has a connection through marriage to the Dover family, and Cantor Levinson is a distant cousin of Joe Lichtenstein. Cantor Levinson served as chazzan of Machzikei Hadas for several decades.

A different Levinson family stems from Abraham (d. 1938), and Sophia (nee Berman, d. 1943) Levinson. Their children were:

- Lillian Grossman, married to Maurice.
- Martin K. Levinson (d. 1996), married to Elizabeth (nee Friedgut d.1989). Martin Levinson was a chartered accountant, who trained many of the Jewish accountants of Ottawa, including my father, Issie Landau. The family also owned the Rialto theater. Children of Martin and Elizabeth are:
  - Helen Perlmutter (d. 1990), married to Israel.
  - Charlotte Burnstine.
  - Sylvia Pasher, married to Amnon.
  - Ruth Fyman, married to Dale.
- Louis (d. 1995), married to Dorothy (nee Caplan, d. 1997), daughter of Meyer (d. 1968). Meyer Caplan was the brother of Ottawa department store pioneer Caspar Caplan (see **Feller**).
- Florence Hurtig (d. 1980), married to Abraham Hurtig (d. 1987). Abraham's brother was the well-known author, activist and political candidate Mel Hurtig.

There were few connections of this Levinson family to other Ottawa families. However, Geni did yield some distant relations through the Friedgut family, based in Western Canada, to my mother Edith **Landau** (through a Simkin cousin in Winnipeg); as well as to Frances (nee Kraft) Mason, wife of Herb Mason (see **Mosion**), and the Richler family (see **Cohen**).

For connections of the Morris and Clara Levinson family to other entries, see Gennis, Greenberg, Macy, Saslove, Schecter.

For connections of the Abraham and Sophia Levinson family to other entries, see: Cohen, Feller, Landau, Mosion.

Jacie and Sandra Levinson
(Ottawa Jewish Bulletin, June 20, 2018)

Cantor Pinchas Levinson of Machzikei Hadas.
(Machzikei Hadas website: https://www.cmhottawa.com/aboutus/clergy)

Martin Levinson outside the Rialto theater a year before it closed in 1978.
(OJA 1-528, OJA 1-529)

LEVITAN

The Levitan family is descended from Morris Levitan (d. 1952), who was married to Rachel (nee Okumjansky, d. 1917), and then to Fannie (nee Isacoff d. 1968). Fannie was a sister of Rose **Molot**, married to Louis.

Children of Morris and Rachel were:

- Harry (d. 1994), married to Frieda (nee **Lesh**, d. 2009), daughter of Samuel and Sarah (nee **Flesher**) **Lesh**.
- Archie (d. 1960), married to Rose (nee **Smolkin**, d. 1990), daughter of John and Anna (nee Ginsburg) **Smolkin**. Their children are:
    o John (d. 2006), married to Lynn (nee Davis), daughter of Barry (d. 2013) and Selma (nee Davidson, d. 2020) Davis.
    o Richard is married to Patty (nee Armitage), and was married to Polly (nee Baker), daughter of Harry (d.1985) and Elsie (nee Goldenberg. d. 2006) Baker (see **Pleet**). Richard and Polly's daughter, Lenora **Zelikovitz**, is married to Evan, son of Leon and Zelda **Zelikovitz**.
    o Susan Goldstein, married to Myron.
    o Marcia Gur-Arie married to Yehuda.
- Leo (d. 1972).
- Rose **Fine** (d. 2006), married to Sidney (d. 1967), son of Abraham Israel Joseph and Ada Tzeepa **Fine**.

Children of Morris and Fannie are:

- Bessie **Greenberg** (d. 1984), married to Gilbert (d. 1980), son of Roger and Rose (nee Bezumny) **Greenberg**.
- Dr. Benjamin Levitan.
- Elliott (d. 2019), married to Sally (nee Brill, d. 2023), daughter of Joseph and Ethel (nee Weinman, d. 2004, also married to Morris Benoway d. 1977) Brill. Ethel's sister was Mary Steinberg, married to Bennet **Steinberg**, son of Yehuda Leib and Leah Tsirel **Steinberg**. Elliot and Sally's daughter Annie is married to Leonard, son of William (d. 2006), and Malca (nee Davidson) Kahansky. Malca Kahansky's sister was Selma Davis (d. 2020), married to Barry Davis (d. 2013). As noted above, the daughter of Barry and Selma Davis, Lynn, was married to John Levitan. Thus two Levitan first cousins -- Annie and John -- married two first cousins -- Leonard Kahansky and Lynn Davis.

A different Levitan family is descended from Archie and Edith (nee Rubin) Levitan. See details under Rubin.

For connections to other entries see Fine, Flesher, Greenberg, Lesh, Molot, Pleet, Smolkin, Steinberg, Zelikovitz.

LICHTENSTEIN

The Lichtenstein family descends from Joseph and Jean (nee Newton, d. 2013) Lichtenstein. Joe Lichtenstein is a Holocaust survivor from Satu Mare, Romania (Szatmar, Hungary at the time) who served as a kosher butcher in Ottawa for many decades. Joe Lichtenstein is a distant cousin of Cantor Pinchas Levinson – both are descended from Rabbi Hillel Lichtenstein of Kolomyya (1815-1895). Their children are:

- Ruth Halperin, married to David, son of Saul Halperin (d. 1994), and Girda (nee Tyber, d. 2006), and grandson of Joseph and Dora (nee **Swedlove**) Halperin.
- Barbara Geller, married to Howard.
- Cayla, married to Harold Biderman. Harold's first wife Heather (nee Posner) is a second cousin of Mark Silver, married to my second cousin Shawna (nee Sosnovich). Shawna is the granddaughter of Sylvia Sosnovich, sister of Edith **Landau**'s father Louis Goldberg.

Jean Lichtenstein was the sister of Dennis Newton (d. 1992), married to Maureen (nee **Gershon**, d. 2005), daughter of David and Tilly **Gershon**. After Dennis' death, Maureen married Israel **Shinder** (d. 2014), son of Jack and Nellie **Shinder**. Jean Lichtenstein and Dennis Newton were cousins of Joan (nee Harris) **Mosion**, married to Rudy, and Daphne (nee Newton) **Kronick**, married to David.

For connections to other entries, see Gershon, Kronick, Landau, Mosion, Shinder, Swedlove.

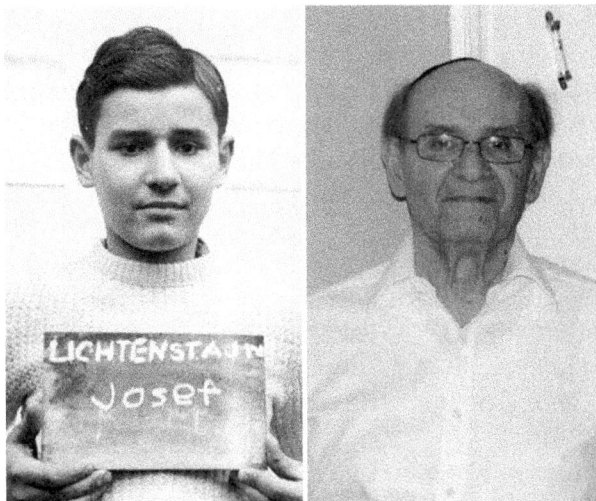

Joe Lichtenstein, on the left in a DP camp, and on the right, later in life in Ottawa.
(United States Holocaust Memorial Museum:
https://rememberme.ushmm.org/updates/josef-lichtenstajn-identified1)

LIEFF

The Lieff family descends from Avraham Chayim Lifschitz. The family members who immigrated to Ottawa changed their surname to Lieff. Children of Avraham Chayim Lifshitz were:

- Bernard Lieff (known also as Barnett, d. 1941), married to Esther Malca (nee Pomerantz, changed to **Palmer**, d. 1936), daughter of Nathaniel and Murian Hannah Pomerantz. Bernard taught at the Ottawa Talmud Torah for 35 years. Their children were:
  - The Honourable Abraham Lieff (d. 2007), married to Sadie (nee Lazarovitz, d. 1999). Abraham Lieff was involved in many Jewish organizations in Ottawa. He served as president of the Jewish community council from 1953-1955, and of the Ottawa Vaad Ha'ir from 1953-1956, and of Agudath Israel Synagogue from 1946-1963. He was the first Jew to serve as Justice on the Ontario Supreme Court (1963-1973). Their children are:
    - Miriam, who was married to Horace Cohen, son of Samuel and Shirley Cohen of Lanark, Ontario. Horace Cohen owned thee Cohen and Lord Insurance Agency. This Cohen family is not related to the other Ottawa Cohen families. Children of Horace and Miriam are: Stephen married to Pernille; Lisa; Sharon married to Eric Barker.
    - Lois. Her children are: Brenda Adessky is married to Kenneth, nephew of Irving and Zelda (nee Soloway) Adessky (see **Greenberg**); Ellin Bessner, married to John Friedland.
  - Louis (d. 1993), married to Jeanne (nee **Gottdank**, d. 2003), daughter of David (d. 1922), and Rachel (d. 1938) **Gottdank**.
  - Elizabeth Narod (d. 1994), married to Milton (d. 2001).
  - Hyman (d. 1987), married to Pearl (d. 1997).
  - Max (d. 2002), married to Dorothy (nee Brovender, d. 2019).
  - Morris (d. 1987), married to Pearl (nee Jacobs. d. 1995)

- o Joseph (d. 2012), married to Evelyn (nee Sobcuff). Joe Lieff served as president of the Ottawa Jewish Community Council from 1981-1983. Their children are Elissa married to David Resnick; Norman married to Francie Greenspoon; Susan married to Joel; Alan married to Ann.
- Leon (d. 1957), married to Minnie (nee Doctor, d. 1960), daughter of Rabbi Louis and Dena Chaya Doctor (see **Florence**). Their children were:
  - o Abraham.
  - o Esther Shaver (d. 1979), married to Reuben (d. 1960), son of Louis and Annie (nee **Taller**) Shabinsky.
  - o Bessie Cohen (d. 1996), married first to Sam Ellis, and then to Samuel Cohen. Their daughter Ellen Cardash is married to Marty Cardash, son of Sam and Celia Cardash (**Kardish**).
  - o Eva Grossman
- Moses (d. 1944) married to Bertha (nee Steinberg d. 1944). Their children were
  - o Meyer (d. 1974), married to Ida (nee **Shore** d. 1944), daughter of Moses and Sarah Shore.
  - o Chaya Rachel (d. 1944).
  - o Samuel (d. 1969), married to Libby (nee **Kardish** d. 2002), daughter of David **Kardish**. Their children are:
    - ▪ Murray, married to Judy.
    - ▪ Bernice **Feller**, married to Robert, son of Henry and Gertrude (nee **Victor**) **Feller**.
    - ▪ David, married to Zena (nee Koffman), daughter of Milton and Beatrice (nee **Bordelay**) Koffman (see **Gennis**).

For connections to other entries see Bordelay, Feller, Florence, Gennis, Gottdank, Greenberg, Kardish, Palmer, Shore, Taller, Victor.

I. L. COHEN
President, 1930-1931

A. H. LIEFF K.C.
President, 1943-1944

through the thirties and with its Nazi and Fascist activities and even unto the present time with its periodic manifestations of small items of Jewish hatred, B'nai B'rith has been particularly active in combatting most successfully these infamous items of vile propaganda. What is important re this matter as it concerns B'nai B'rith is the manner that has been adopted in fighting anti-Semitism. This has usually taken the form of a dignified and firm stand re the question in hand without the need of a lot of ballyhoo, fanfare and widespread publicity. It is this particular method of dealing with anti-Semitism that has often lead many to think that nothing was being done, but the facts are definitely not so. It might also be observed that when it was necessary that a firm stand was required to fight racial intolerance, B'nai B'rith on the local, regional and national level did not hesitate to speak out bluntly and to the point.

It should be worthy of mention that a number of the leaders of Ottawa B'nai B'rith have and are playing a very important part in the wider sphere of B'nai B'rith activity which includes the Canadian Conference of B'nai B'rith, District No. 1, of which Ottawa is a member Lodge and in the international realm which is the responsibility of the Supreme Grand Lodge in Washington. At least three names must be mentioned in this connection, namely, Dr. Harry Dover, the late Ben Goldfield, K.C., and Maxwell B. Abrams. Dr. Dover was in fact one of the guiding spirits during the pioneer days of the Canadian Conference. The late Mr. Goldfield, K.C., and Mr. Abrams were and are known as "Mr. B'nai B'rith," so intense a part have they both played in the affairs of Canadian B'nai B'rith.

One cannot complete this brief account without mention of the work accomplished in the 25th year of B'nai B'rith activity in Ottawa under the inspired leadership of Mr. J. C. Horwitz. Not only did the local lodge grow tremendously in active membership but the work was accomplished by some twenty-five odd committees, each of whom under its own chairman could relate much towards the realization of the aims and purposes of B'nai B'rith. This innovation by Mr. Horwitz of dividing the work of B'nai B'rith amongst committees has proven its worth and will likely continue now as a permanent feature of the future.

So ends this brief history of B'nai B'rith.

10

Page 5 of "History of B'nai B'rith in Canada's Capital" which appeared in the 25th anniversary souvenir booklet of the Ottawa Lodge No. 885, 1946.

The Lieff men in uniform, 1944.L-R: Joseph Lieff - Navy; Hyman Lieff - Air Force; Max Lieff - Army Service Corps. (OJA 1-580-05)

LITHWICK

The Lithwick family descends from Naphtali Hertz (d. 1926), and Esther Baila (nee Lerner, d. 1930) Lithwick. Esther Baila's nephew was Jacob **Freedman**, married to Leah. Children of Naphtali Hertz and Esther Baila were:

- Feige Chaya Silverstein, married to Yisrael.
- Shaul Isaac (d. 1921), married to Necha (nee Krupnick, d. 1923). Their son Abraham (d. 1953) was married to Dora (nee Rosenberg, d. 1980). Abraham and Dora Lithwick were very active in the Hillel Lodge, and the chapel in the former Hillel Lodge on Wurttemberg St. was named for them. Children of Abraham and Dora were:
  - Sarah Green (d. 2007), married to Murray Sidney Green (d. 2001).
  - Sidney (d. 2008), married to Ida (nee Witchel).
  - Norman (d. 2006).
  - Harold (d. 1972).
- Max (d. 1958), married to Dora (nee Ness. d. 1960). Note that this Dora Lithwick is to be differentiated from her niece, Dora Lithwick, who was married to Abraham. Children of Max and Dora are:
  - Hyman (d. 1990), married to Freda (nee **Swedlove**, d. 2013), daughter of Zelig and Rachel (nee Achbar) **Swedlove**.
  - Sydney (d. 2012), married to Geraldine (nee Grover, d.2001). Sydney Lithwick was a well-known architect, who designed both Beth Shalom and Agudath Israel synagogues.

- o Libby Glube (d. 2009), married to Stanley (d. 1998). Stan Glube owned Factory Surplus on the Byward Market together with his brother-in-law Hy Lithwick. Children of Stan and Libby Glube are:
    - Malcolm, married to Vera (nee Gottlieb). Their daughter Sharon is married to Sol **Reichstein**, son of Hyman and Marlene **Reichstein**.
    - Norman, married to Arlene.
    - Allan, married to Rhona.
    - Bryan, married to Bev.
  - o Val (d. 2004), first married to Ruth (nee Ain, d. 1984), and then to Annette Lesonsky (nee **Feller** d. 2001), who was originally married to Lou Lesonsky (d. 1976). Annette was the daughter of Moe and Germaine (nee Zittrer) **Feller**. Ruth's brother Kenneth Ain, is the father of Susan Kriger, married to David, son of Akiva and Shirley (nee Movsovich), Kriger (see **Glustein** and **Smolkin** entries).
- Shamma (d. 1964), married to Hinda (nee Guz, d. 1958). Hinda is the sister of Elka **Kimmel**, married to Jacob Leib **Kimmel**. Children of Shamma and Hinda were:
  - o Arnold (d. 1980), married to Rose (nee Esar, d. 1995). Their children are:
    - Harvey, married to Yvonne (nee Bahar).
    - Barry, married to Marieta (nee Pareno).
    - Irwin, married to Monique (nee Topol).
  - o Riva Kroll, married to Abraham.
  - o Irving (d. 1988), married to Ellen (nee Blair, d. 2009). Their children are:
    - Norton (d. 2017).
    - Vicky Weiss, married to Earl.
  - o Lev Litvak, married to Anna. This branch of the family never left the Soviet Union, and lived in Leningrad. Lev's son Emmanuel (d. 2006) was married to Vera (nee d.. 2012). Vera's sister Nina was married to the son of Hassia Rashevsky (nee **Kimmel**), daughter of Jacob Leib and Elka (nee Guz), **Kimmel** – thus forging another connection between the Lithwick, Guz, and **Kimmel** families. David **Kimmel** informs me that the Lithwick and **Kimmel** branches who were connected through the Guz connection lived together in their parents' house in Rovno, later in Leningrad, and remained very close when they arrived in Ottawa.
- Mary Greenblatt (d. 1959), married to Harry (d. 1959). Their children were:
  - o Stella Lerner (d. 1974), married to Abraham.
  - o Bea Moscovitch Grant (d. 1981), married to Joseph (d. in the 1950s), and then to Jack Grant.
  - o Dr. Joseph Greenblatt (d. 1982), married to Frances (nee Trachtenberg, d. 2012).
- Naomi Coopersmith (d. 1964), married to Benjamin (d. 1948). Their children were:
  - o Gertrude Farber (d. 1974) married to Max (d. 1990). Max Farber, a Holocaust survivor, was first married to Zisele, and had two sons, David and Yitzchak, who all perished in the Holocaust. After Gert's death, Max married Bess Chalefsky (nee Schneiderman, d. 2005). The son of Max and Gert, Bernie Farber, served as executive director of the Canadian Jewish Congress. He is married to Karyn Bosloy, daughter of Syd and Noreen Bosloy (see **Gosewich**). Max Farber had three nephews in Ottawa: Norman Fishbain (d. 1994), married to Alice (d.2012); Israel Fishbain (d. 1993),

married to Luba (d. 2004) (owners of Foster's Sports Center); Sam Fishbain (d. 1995), married to Sandra.

- o Bertha Klugsberg (d. 2006), married to Abraham (d. 2008).
- o Saul (d. 1993), married to Selma (nee Seidler, d. 1993). Selma's sister was Gusta **Sugarman** (d. 1994), married to Philip (d. 1991), son of Hyman and Jessie **Sugarman**.

- Moshe (Max, also known as M.Z., d. 1953), married to Manya (nee Greenberg). Their children were:
  - o Leema Magidson, (d. 2012) married to Sam (d. 1989), son of Aaron and Hasse (nee Ness) Magdson. Hasse is the sister of Dora Lithwick, married to Leema's uncle Max – forging a double connection between the Magidson and Lithwick families. Sam and Leema's daughter Roslyn **Kimmel** is married to Arnold, son of Arthur and Sarah (nee **Hanser**) **Kimmel**. Sam and Leema's son Stanley is married to Ellen (nee Polsky), daughter of Bill and Ruth (nee Tavel) Polsky (see **Palmer**).
  - o Sylvia Leibner, married to Alex.
- Ente Aisenberg (d. 1973), married to Harry (d. 1973). Their children were:
  - o Sydney (d. 1980), married to Judy (d. 2021). Syd Aisenberg was a partner with my father in the Landau & Aisenberg accounting firm before moving to Toronto. After Syd's death, Judy married Theodore Wolfe (known as Ted, d. 2004), who was formerly married to Mildred (nee Goldsmith, d. 1980). Ted was the son of Moses Wolfe (d. 1948), and the brother of Irving (known as Chick, d. 2009), married to Louise (d. 2013); Nathan (d. 1991), married to Dora (nee Golden, d. 2007); Edward (d. 1980); Harry; Alexander (d. 1974), married to Marianne (d. 2006); Bella. Mildred Wolfe's sister was Nancy **Saslove** (d. 2003), married to Edgar **Saslove**.
  - o Irene **Swedlove** (d. 2009), married to Joseph (d. 1989), son of Sam and Fanny (nee **Cohen**) **Swedlove**.

For connections to other entries, see Cohen, Feller, Freedman, Glustein, Gosewich, Kimmel, Palmer, Reichstein, Saslove, Smolkin, Sugarman, Swedlove.

Harry Aisenberg [married to Ente, nee Lithwick] and Harry Small standing outside H. Aisenberg Fruits & Vegetables, 30 Byward Market, circa 1930. (OJA 2-059)

Abraham and Dora Lithwick (OJA 1-413)

LITWACK

See Glustein.

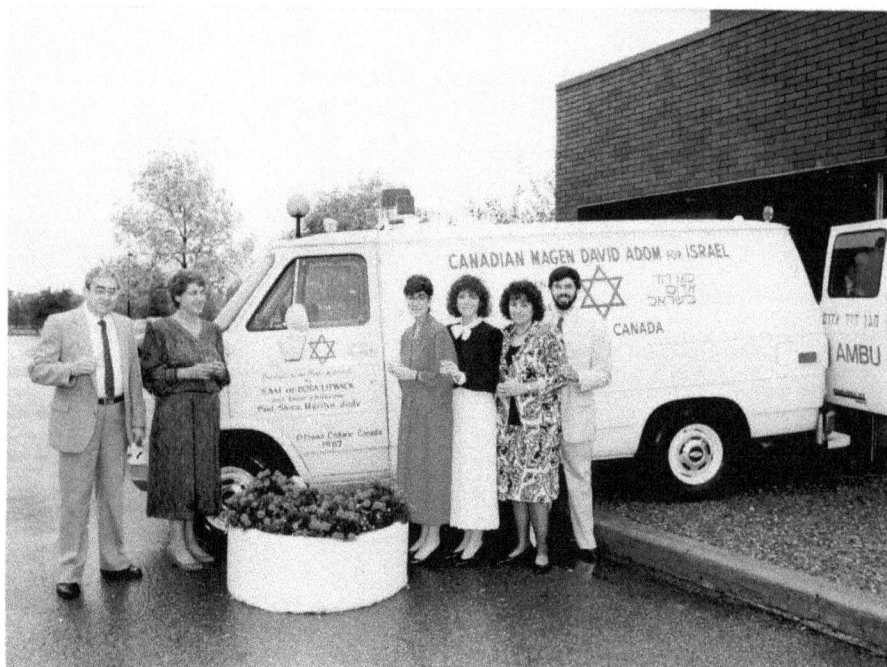

L-R: Sam, Dora, Marilyn, Judy, Shira, and Paul Litwack. Ambulance dedication ceremony, September 13, 1987. (OJA Facebook Page)

LOEB

The Loeb family is descended from Moses (d. 1951), and Rose (d. 1963) Loeb. Their children were:

- Dr. Lazarus (d. 2005), first married to Rhoda (nee **Saslove**), daughter of Samuel and Lillian (nee Radnoff) **Saslove**, and then married to Jacqueline.
- Bertram (d. 2006), married to Blanche (nee Spieler, d. 1993). Bertram was the founder of the IGA supermarket chain. Blanche was the sister of Theodore Spieler, married to Goldie (nee **Leikin**) Spieler.
- Dr. Henry (d. 1949).
- Norman (d. 2005), married to Amelia (nee Brownstein, d. 1979).
- Jules (d. 2008), married to Fay (nee **Zelikovitz**, d. 2017), daughter of Solomon and Sonia **Zelikovitz**.
- David (d. 2016), married first to Joyce (nee Glickman, d. 1995), daughter of Dr. Abraham and Jennie (nee **Freedman**) Glickman, and then to Adele (nee Light). David Loeb served as President of Parliament Lodge B'nai B'rith, President of Agudath Israel Congregation, President of the Jewish Community Council, President of the Jewish Community Foundation, Chairman of United Jewish Appeal, Chairman of Israel Bonds of Ottawa, and Chairman of the United Way of Ottawa-Carleton. Children of David and Joyce are:
  - Kenneth.
  - Mitchell.

- o Arthur, who was married to Lori (nee **Fine**). Lori later married Mendy **Taller**, son of Samuel and Bessie (nee **Cantor**) **Taller**. Arthur's second wife is Karen (nee Shiller).

For connections to other entries, see Cantor, Fine, Freedman, Leikin, Saslove, Taller, Zelikovitz.

The Loeb Brothers. From L-R standing: Jules and Henry; seated: Lazarus, Bertram (Bert), Norman, and David. (OJA 1-443)

MACY

The Macy family is descended from Samuel (d. 1969), and Freda (nee Kishinofsky, d. 1986) Macy. The original family name was Mausberg. Their children are:

- Murray (d. 2020), first married to Myrna (nee Katz), daughter of Joseph and Esther (nee Parnass, d. 2016) Katz, and then to Mary. Esther Katz's sisters were Bas Sheva, married to Joseph **Appotive**, and Fruma, married to Rudy **Appotive**. Joseph and Rudy are both sons of Avraham and Sarah (nee **Viner**) **Appotive**.
- Ruth **Viner** (d.2020), married to Joseph (d. 2014), son of Irving and Clara (nee **Halpern**) **Viner**. Their daughter Susan is married to Gilad Vered, son of Zeev and Sara Vered (see Soloway branch of the **Greenberg** family).
- Sandra **Levinson** (d. 2017), married to Jacie (d. 2016), son of Morris and Clara (nee **Schecter**) **Levinson**.

- Shirley **Molot**, married to Michael, son of Reuben and Sylvia (nee Saipe) **Molot**. Sylvia is the sister of Roy Saipe, married to Helen (nee **Dworkin**), and Bertha (nee Saipe) **Dover**, married to Jacob **Dover**.

For connections to other families, see Appotive, Dover, Dworkin, Greenberg, Halpern, Levinson, Molot, Schecter, Viner.

MARCOVITCH / MARCUS

The Marcovitch family is descended from Abraham (d. 1970), and Freida (nee Haimovici, d.1950) Marcovitch. Many branches of this family changed their surname to Marcus. Children of Abraham and Frieda were:

- Nathan Marcus (d. 1982) married to Sarah (nee **Froman**, d. 1986), daughter of Simeon and Tobya **Froman**. Their daughter Gertude Greenberg is married to Fred. Andrea Zagerman, daughter of Fred and Gert, is married to John, son of Herbert and Corinne (nee Ross) Zagerman (see **Krantzberg**). Fred Greenberg's brother was Harry Greenberg, married to Sarah. Their daughter Tziona is married to Melvyn Yankoo, son of Joseph and Ann (nee **Ellenberg**) Yankoo.
- Lillian **Saslove** (d. 1996), married to Samuel (d. 1986), son of Jacob and Hanna Zaslovsky / **Saslove**. Their children are:
  - Barry, who was married to Nili.
  - Dorothy **Karp** (d. 2019), married to Maurie (d. 2009), son of Max and Dora Kapinsky.
  - Carol, first married to David Shaikin, and then to Harvey Goodman.
- Rachel Tuckman (d. 1984), married to Benjamin (d. 1969), son of Tevel (d. 1945), and Miriam (d. 1929) Tuckman. Their children are:
  - Edna **Waserman** (d. 1978), married to Nathan (d. 2006), son of Harry and Rachel **Waserman**.
  - Helen Peters, married to David.
- Tom Marcus, married to Fanny (nee Lazarus, d. 1968).
- Max Marcus (d. 1980) married to Fanny (nee Lifshitz, d. 1979).
- Benjamin (d. 1997), married to Jean (nee Weatherall).
- Samuel (d. 2007), married to Rita (nee Hershorn, d. 1999).

Abraham's brother was Haim Leib Marcus (d. 1932), married to Feige (nee Bleichner, d. 1934). They had many children, only a few mentioned here:

- Max, married to Reta (nee Samuels). Their children are:
  - David (d. 2011), married to Eileen, daughter of Isaac and Helen (nee **Kizell**) Beiles.
  - Perry (d. 2015), married to Myrna (nee Helfgot),. Their daughter Susan is married to Mark Silver. Susan Marcus served as president of Beth Tikva Congregation of Ottawa.
- Harry (d. 1976), married to Doris (nee Swartz, d. 1963). Their daughter Florence (d.2017) was married to Louis Strolovitch. Sharron, the daughter of Florence and Louis Strolovitch, married Richard **Gennis**, son of Max and Hilda (nee **Aaron**) **Gennis**.

For connections to other entries, see Aaron, Ellenberg, Froman, Gennis, Karp, Kizell, Krantzberg, Saslove, Waserman.

MAX

The Max family is descended from Max Max (d. 1939), married to Annie (nee Bromberg, d. 1939). The original family name was Kavalsky. Apparently, people used to refer to Max Kavalsky in Lowertown as Mr. Max, and he eventually adopted that last time (source: Michael Polowin). Children of Max and Annie were:

- Rose Goldberg (d. 1996), married to Samuel (d. 1965). Their children are:
  - Evelyn **Tradburks – Rivers**, first married to Irwin **Tradburks** (d. 1974), Osias and Minnie **Tradburks**; and then to Irving **Rivers**, son of Jacob and Leah (nee Keller) **Rivers**.
  - Dr. Morley Goldberg.
- Sol (d. 2000), married to Lillian (nee Abrams, d. 2005). Their children are:
  - Mark, married to Yanda (nee Waiser), daughter of Arthur and Gitel (nee **Pollock**) Waiser.
  - Leonard, married to Mina (nee Kapinsky, d. 1998), daughter of Nap and Fay (nee **Torontow**) Kapinsky (see **Karp**). Their daughter Melanie **Polowin** is married to Michael, son of David and Betty (nee Cowan) **Polowin**.
  - Ann Levencrown, first married to Richard Slone (d. 1971), and then to Leonard Levencrown. Richard and Ann's daughter is Stacey **Cantor**, married to Mark, son of Danny and Bev (nee Segal) **Cantor**. Leonard and Ann's daughter is Amanda.
- Arthur (d. 2012), married to Sara (nee Wise, d. 2000), and originally married to Hannah (nee **Polowin**, d. 2003), daughter of Jacob and Dina (nee Gordon) **Polowin**.
- Sasa **Dover** (d. 1987), married to Robert (d. 1970), son of Henry and Nettie (nee Feinberg), **Dover**. Their children are:
  - Helen **Polowin**, married to Gerald, son of Benjamin and Bessie **Polowin**.
  - Mark, married to Ann (nee Abrahamson), son of Arnold and Bella (nee **Vechsler**) Abrahamson.

For connections to other entries, see Cantor, Dover, Karp, Pollock, Polowin, Rivers, Torontow, Tradburks, Vechsler.

MIRSKY

The Mirsky family is descended from Nachman Yehuda Mirsky. Two of his sons, Rev. Jacob Mirsky, and Harris Mirsky, were the ancestors of Ottawa families. Rev. Jacob Mirsky was a cantor and spiritual leader in Ottawa for many years.

Rev. Jacob Mirsky (d. 1942) was married to Sarah (nee Jaffe, d. 1900), and then to Fanny (nee Bach, d. 1943). Fanny was the brother of Benjamin Nathanson, whose son Joseph was married to Harriet (nee **Dover**), son of John and Minnie (nee Cohen) **Dover**. Children of Jacob and Sarah were:

- David (d. 1962), married to Sadie (nee Vineberg, d. 1939). David was the founder of the Pure Spring soft drink company. Their children were:
  - Norman (d. 1986), married to Anne (d. 2003), daughter of Leon and Rae (nee **Feller**) Fine. Their son Stephan is married to Millie (nee **Bilsky**), daughter of Lawrence and Esther (nee Rabin) **Bilsky**.
  - John (d. 1962), also known as Jack, married to Marion Rosenfeld.
  - Mervin (d. 2010), married to Barbara Jean (nee Martin, d. 2009).
- Rose Pearlman (d. 1982), married to Mendel (d. 1961). Their son Dr. Lyon Pearlman (d. 1997), married to Naomi (nee Perchanok, d. 2007), was a prominent pediatrician in Ottawa. Their daughter Elaine Goldstein is married to Franklin Goldstein, son of Sam and Miriam (nee London) Goldstein (Miriam is a cousin of A. J. Freiman – see **Bilsky**).
- Abraham (d. 1914).
- Dr. Samuel (d. 1976), married to Hazel (d. 1984)
- Reva Sklar.

Harris (Harry) Mirsky (d. 1965) was married to Ida Cayla (nee Cohen, d. 1941). Their children were:

- Lazarus (d. 2007), married to Gertrude (nee **Tradburks**, d. 1967), daughter of Osias and Minnie **Tradburks**. Laz' second marriage was to Sibyl (nee Moscovitch, d. 2006). The Moscovitch family, based in Winnipeg, are cousins of the **Feller** family. Children of Laz and Gertrude are:
  - Kenneth, married to Linda (nee Cohen), daughter of Lefty and Jenny (nee **Kardish**) Cohen.
  - Cayla **Baylin**, married to Michael (d. 2015), son of Sam and Carolyn (nee Progosh) **Baylin**.
- Libby Moraff, married to John (d. 1964).
- David (d. 1983), married to Esther (nee **Gottdank**, d. 1988), daughter of David and Rachel **Gottdank**.
- Louis (d. 1988), married to Rose (d. 1961).
- Ann Seigal, married to Murray.
- Rose.

For connections to other entries, see Baylin, Bilsky, Dover, Feller, Gottdank, Kardish, Tradburks.

Louis Mirsky behind the counter of the Party Palace Deli on Elgin Street, in the late 50s -mid 60s. (OJA 1-708-01)

Jacob Mirsky (1859-1942) - Ottawa's First Rabbi. (OJA 1-945-01)

L-R: Peter, Jane, Michael, Brian and Philip, with parents Mervin and Barbara Mirsky in front. Photo by Jon Joosten Photography, ca.1976.
(M-023, Ottawa Jewish Archives)

The newspaper clipping in the photo reads:

part American. Max Geums of Ottawa,
President of the Region attended the
meeting.

* * *

DR. L. PEARLMAN ARRIVES

The Jewish c'tizenry of Ottawa are
proud of the recent addition to the city's
medical corps of Dr. Lyon Pearlman, son
of Mr. and Mrs. M. Pearlman, and
grandson of Ottawa's beloved Rev. J.
Mirsky.

Dr. Pearlman, whose specialty is
Pediatrics, returns to his home c'ty after
several years of excellent post-graduate
practice and training under some of the
leading child-special'sts in the United
States. He will formally open offices at
151 Metcalfe Street on October 1st. In
extending s'ncere good wishes for his
success, the "Bullet'n" is confident that
the city's health records will mark as a
Yom Tov for Ottawa children, the day
Dr. Pearlman began his medical minist-
rat'ons.

* * *

AIR-MINDED

Jack Arron son of Mr and Mrs L L

Photo 1) Lyon Pearlman along with his parents, Mendel and Rose [nee Mirsky] – 1919 (OJA 1-190)

Photo 2) Dr. Lyon Pearlman - 1994

Photo 3) The original notice in the October 7, 1938 edition of the Ottawa Jewish Bulletin giving notice of the opening of Dr. Pearlman's practice.

(Note: Dr. Pearlman was my pediatrician during my childhood.)

MOLOT

The Molot family is descended from Louis (d. 1946), and Rose (nee Isacoff, d. 1960), natives of Minsk. Louis Molot was the founder of Molot furs. Rose was a sister of Fannie **Levitan**, married to Morris. Children of Louis and Rose are:

- David (d. 2008), married to Lottie (nee Langstadt, d. 2009), daughter of Julius (d. 1959), and Paula (d. 1975) Langstadt. Dave, Abe, and Rube Molot owned Molot Pharmacies. Children of Dave and Lottie are:
  - Helen Held, married first to Martin Green, and then to Ricky Held.
  - John, married first to Erryl Myers (d. 2013), and then to Debra Aronson.
  - Lewis, married to Linda Kamerman.
  - Morris (d. 1970).
- Abram (d. 1977), married to Edith (d. 1975). Their children are:
  - Henry, married to Maureen (nee Appel), daughter of Toby (d. 2008) and Rebecca (nee Morris. d. 1967) Appel. Toby was later married to Freda Appel (nee Swetsky, d. 2007). Toby was the son of Max (d. 1960), and Chasia Feiga (d. 1954) Appel. Toby was the brother of Moses (d. 1979), married to Mollie (nee Karon, d. 2004), and Nell Gluck (d. 2003), married to Dr. Elliot Gluck (d. 1999).
  - Barbara **Sugarman**, married first to Sol Schmelzer, and then to Laurence **Sugarman** (d. 1991), son of Hyman and Jessie (nee Phillips) **Sugarman**. Laurence was first married to Shirley (nee **Polowin**, d. 1984), daughter of Jacob Oscar and Dina (nee Gordon) **Polowin**.
- Reuben (d. 1986), married to Sylvia (nee Saipe, d. 2008). Sylvia is the sister of Roy Saipe, married to Helen (nee **Dworkin**), and Bertha (nee Saipe) **Dover**, married to Jacob **Dover**. Their children are:
  - Michael is married to Shirley (nee **Macy**), daughter of Sam and Freda (nee Kishinofsky) **Macy**.
  - Mark, originally married to Nancy, then to Juquita.
  - Judy Piazza, originally married to Larry, son of Sam and Tillie (nee Steinberg) **Kardish**, and then to Vince Piazza.
- Sam, married to Lee (nee Stern). Their children are:
  - Beverly.
  - Martin, married to Marcia.
- Lazar (d. 1980), married to Ruth (d. 1998). Their children are:
  - Florette Brill, married to Marvin.
  - Marilyn Goldsmith, married first to Gilbert Portnoy, and then to Sid Goldsmith.
- Solomon (d. 1997), married to Louella (d. 2011). Their children are:
  - Leslie Kirshenblatt, married to Marvin.
  - Russell, married to Dawn (nee Wolfson).
  - Pamela, was married to Ron Berman.
- Edith Sonken (d. 2008), married to Saul (d. 1978). Saul Sonken is a cousin of Fannie **Betcherman**, married to Abraham, and Sylvia (nee **Gould**) Smith, married to Kalman. Children of Saul and Edith are:
  - Rhoda Shabinsky, married to Marvin (d. 2021), son of Bennie and Alice (nee Bergman) Shabinsky (see **Taller**).
  - Rosalind Lewin was married to Julian, son of Nathan (d. 1996) and Tema (nee Kleinplatz) Lewin. Nathan Lewin was a respected teacher at Hillel Academy for many decades, and Tema served as the librarian at the Jewish Community Center.

For connections to other families, see Betcherman, Dover, Dworkin, Gould, Kardish, Levitan, Macy, Polowin, Sugarman, Taller.

MOSION

The Mosion family is descended from Max Wolfe (d. 1941), and Fannie (nee Rosen). Their children were:

- Sylvia **Rubin** (d. 1979), married to Louis (d. 1995), son of Jacob Moses and Zishe (nee **Coplan**) **Rubin**.
- Abraham (d. 1971), married to Betty (nee Gutteit, d. 2020), daughter of Isaac and Rachel (nee Lerner, see **Gandall**). Betty was a first cousin of Libby **Steinberg**, married to Jack.
- Herb Mason (d. 1971), married to Sadie (known as Stish, nee **Craft**, d. 1974), daughter of Hyman (d. 1947), and Annie (nee Michelin, d. 1967) **Craft**. Their son Morley Mason (d. 2017) was married to Marcia (nee **Kardish**), daughter of Louis and Mary (nee Udashkin) **Kardish**, and then to Cathy. Morley Mason served as the director of Camp Bnai Brith of Ottawa for many years.
- Rudolph (Rudy, d. 1990), married to Joan (nee Harris, d. 1999). Joan Mosion was known to all Hillel Academy Central Branch students from the 1960s and 1970s as the office manager. Their son Max is married to Elizabeth, daughter of Al and Shirley (nee Zagerman) Cohen (see **Cantor** and **Krantzberg**). Joan Mosion was a cousin of Jean (nee Newton) **Lichtenstein** and Dennis Newton.
- Benjamin (d. 1967).

For connections to other entries, see Cantor, Coplan, Craft, Gandall, Kardish, Krantzberg, Lichtenstein, Rubin, Steinberg.

This ca. 1930's photo shows the Max Mosion and family standing outside of their shop, The Dominion Bakery, which was located at 419 St. Patrick Street. On the right is a receipt from the Breakfast Club, a group of 13-16 year old boys who would meet on Sunday mornings. (OJA 2-047)

MURRAY

The Murray family is descended from Joseph and Bertha (d. 1953) Murray. The surname is pronounced with the stress on the final syllable. The children of Joseph and Bertha were:

- Bessie **Greenberg** (d. 1994), married to Samuel (d. 1970), son of Max and Bayla **Greenberg**. See **Greenberg** for connections to the **Betcherman**, **Dover**, **Froman**, **Slover**, **Taylor**, **Viner** and Zunder families.
- Boruch (d. 1955), married to Esther (nee Cratzbarg, d. 1997), daughter of Sam and Bessie (nee Krupnick, d. 1938) Cratzbarg. Esther was the sister of Libby **Kardash**, wife of Pinney **Kardash**; and Joseph Cratzbarg (d. 1987), married to Anne (d. 1994). Joseph and Anne's son is Sidney, married to Sandy. Sid and Anne's daughter, Hillary, is married to Ian Raskin, son of Carl and Lorna (nee Gerson) Raskin. Children of Boruch and Esther Murray are:
  o Joseph (d. 2018), married to Jessie (nee Reiman, d. 2015).
  o Abraham (d. 2014), married to Ethel (nee Levinson, d. 2012), daughter of Harry (d. 1982) and Fanny (nee Prusky d. 1980) Levinson.
  o Gordon (d. 2017), married to Bertha.
- Libba Breatross (d. 1980), married to Usher (d. 1951). Their children were:
  o Tili Wilner Atlas (d. 2011), married to Dr. Saul Wilner, and then Dr. Moe Atlas.
  o Joseph (d. 2016), married to Deborah (nee Flatt), daughter of Max (d. 1982) and Leah (d.1990) Flatt. Debbie's brother is Marvin Flatt, married to Lila (nee Selector, d. 2015). Marvin's cousin Ab Flatt is an uncle of Lisa (nee Wolfe) **Aaron**, wife of Leslie **Aaron**, son of Irving and Ruth **Aaron**.
- Gittel Liff (d. 1970), married to Abraham (d. 1979). Their son Joseph was married to Rebecca (nee Schlossberg, d. 2013), daughter of Isaac and Sadie (nee Weinman) Schlossberg. Sadie's sister was Yetta **Landau**, married first to my great uncle Shea (Sam) **Landau**, and then to Sam **Shinder**. Rebecca's sister Bessie Bromberg was married to Morty (d. 1993), father of Sheldon Bromberg, whose wife Alyse (nee Morris) is the granddaughter of Raphael and Bessie (nee Rubin) Morris (see **Rubin** and **Coplan**).

For connections to other entries, see Aaron, Betcherman, Coplan, Dover, Froman, Kardish, Landau, Rubin, Shinder, Taylor, Viner.

A family gathering for Passover in the home of Mr. and Mrs. Boruch Murray, 1953.

Seated at table L-R: Bess Kardash, Libby Kardash, Esther Murray, Betty Cratzbarg (nee Rose) (seated with father) Joe Cratzbarg, Anne Cratzbarg, Sid Cratzbarg (seated with brother) Abe Liff, Gittel Liff, Tilly Liff. Standing L-R: Sid Kardash, Pinny Kardash, Boruch Murray, Gordy Murray, Joe Murray, Abe Murray, Joe Liff. (OJA 1-1225)

NEWMAN

See Fine, Gorelick, Leikin.

OSTERER

See Glustein.

From L-R: Leo Osterer is pictured at the opening of the Beth Hamidrash Chapel (Abraham and Dora Lithwick Chapel) at Hillel Lodge in 1975; in the centre is a watercolor of Osterer's Store painted by Ben Babebiocky in 1984; and the 136 Florence Street building as it appeared on March 19th, 2016. (OJA 4-446-03)

Joseph Osterer playing softball in the streets of Lowertown - ca. 1940
(OJA 1-941-14)

PALMER

The Palmer family is descended from Moses (d. 1946), and Rose (nee **Greenberg**, d. 1967). Rose is related to the main Ottawa **Greenberg** family. Moses is the sister of Esther **Lieff** (d. 1936), married to Bernard **Lieff** (d. 1941). The original family name was Pomerantz. Children of Moses and Rose were:

- Abraham (d. 1997), married to Bertha (nee **Leikin** d. 2009), daughter of Yosef **Leikin**, and sister of Harry **Leikin**. Their son Joel was married to Barbara (nee **Gould**), daughter of Kalman and Sylvia (nee Smith) **Gould**. Their daughter Sunny Tavel is married to John Tavel, son of Charles (d. 1982), and Rae (d. 1969) Tavel. Charles and Rae's daughter Ruth Polsky was married to Bill Polsky – whose daughter Ellen is married to Stan Magidson, son of Sam and Leema (nee **Lithwick**) Magidson, Abraham Palmer was active in many Jewish organization in Ottawa. He was a founder of the Modern Jewish School, and was president of the Jewish Community Council of Ottawa from 1970-1972. Abraham Palmer is a cousin of Abraham Held (see **Pollock**).
- Benjamin (d. 2006), married to Pat.
- Morris (d. 1991). Second wife is Hennie (nee Ross), who was originally married to Philip **Gosewich**.
- Jack (d. 1937).
- Betty Stotland.
- Jen Rubin.
- Rachel Segal Ages.
- Molly Phomin (d. 2011), married to Barney (d. 1975)

William Palmer (d. 1989), a lone Holocaust survivor, was a cousin of this family.

For connections to other entries, see Gosewich, Gould, Greenberg, Leikin, Lieff, Lithwick, Pollock.

PETIGORSKY

The Petigorsky family descends from Mordechai Eliezer (Max, d. 1921), and Esther (nee Fertig, d. 1931). Some members of the family spelled the name as Petegorsky. Children of Mordechai and Eliezer and Esther were:

- Oscar (d. 1971), married to Nina (nee Cheigowsky, d. 1969). Their children were:
  - Lena **Schecter** (d. 2005), who was married to Sydney (d. 2007), son of Lazarus and Minnie **Schecter**. Sydney later married Shirley (nee Starker, d. 2001). Lena and Syd's daughter Estelle Gunner is married to Sol, son of Levi and Rachel Gunnerotsky. Levi's sister Dora **Slack** was married to Harry **Slack**.
  - Samuel (d. 2005). Sam Petigorsky served as head of the Chevra Kadisha for many years.
  - Minna (d. 2005).
  - Ann (d. 1988).
  - Leon (d. 1964).
  - Joseph (d. 1991), married to Miriam (nee **Polowin**, d. 2000), daughter of Jacob and Dina **Polowin**.
  - Cecilia Tennenbaum, married to Nathan.
- Leon Petegorsky (d. 1966), married to Beckie (nee Wolinsky, d. 1991), daughter of Benjamin and Sarah Wolinsky. Beckie was the sister or Rachel **Bessin** Hochman, the wife of Moses **Bessin**; and Joseph Wolinsky, married to Minnie (nee **Shaffer**). Their children of Leon and Beckie Petegorsky are:

- o Beverly, married to Marvin Chodikoff (d. 1965), son of Israel (d. 1963) and Anne (nee **Freedman** d. 1931) Chodikoff.
  - o David (d. 1956), married to Carol (nee Coan). David was a well-known professor, who was also executive director of the American Jewish Congress, and a member of the executive committee of the World Jewish Congress. There is a David W. Petegorsky chair of Political Science at Yeshiva University.
  - o Ethel Geffen (d. 2004) married to Dr. Abraham Geffen.
  - o Jeanette Pelcovits (d. 2009), married to Dr. Nathan Pelcovits (d. 1997). Nathan Pelcovits worked for the US State Department, and specialized in United Nations peacekeeping and political affairs.
- Tevya (also known as Tobias or Tom, d. 1967), married to Elizabeth (nee Nemerovsky, d. 1947). Their children were:
  - o Sally Jason, married to Harry Jason (original name Yashinofsky, d. 1976).
  - o Leo (d. 1957), married to Rachel (nee Glushtein), daughter of Hyman and Pearl (nee Dutnoff) Glushtein (see **Glustein**).
  - o Rose Steinberg, married to Robert.
  - o Muriel **Flesher** (known as Micki, d. 1989), married to Frank (d. 1989), son of Israel and Etta **Flesher**.
  - o David.
  - o Harry.
  - o Ben Peters (d. 2006), married to Bella (nee Cohen d. 1984).
  - o Molly.
- Miriam **Dworkin** (known as Minnie, d. 1973), married to Max (d. 1979). Their children were:
  - o Ann Silver (d. 1984), married to Max.
  - o Zelda **Roodman** (d. 1999), married to Herman (d. 2001), son of Louis and Frieda **Roodman**. Their daughter Joy **Karp** is married to Richard, son of Ben and Etta (nee **Shulman**) **Karp**.
  - o David, married to Bonnie.
- Rabbi Simon Petegorsky, married to Sarah (nee **Lachovitz**), daughter of Max (d. 1950), and Gitel (nee **Weiner**, d. 1942) **Lachovitz**. Rabbi Petegorsky served as the rabbi, cantor, teacher, shochet, mohel and chaplain in Kingston, Ontario, from 1922-1934.

For connections to other entries, see Bessin, Dworkin, Flesher, Freedman, Glustein, Karp, Lachovitz, Polowin, Roodman, Schecter, Shaffer, Shulman, Slack, Weiner.

Oscar Petigorsky standing outside his leather and shoe findings store located at 289 Dalhousie Street - ca. 1940 (OJA 1-698-04)

PLEET

The Pleet family is descended from Leo (d. 1941) and Rachel (d. 1944). Rachel (Rechil) is the sister of Rachel Stein (d. 1948), married to Max (d. 1928). Children of Leo and Rachel were:

- Archie (also known as Aaron, d. 1988), married to Edith (d. 1976). Their children are:
    - Roslyn **Gould** (d. 2014) married to Norman (d. 2011).
    - Morton (d. 2019), married to Sylvia (nee **Greenberg**, d. 2019), daughter of Menashe and Leika (nee Zunder) **Greenberg**. Their son Jeffrey is married to Felice (nee Singerman), daughter of Sydney and Rae Singerman, and sister of Aviva **Diener**, married to Seymour; and Barbara **Diener**, married to Joel.
    - Larry (d. 2011), married Nancy (nee Goldenberg, d. 2019), daughter of Max Goldenberg. Max Goldenberg is the brother of Edward (d. 1986); Harry (d, 1973), married to Helen (d. 1988); Elsie Baker (d. 2006) married to Harry (d. 1985). Harry and Elsie Baker's daughter Polly **Levitan** was married to Richard **Levitan**, daughter of Archie and Rose (nee **Smolkin**) **Levitan**.
- Harry (d. 1985), married to Clara (d. 1928), and then to Bertha (nee Schwartz, d. 1998). Children of Harry and Clara are:
    - Esther Sadavoy (d. 2005), married to Robert (d. 1967), son of Jacob (d. 1940) and Dora (d. 1961). Robert Sadavoy was the brother of Sam (d. 1972); and Benjamin (d. 1978), married to Bella (d. 2002).

- o Jack.
- Children of Harry and Bertha are:
  - o Pinchas, married to Barbara.
  - o Michael.
- Abraham David (d. 1960) married to Rose (nee Shore, d. 1971), daughter of Moses and Sarah Shore. Their children were:
  - o Jack (d. 2010), married to Miriam (nee Kahn).
  - o Gertrude Kotlarsky (d. 1984), married to Harry (d. 2007).
  - o Lila Bookman (d. 2006), married to Abraham (d. 2015) son of Jacob and Bertha (nee **Gorelick**) Bookman. Their son Rick is married to Margot (nee Wolf), daughter of George Wolf (d. 1999), and Brenda; and granddaughter of George Wolf Sr. (d. 1979) and Augusta (d. 1942). George Wolf Sr. was the founder of Ottawa Leather Goods.
- Meyer (d. 1962), married to Bessie (d. 1940). Their daughter Clara Koffman (d. 1973), was married to Sammy (d. 1985), son of Sam and Pearl (nee **Gennis**) Koffman.
- Isaac.
- Pinny.
- Sarah Goren (d. 1945), wife of Chaim Nachum (d. 1929).
- Goldie Oiring, married to Solomon.

For connections to other entries, see Diener, Gennis, Gorelick, Greenberg, Levitan, Shore, Smolkin.

Warrant Officer Jack Pleet in World War II Army uniform, 1941. (OJA 1-784)

POLLOCK

The Pollock family is descended from Peisach and Esther Gitel Polyak. They had many children, but only those with direct connections to Ottawa are noted here. Their children include:

1. Pinchas (d. 1906) married to Rivka (nee **Gencher**), daughter of Mayer Dov and Tsipora **Gencher**. Rivka's sister was Shaindel (Sarah) **Greenberg**, married to Isaac. Shaindel and Isaac are the ancestors of the one of the large **Greenberg** clans of Ottawa. Children of Pinchas and Rivka were:

- Pitzi **Taylor** (also known as Fanny, d. 1983), married to Albert (d. 1961), son of Yitzchak **Taylor**. Their children are:
  o Gerald (d. 2010), married to Barbara.
  o Sheldon, married to Cynthia, and then to Corrinne (nee Rothman).
  o Samuel (d. 1945 as an infant).
- Nathan **Greenberg** (d. 1983), married to Sarah (d. 1984). Nathan was sponsored by his aunt and uncle Sheindel and Isaac **Greenberg** when he arrived in Canada, and took on their surname. Children of Nathan and Sarah are:
  o Gertrude Budovich married to Sam. The Budovich family is based in the Maritimes. Sybil Budd (nee **Goldfield**), daughter of Benjamin **Goldfield**, is also married into the Budovich family.
  o Irving (d. 2007), married to Evelyn (nee Feldman), daughter of Israel (d. 1963) and Sally (d. 1985) Feldman. Evelyn's sister Jaquelin Holzman was first married to John Holzman (d. 2010), and then to John Rutherford. Jaquelin Holzman served as mayor of Ottawa from 1991-1997. Irving and Evelyn's son Peter is married to Lori (nee **Sherman**), daughter of Louis **Sherman** and Barbara (nee **Roodman**) Gutmajer.
- Gordon (d. 1954), married to Eva (nee **Gencher**, d. 2006) daughter of Jacob Joseph and Pessie (nee Soloway) **Gencher**. Gordon and Eva were cousins through the **Genchers**. Eva's second husband was Cantor Hyman Gertler (d. 1975), who served as cantor of Beth Shalom Synagogue during the 1950s and 1960s. Children of Gordon and Eva are:
  o Thelma Berezin (known as Tami, d. 2011), married to Robert (d. 2002), son of Samuel (Berezin (d. 1932). Their daughter Susan Danoff is married to Frank, son of Samuel and Dora (nee **Roodman**) Danoff. Robert's brother was Moe, married to Zelda (nee **Ages**), daughter of Zalman and Esther (nee **Bodnoff**) **Ages**.
  o Bernard, married to Anita.
- Jack (d. 1966), married to Sarah (nee Held, d. 1968), daughter of Mayer Held (d. 1950), and Yenta (d. 1944). Mayer and Yenta's other children were Abraham (d. 1977), married to Esther (d. 1983); Benjamin (d. 1994), married to Freda (d. 1996) – their daughter Laya Abramowitz (d. 2016) was married to Michael Abramowitz; and their daughter Claire Zloten was married to Murray Zloten (d. 2010); Louis (d. 1944). Children of Jack and Sarah Pollock are:
  o Gitel Waiser, married to Arthur (d. 1984). Their daughter Yanda **Max** is married to Mark, son of Sol and Lillian (nee Abrams) **Max**.
  o Dr. Pinhey (d. 2015), married first to Florie (nee Adelson), and then to Sandy. Dr. Pollock was a well-known cardiologist.

- Sam (d. 1936), married to Mary (nee Kadish).

, 2. Dov Ber Pollock. His children were:

- Annie Goldenberg (d. 1999), married to Harry (d. 1981). Their daughter Barbara was married to Louis (d. 2013), son of Harry and Rachel Lesha (nee **Polowin**) **Fine**.
- Doris Hersenhorn (d. 1988), married to Harry.
- Bella Robitaille (known as Babe, d. 1993), married to Peter (d. 1996), son of David (d. 1944) and Fanny Robitaille (d. 1951). Peter Robitaille (original name Rabinovitch) is the sister of Belle Sadowski (d. 1988), married to Moses (d. 1951). Belle and Moses are the grandparents of Debra (nee Sadowski) **Viner**, married to Gary, son of Joseph and Ruth (nee **Macy**) **Viner**.
- Pearl Harris (Patricia, d. 1982, married to Hy Harris (d. 1987), son of Hershel and Ada Segalowitz (see **Cohen**).
- Lilyan Saxe (d. 1985), married to Joseph (d. 1985).

3. Libby Dubinsky (d. 1944), married to Benjamin (d. 1946). Their children were:

- Sarah **Shore** (d. 1987), married to Joseph (d. 1954), son of Moses and Sarah Freda **Shore**.
- Faye Azmier, married to Joe.
- Oscar.
- Issy (d. 1987).
- Charles (d. 1986), married to Annie (d. 1994).
- Philip (d. 1985), married to Flora (d. 1994).
- Abraham (d. 2003), married to Beatrice (nee **Weiss**), daughter of Barney and Henrietta **Weiss**.
- Lillian (d. 2005).

For connections to other entries, see Ages, Bodnoff, Cohen, Fine, Gencher, Greenberg, Macy, Max, Polowin, Roodman, Sherman, Shore, Taylor, Viner, Weiss.

Ottawa mayor Jacquelin Holtzman (mayor from 1991-1997), with Queen Elizabeth. (see Nathan Greenberg branch of the Pollock family) (OJA 1-805-03)

Mr. & Mrs. Nathan Greenberg married at the Billings Bridge Town Hall, March 20, 1920. (OJA 1-176)

POLOWIN

There are two branches of the Polowin family, descended from the brothers Avraham David Polowin, and Yitzchak Polowin..

The children of Avraham David Polowin were:

- Oscar (d. 1959), married to Sonia (d. 1955). Their children were:
  - Rachel Lesha **Fine** (d. 1936), married to Harry **Fine**, son of Abraham Israel Joseph and Ada Tseepa **Fine**.
  - Jacob Victor Polowin (d. 1976), married to Rose (nee Shandler, d. 1988).
- Benjamin (d. 1966), married to Bessie (d. 1985). Their children are:
  - David (d. 2000), married to Betty (nee Cowan d. 2002). Their children are:
    - Jeffrey.
    - Stephen.
    - Michael, married to Melanie, daughter of Leonard and Mina (nee Kapinsky, see **Karp**) **Max**.
  - Ann (d. 2009).
  - Charles (Chuck, d. 2021), married to Malca (nee **Taylor**), daughter of Samuel and Bertha (nee **Slover**) **Taylor**.
  - Hyman Samuel (d. 1987), married to Gladys.
  - Sheila Hammer (d. 1981), married to Arni (d. 1983).
  - Gerald, married to Helen (nee Dover), daughter of Robert and Sasa (Sara, nee **Max**) **Dover**.
  - Freda Grill, married to Manny.
  - Alex (d. 2022), married to Kathleen (d. 2014).

The son of Yitzchak was Jacob Oscar (d. 1935, married to Dina (nee Gordon d. 1966). Children of Jacob and Dina were:

- Miriam **Petigorsky** (d. 2000), married to Joseph (d. 1991), son of Oscar and Nina (nee Cheigowsky) **Petigorsky**.
- Esther Abeles (d. 2010, married to Daniel (d. 2012).
- Hannah **Max** (d. 2003), originally married to Arthur (d. 2012). Arthur later married Sara (nee Wise, d. 2000).
- Bea Schaffer.
- Sarah (d. 1932).
- Leah Abeles, married to Joseph.
- Deborah (d. 1993), married to Phillip **Swedlove** (d. 1993), son of Sam and Fanny (nee **Cohen**) **Swedlove**.
- Shirley **Sugarman** (d. 1984), married to Laurence (d. 1991), son of Hyman and Jessie (nee Phillips) **Sugarman**. After Shirley's death. Laurence married Barbara (nee **Molot**), daughter of Abram and Edith **Molot**.
- Dr. Moses (d. 1995).
- Rena (d. 2003).

For connections to other entries, see Cohen, Dover, Fine, Karp, Max, Molot, Petigorsky, Slover, Sugarman, Swedlove, Taylor.

POTECHIN

The Potechin family descends from Isidore (d. 1991), and Mary (nee Bernstein, d. 2006 at age 105). Their children are:

- Norman (d. 2013), married to Evelyn (nee Perlove, d. 2013). Their son Bram is married to Dodie (nee **Taller**), daughter of Max and Sally **Taller**.
- Leonard, married to Mary (nee Steinberg), daughter of Frank and Laura (nee **Lachovitz**) Steinberg. (See **Lachovitz** for connections to the **Kardish** and **Petigorsky** families.) Children of Len and Mary are:
  - Gail Scher is married to Joel. Joel and Gail Scher are the parents of Rabbi Idan Scher, married to Shifra. Rabbi Scher is currently the rabbi of Machzikei Hadas Congregation of Ottawa.
  - Laurie Gordon is married to Steven, son of Harold (d. 2003) and Miriam (nee Lurie, d. 2007) Gordon. Steven and Laurie are the parents of Erin, married to Rabbi Ari Galandauer, who served as the rabbi of Young Israel of Ottawa for several years. Thus, Rabbi Scher of Machzikei Hadas and Rabbi Galandauer of Young Israel are first cousins by marriage. Siblings of Harold Gordon are Jack (d. 2004), married to Adele (d. 2005); Robert; and Esther. Other children of Harold and Miriam Gordon are Elaine Pludwinsky, married to Earl; and Arthur, married to Mary (nee Morello).
  - Reva Goldberg, married to Ernest. Their son Ryan is married Arielle (nee Kreisman), daughter of Irwin and Audrey (nee Malek) Kreisman (see **Shinder**).
- Ernie Potechin (d. 2018), married to Myrna (nee Frank, d. 1999), and then to Kathy.

For connections to other entries see Kardish, Lachovitz, Petigorsky, Shinder, Taller.

Rabbi Idan and Shifra Scher of Machzikei Hadas. Rabbi Scher is the son of Gail [nee Potechin] (https://www.rabbischer.com/about)

PROGOSH

See Baylin, Dworkin.

PULLAN

The Pullan family descends from Bernard and Malkla Pullan. Their children were:

- Lena (d. 1936), married to Abraham Lazarus (d. 1925) **Florence**. See **Florence** for connections to the **Betcherman**, **Lieff**, and Doctor families.
- Elias, married to Bertha (nee Helner). After living in Ottawa for a brief period, they moved to Toronto, where Elias was very active in Jewish communal institutions, including serving as president, treasurer and parnas of Goel Tzedek Synagogue (the precursor of Beth Tzedek), and first president of the Simcoe Talmud Torah.
- Toba Sachs (d. 1950). Toba was married to Samuel. Their children were:
  - Max (d. 1959), married to Jennie (d. 1992).
  - Thomas (d. 1996). Tom Sachs was a communal leader for many decades, who was known for giving the gift of a chumash to all graduates of the Ottawa Talmud Torah.
  - Reva Brownstein.
  - Mollie (d. 1928).
- Henry Mayer. His children were:
  - Lena **Coplan** (d.1953) married to Archie (d. 1937), son of Hyman and Estelle (nee Pameth) **Coplan**.
  - Olive (d. 2005).
  - Anna Metrick (d. 1959), married to Nathan (d. 1980). Their children were:
    - Ted (d. 1992), married to Claire (nee Wyneberg, d. 2000).
    - Lionel (d. 2018), married to Sarah (nee Dorfman, d. 1992).
    - David (d. 2017) married to Vera (nee Saks).
    - Fred married to Cecile.

For connections to other entries, see Betcherman, Coplan, Florence, Lieff.

Bernard Pullan (OJA 1-421-01)

REICHSTEIN

The Reichstein family descends from Hyman and Marlene Reichstein. Hymie is a founder of the Jewish Genealogical Society from Ottawa. Hymie's maternal grandfather was a brother of Shlomo Gershon Tenenbaum, ancestor of the Tanner family (see **Gershon**). The children of Hymie and Marlene are:

- Hildy **Lesh**, married to Steven, son of Norman and Isabel (nee **Kimmel**) **Lesh**.
- Randi, was married to Joseph Huniu, son of Lazar (Larry) and Estelle (nee Spector, d. 2020) Huniu. Estelle is the daughter of Jack (d. 2001), and Ettie (known as Molly, d. 2001) Spector (see **Cherm**).
- Solomon, married to Sharon, daughter of Malcolm and Vera (nee Gottlieb) Glube (see **Lithwick**).

For connections to other entries, see Cherm, Gershon, Kimmel, Lesh, Lithwick.

RIVERS

The Rivers family is descended from Jacob (d. 1949), and Leah (nee Keller, d. 1977). The original name of the family was Riber. Children of Jacob and Leah are:

- Eleanor Wallach, married to Benjamin (d. 1979).
- Thelma Steinman (d. 2004), married to Nathan (d. 1988). Nat Steinman was a first cousin of Sarah **Aaron**, wife of David **Aaron**. Nat and Thelma's children are:

- o Elaine Shapiro, married to Daniel, son of Abraham and Nelly (nee **Hanser**) Shapiro.
- o Gail Victor is married to Stephen, son of Samuel and Rhea (nee Appel) Victor (not related to the larger Ottawa Victor family). Rhea Victor was a sister of Minnie **Gershon**, married to Erwin, and Rose **Ages**, married to Joseph.
- o Adele Tate.
- Eileen Goldberg (d. 2011), married to Benjamin (d. 1998). Benjamin Goldberg's sister-in-law's cousin is Dorothy Browns (d. 2020), married to Morris (d. 2007). Morris and Dorothy's son Shmuel was married to Bonna Haberman (d. 2015), daughter of Jack (d. 1994), and Hazelle (nee Bernstein, d. 1982). Bonna Haberman was the founder of the Woman of the Wall organization in Israel. Benjamin and Eileen's son Howard Goldberg (d. 2000) was married to Ibolya.
- Albert (d. 2002), married to Goldie (nee Schachter, d. 2014).
- Irving (d. 1997), married to Ethel (nee Sandler, d. 1975), daughter of Issie and Malya (nee **Shinder**) Sandler. Irving's second wife was Evelyn (nee Goldberg), daughter of Samuel and Rose (nee **Max**) Goldberg, who was originally married to Irwin **Tradburks**. Irving Rivers was the owner of the well-known Irving Rivers store on the Byward Market. Children of Irving and Ethel are:
  - o Jacqui Vital, married to Yaron. They live in Israel. Their daughter Adi Vital-Kaploun, may G-d avenge her blood, was brutally murdered on Oct 7, 2023 in Kibbutz Holit, near the Gaza border, during the vicious Hamas massacre on Simchat Torah. Adi's husband, Anani, is a great nephew of Rabbi Yaakov and Dreizel Kaploun. Rabbi Kaploun served as the principal of Hillel Academy of Ottawa for several years, starting in 1974.
  - o Ellen was married to Howard Osterer (d. 2014), son of Joseph and Blanche (nee **Betcherman**) Osterer (see **Glustein**). Their daughter Erin **Smith** is married to Aaron **Smith**, son of Leslie and Maureen **Smith** and grandson of the well-known Ottawa caterer Jack and Inez **Smith**.
  - o Ilsa Kamen, married to Howard.
- Goldie **Cantor**, married to Morris (d. 2002), son of Hyman and Ida **Cantor**.

For connections to other entries see Aaron, Ages, Betcherman, Cantor, Gershon, Glustein, Hanser, Max, Shinder, Smith, Tradburks.

The Rivers family posed for this photograph circa 1949 on what appears to be Nepean Point. L-R standing is Morris Cantor, Goldie Rivers, Nat Steinman, Ben Wallach and Ben Goldberg; seated on the bench is Goldie Cantor, Albert Rivers, Thelma Steinman, Jacob Rivers, Leah Rivers, Eleanor Wallach, Eileen Goldberg and Irving Rivers; and seated on the grass are Fred Wallach, Gail Victor (Steinman), Howard Goldberg and Elaine Shapiro. (Photograph by Malak, OJA 1-582-07)

The Rivers family donating a TV to the Hillel Lodge in honour of Leah Rivers' 80th birthday – 1967. L-R: Irving Rivers, Ethel Rivers, Nathan Steinman, Thelma (Rivers) Steinman, Goldie Rivers, Albert Rivers, Goldie (Rivers) Cantor, Leah Rivers (with hand on TV), Ben Goldberg, Eileen (Rivers) Goldberg. (OJA 1-582-01)

ROODMAN

The Roodman family is descended from Simon Roodman. Children were:

- Moses (d. 1949), married to Basheva (nee Camen, d. 1935), and then to Esther (d. 1968). Children of Moses and Basheva were:
  - Jacob (d. 1996), married to Elizabeth (nee **Taller**, d. 1997), daughter of Jacob and Ethel **Taller**.
  - Samuel (d. 1963), married to Bessie (nee Cohen, d. 1955).
  - Bella Wolfe (d. 1995), married to Norman (d. 1991), son of Nathan Wolfe (d. 1951).
  - Joseph (d. 1979).
  - Julius (d. 1932).
  - Max (d. 1982).
  - Dr. Harry (d. 1974), married to Beatrice (nee Levy, d. 1982). Their children are:
    - Barbara, married to Louis **Sherman**, son of Harry and Sylvia **Sherman**; and then to Isaac Gutmajer (d. 2012). Lori Greenberg, daughter of Louis and Barbara Sherman, is married to Peter, son of Irving and Evelyn (nee Feldman) **Greenberg** (see **Pollock**).
    - Michael (d. 2014), married to Anita (nee **Kathnelson**), daughter of Hiram and Lillian (nee Nadler) **Kathnelson**.

- o Rabbi Solomon (d. 2001), who served as rabbi in Louisville Kentucky.
  o Rabbi Daniel.
  o Dora Danoff (d. 1995), married to Samuel (d. 1973). Their son Frank is married to Susan (nee Berezin), son of Robert and Tami (nee **Pollock**) Berezin. Samuel's brother Gus Dutnoff was married to Eva (nee **Glustein**); his sister Pearl was married to Hyman **Glushtein**, and his sister Dora was married to Israel **Ellenberg**
- Louis (d. 1952, married to Freida (nee Zimmerman, d. 1943). Their children were:
  o Joseph (d. 1968), married to Ida (nee Greenberg, d. 1977), daughter of Harry and Shlima Greenberg.
  o Ida Gaffen (d. 2008), married to Samuel (d. 1993). Samuel's brother was Robert (d. 1997).
  o Archie (d. 1982), married to Lillian (nee Feldstein, d. 1983).
  o Phillip (d. 1979).
  o David (d. 1949).
  o Betty Greenberg (d. 1997), married to Harry (d. 1969).
  o Herman (d. 2011), married to Zelda (nee **Dworkin**, d. 1999), daughter of Max and Miriam (nee **Petegorsky**) **Dworkin**. Their daughter Joy **Karp** is married to Richard, son of Ben and Etta (nee **Shulman**) **Karp**. Herman's second wife was Penny Bar-Noy (d. 2010, whose daughter Marion is married to Alan Brass (see **Landau** for a connection through a mutual set of cousins to my mother Edith **Landau**).
  o Frances (d. 1979).
  o Susan (d. 1986).
- Rachel Lee, married to Isiak Lee.

For connections to other entries, see Dworkin, Ellenberg, Glustein, Greenberg, Karp, Kathnelson, Landau, Petigorsky, Pollock, Sherman, Taller.

RUBIN

The Rubin family is descended from Jacob Moses (d. 1957) and Zishcha (nee **Coplan**, d. 1949) Rubin of Minsk, Zischa was the daughter of Hyman and Estelle Lillian (nee Pameth) **Coplan**. Children of Jacob Moses and Zischa were:

- Samuel (d. 1933), married to Rebecca (nee Feldman, d. 1936).
- Edith Levitan (d. 1982), married to Archie (d. 1971). Their children were:
  o Sarah Saper (d. 2005), married to David (d. 1977).
  o Elliott (d. 1990), married to Cecelia (nee Monson, d. 2011), daughter of Harry (d. 1926). Their son Brian is married to Cheryl (nee **Kardish**), daughter of Sam and Tillie (nee Steinberg) **Kardish**.
  o Estelle Abelson (d. 2004), married to Alan, son of Jess (d. 1975), and Mollie (nee Gray, d. 1979) Abelson. Jess Abelson was the son of Wolf (d. 1938), and Julia Abelson (nee Rosenblum, d. 1951). Jess Abelson played for the Ottawa Rough Riders in 1913-1914. Other children of Jess and Mollie are Sylvia Gellman, married to Lawrence; Lawrence (known as Duke, d. in action 1943); Stanley (d. 2014) married to Malca; and Robert, married to Lois.

- Michael (d. 1996), married to Lillian (nee Lipman, d. 1989), and then to Frances (nee **Kizell**, d. 2000), daughter of Jacob and Esther (nee **Dover**) **Kizell**.
- David (d. 1986), married to Mary (nee Levy, d. 2004).
- Harold (d. 1971), married to Laura (nee Finkelstein. d. 1984), daughter of Henry and Sarah (nee **Slover**) Finkelstein. Harold's autobiography was published by the Ottawa Jewish Historical Society as *Those Peksy Weeds*.
- Louis (d. 1995), married to Sylvia (nee **Mosion**, d. 1979), daughter of Max Wolfe and Fanny (nee Rosen) **Mosion**.
- Alex (d. 2011), married to Phyllis (nee Waterman).
- Bessie Morris (d. 1995), married to Raphael (known as Fred, d. 2987). Their granddaughter Alyse Bromberg (nee Morris), daughter of Morton and Susan (nee Kramil) Morris, is married to Sheldon Bromberg, son of Morton (d. 1993), and Bessie (nee Schlossberg) Bromberg. Bessie Bromberg is the sister of Rebecca Liff, married to Joseph, son of Abraham and Gittel (nee **Murray**) Liff.

For connections to other entries, see Coplan, Kardish, Kizell, Mosion, Murray, Slover.

17-year-old Harold Rubin standing along Rideau Street in 1928.
(OJA 1-579-05)

In 1931, Harold Rubin was a young and avid swimmer from Ottawa who entered himself into the CNE's swim and traveled to Toronto to compete. As a Jewish participant he was required to wear the Star of David on the front of his suit. This he did with great pride! (OJA 1-579-06)

Jess Abelson was the Captain of Brittania Canoe Club. The Brittania Canoe Team won the Canadian 1 Mile War Canoe Championships, 1914. (See Edith Levitan branch of the Rubin family in entry above) (OJA 1-393)

The 1913-1914 Y.M.C.A. Basketball Canadian Champions, Ottawa Team. J.Abelson pictured in middle, right of center. (OJA 1-723)

SADINSKY

The Sadinsky family descends from Nesanal (d. 1937) and Sara Feiga (d. 1942). Their children were:

- Nathan (d. 1965), married to Hilda (nee **Flesher**, d. 1939), daughter of Meyer and Kayla Flesher.   Nathan's second wife was Anne (nee Zagerman), a sister of Morris Zagerman (see below – a brother and a sister married a brother and a sister). Children of Nathan and Hilda children are:
  - o Stanley.
  - o Eileen Tanner, married to Nathan, son of Charles and Lillian Tanner (see **Gershon**).
- Hyman (known as Louis, d. 1923), married to Rachel (known as Rose, d. 1977). Their children were:
  - o Joseph (d. 1973), married to Molly (nee **Craft**, d. 2004), daughter of Hyman and Anne (nee Michelin) **Craft**. Their daughter Carol Sadinsky Spiro (d.

2010) was married to Stanley **Kimmel**, son of Phillip and Ettie (nee **Shulman**) **Kimmel**.

- o Edward (d. 1976), married to Esther (d. 2009). Their son Ian was married to Deanna (nee **Karp**), daughter of Harry and Ruth (nee Keyfitz) **Karp**, and is currently married to Joan (nee Bercovitch).
- o Edith (d. 1985).
- o Mildred (d. 2004).
- o Adelaide Cowan (d. 2014), married to Lawrence (d. 2000), son of Abraham and Esther (nee **Froman**) Cowan.
- o Archie married to Rose.
- Mildred Zagerman (d. 1971), married to Morris (d. 1967) (see **Krantzberg**). Morris Zagerman is a sister of Anne Sadinsky, second wife of Mildred's brother Nathan. Children of Mildred and Morris are:
  - o Joel (d. 1944).
  - o Herbert, married to Corinne (nee Ross). Their son John is married to Andrea (nee Greenberg), daughter of Fred and Gert (nee Marcus, see **Marcovitch**) Greenberg.
  - o Norman, married to Valerie (d. 1976), and then to Carole (nee Saxe), daughter of Harry and Frances (d. 2004) Saxe. Carole was formerly married to Stanley Arron (see **Weinstein**).
  - o Shirley Cohen, married to Al Cohen (d. 2010) (see **Cantor**). Their daughter Elizabeth **Mosion** is married to Max, son of Rudy and Joan **Mosion**.

For connections to other entries, see Cantor, Craft, Flesher, Froman, Gershon, Krantzberg, Karp, Kimmel, Marcovitch, Mosion, Shulman Weinstein.

SASLOVE

There are two distinct Saslove familes in Ottawa, which are believed to not be related (source: a discussion with Sheila Baslaw, who mentioned to me that she established this through a discussion with Betty Ballon, of the other Saslove family. Both families, however, originate from the same area of Uman, Ukraine.)

Saslove Family A

This family descends from Jacob (d. 1951), and Hanna (nee Brodsky, d. 1947) Saslove. The original surname of this family was Zaslovsky. Children of Jacob and Hanna were:

- Samuel (d. 1986), married to Lillian (nee **Marcovitch**, d. 1996), daughter of Abraham and Freda (nee Haimovici) **Marcovitch**. Their children are:
  - o Barry, who was married to Nili.
  - o Dorothy **Karp** (d. 2019), married to Maurie **Karp** (d. 2009), son of Max and Dora Kapinsky.
  - o Carol, first married to David Shaikin, and then to Harvey Goodman.
- Morris (d. 1980), married to Edythe (nee **Taller**, d. 1964), daughter of Jacob and Ethel **Taller**. Morris' second marriage was to Anna Lazear (nee Kentorowitz, d. 2002), his son-in-law's mother. Anna's brother was the deputy mayor of Newark, NJ. Children of Morris and Edythe are:

- o Marion Shapiro (d. 2003), married to Al (d. 2004). Al Shapiro was the choir director of Beth Shalom synagogue for many years.
- o Norma Lazear, married to Philip, son of Samuel (d. 1959) and the aforementioned Anna (d. 2002). Samuel and Anna Lazear's other children are Arthur (d. 2001), married to Ann (nee Tarantour, d. 2021), daughter of Maurice Tarantour (d. 1975), and Sylvia (d. 1950). Maurice second wife was Lillian (nee Cohen) Fried (see Berezin branch of **Ages**); and Sonia **Shaffer**, married to Sheldon, son of Abraham and Mary **Shaffer**.
- o Joyce **Kimmel**, married to Milton, son of Philip and Ettie (nee **Shulman**) **Kimmel**.
- o June Kurland, married to Jerry.
- Abraham (d. 1988), married to Anne (nee **Taller**), son of Jacob and Ethel **Taller** (i.e. two Saslove brothers married two **Taller** sisters). Their son Stephen is married to Brenda (nee **Sugarman**), daughter of Phillip and Gusta (nee Seidler) **Sugarman**.
- Mary Slipacoff (d. 1984), married to Charles (d. 1995), son of Samuel (d. 1976), and Dora (d. 1943) Slipacoff. Their children are:
  - o Harvey, married to Karen (nee Brownstein)
  - o David, married to Joan (nee **Fine**), daughter of David and Rose (Nee Smurlick) **Fine**.
  - o Jerry married to Norma (nee Lobel), daughter of Maxwell and Frieda Lobel (see **Lesh**).
- Betty Ballon (d. 2011 at the age of 103), married to Jack (d. 1992). Their children are:
  - o Henry, married to Frances (nee **Levinson**), daughter of Morris and Clara (nee **Schecter**) **Levinson**.
  - o Fred (d. 2019), married to Esther (nee Davis), daughter of Benjamin (d. 1959), and Rochelle (nee Volfzon, d. 1982) Davis. Other children of Benjamin and Rochelle Davis are Morton (d. 1980); and Frieda Edelson (d. 1976) married to Jack (d. 2017), son of Benjamin (d. 1988) and Alice (nee Coblentz, d. 1988) Edelson. Jack Edelson ran a kosher catering business in Ottawa for many years. Jack Edelson's second marriage was to Annette. Alice Edelson's mother Chaya Coblentz was a second wife of Yakov Schecter, father of Bessie **Greenberg**. Jack Edelson' siblings are: Samuel (d. 2004), married to Rose (nee Manheim, d.2003); Dina (d. 2010); Lillian Katznelson (d. 2008), married to Harry (d. 1965); Vivian Caplan (d. 2012), married to Donald (d. 2007); Joyce; Elihu (d. 2013), married to Helen (nee Wiseman).
  - o Sheila.
  - o Lawrence, married to Jeraldine.
  - o Madelaine.
- Benjamin Saslow.
- Eliezer Zaslavsky.

For connections to other entries for the first Saslove family, see Ages, Greenberg, Fine, Karp, Kimmel, Lesh, Marcovitch, Schecter, Shaffer, Shulman, Sugarman, Taller.

Saslove family B

This family descends from Moshe. The original family name was Saslovsky. Children were:

- Shika, married to Chia. Their children were:
  - Samuel (d. 1986), married to Lillian (nee Radnoff, d. 1964), daughter of Yekutiel Radnoff (original name Radnoffsky). Sam's second wife was Ettie Gelfand-Saslove (d. 1999), whose first husband was Hyman Gelfand. Lillian's brother was David Radnoff (d. 1986), married to Freda (nee Kilinovsky, d. 2005), daughter of Meyer (d. 1946) and Buneh (d. 1947) Kilinovsky. Freda (Kilinovsky) Radnoff's brothers were Reubin Kalin (d. 2003), married to Anne (d. 1988), and Norman Kalin (1963), married to Estelle (d. 1975). Lillian's sister was Fannie Saslove, married to Samuel's uncle Nathan (see below: a Saslove uncle and nephew married two Radnoff sisters). Children of Samuel and Lillian Saslove are:
    - Sheila **Baslaw**, married to Morton (d. 2016), son of Murray and Libby (nee Finn) **Baslaw**. Murray's second wife was Pearl (nee **Goldfield**) **Baslaw**.
    - Norman, married to Sally.
    - Rhoda **Loeb**, who was married to Dr. Lazarus **Loeb** (d. 2005), son of Moses (d. 1951), and Rose (d. 1963) Loeb. Laz Loeb's second wife was Jacqueline. Rhoda's second husband was Stan Hock, son of Samuel (d. 2002), and Beatrice (nee Sabbath, d. 2013) Hock.
  - Moe.
  - Sonia.
  - Lill.
  - Fania.
  - Gittlle.
  - Ruth.
- Yisrael (d. 1934), married to Anna (nee Malchusky). Their children were:
  - Saul (d. 1991), married to Lillian (nee Ginsberg, d. 1989). Their children are:
    - Zelda **Greenberg** (d. 2009), married to John (d. 2007), son of Morris and Bertha (nee **Gennis**) **Greenberg**.
    - Nina **Dover**, married to Mark, son of Jacob and Bertha (nee Saipe) **Dover**.
    - Edgar (d. 2016) married to Nancy (nee Goldsmith, d. 2003). Nancy was the sister of Mildred Wolfe (d. 1980), married to Ted (d. 2004, see **Lithwick**).
    - Herbert (d. 2002), married to Anita (d. 2020). Herb Saslove was co-owner of Saslove furniture.
  - Adolph (d. 1942) married to Sarah (nee **Torontow**, d. 1964), daughter of Abraham Raphael and Ethel Rhoda (nee Solomon) **Torontow**. Their children are:
    - Edward (killed in action in 1945).
    - Ralph (d. 2018), married to Sylvia (nee **Weiner**, d. 2006), daughter of Israel and Anne **Weiner**. Their daughter Andrea was married to Mark **Shore**, son of David and Debi **Shore**.

- ▪ Martin, married to Anna Ruth (nee Hart, d. 2016).
- Nathan (d. 1930), married to Fannie (nee Radnoff, d. 1966), sister of the aforementioned Lillian Saslove, who married Nathan's nephew. Their daughter Ruth Greenberg (d. 2010), was married to Earl (d. 1992). Their other daughters were May, Lillian, and Kay.

For connections to other entries for the second Saslove family, see Baslaw, Dover, Gennis, Goldfield, Greenberg, Lithwick, Loeb, Shore, Torontow, Weiner.

One-year-old twins, Edward and Herbert Saslove, sitting on the family automobile – 1929 (OJA 1-070)

SCHECTER

The Schecter family descends from Lazarus (d. 1969), and Minnie (d. 1969) Schecter. Their children were:

- Ann (d. 2006).
- Jack Irving (d. 1953).
- Clara **Levinson** (d. 1969), married to Morris (d. 1974). Their children are:
  - Jacie (d. 2016), married to Sandra (nee **Macy**, d. 2017), daughter of Sam and Freda **Macy**.
  - Barbara **Greenberg** (d. 2016), married to Sydney (known as Snooki, d. 2013), son of Morris and Bertha (nee **Gennis**) **Greenberg**.
  - Frances Ballon, married to Henry, son of Jack and Esther (nee **Saslove**) Ballon.
- Dr. Nathan Schecter (d. 2007), married to Tessie (nee **Bessin**, d. 2000), daughter of Moses and Rachel (nee Wolinsky) **Bessin**.
- Sydney (d. 2007), married to Lena (nee **Petigorsky**, d. 2004) daughter of Oscar and Nina (nee Cheigowsky) **Petigorsky**. Sidney later married Shirley (nee Starker, d. 2001). Lena and Syd's daughter Estelle Gunner is married to Sol, son of Levi and Rachel Gunnerotsky. Levi's sister Dora **Slack** was married to Harry **Slack**.
- Rebecca Gelman (d. 1993), married to Ben. Their daughter Vivian **Taller** (d. 2010) was married to Herbert, son of Samuel and Bessie (nee **Cantor**) **Taller**.

For connections to other entries, see Bessin, Cantor, Gennis, Greenberg, Levinson, Macy, Petigorsky, Saslove, Slack, Taller.

SCHREIBER

The Schreiber family is descended from Rev. Samuel (d. 1995), and Leah (nee Schiff, d. 1984) Schreiber. Reverend Schreiber was a chazzan, shochet, and teacher at the Bnai Jacob (James Street) Synagogue for many years. Their children are:

- Molly **Sherman** (d. 1997), married to Sol, son of Harry and Sylvia **Sherman**.
- Marvin (d. 2000), married to Rita (nee Spiegel). After Marvin's death, Rita married Seymour Brudner, who was the former father-in-law of Asher Breatross, son of Joseph and Debbie (nee Flatt) Breatross (see **Murray**).
- Marlene Briskin married to Julius (d. 2005).
- Riva **Freedman**, married to Jarvis (d. 1985), son of Michael (d. 1978) and Anna (nee Smith, d. 1943) **Freedman**. After Jarvis' death, Riva married David Rotenberg, who served as member of provincial parliament in North York from 1977-1985. Children of Riva and Jarvis are:
  - Jacob, married to Esther (nee Koreen), daughter of Dr. Joseph and Esther (nee **Greenberg**) Koreen.
  - Jonathan Ben-Choreen, married to Aviva.
  - Roseann, originally married to Harry Prizant, and then married to Sydney Goldstein.

Samuel Schreiber's sister Rechel Borenstein was married to Yossel. Yossel Borenstein's brother Rev. Nathan (Nachman) Borenstein (d. 1981), served as the cantor of Machzikei Hadas Synagogue on Murray Street, and also as a shochet. He was married to Mollie (Malka, nee Horshovski, d. 1998). Their grandson Ari Sacher, who is a scientist with the Iron Dome project in Israel, is married into the Kurtz family (see **Bessin** for how the Kurtz family of Toronto connects to Lang, Diena, and Tenenbaum).

For connections to other entries see Bessin, Freedman, Greenberg, Sherman.

SHAFFER

The Shaffer family is descended from Samuel Shaffer (d. 1917), and Mary (nee Katz, d. 1933). Their children were:

- Minnie Wolinsky (d. 1952), married to Joseph (d. 1980), son of Benjamin (d. 1918) and Sarah (d. 1953) Wolinsky. Joseph's sister Rachel **Bessin** Hochman was married to Moses **Bessin**, and his sister Rebecca **Petegorsky** as married to Leon **Petegorsky**. Joseph's second wife was Lena (nee Astor) Shapiro Wolinsky.
- Benjamin (d. 1957), married to Martha (nee Miller, d. 1960).
- Estelle Diamond Wener (d. 1967), married to Benjamin Diamond (d. 1936), and then to Jack Wener (d. 1972). Family moved to southern California.
- Abraham (d. 1965), married to Mary (nee **Baslaw**), daughter of Morris and Ida (nee Yarofsky) Boslow. Their children are:
    - Irving (d. 1986), married to Browna (nee Finsten, d. 2009).
    - Harold (d. 1979), married to Frances (nee Sanders, d. 2014 at the age of 103).
    - Beatrice Zagon (d. 1988), married to Bertram. Their son James (d. 2002), was married to Sandra, daughter of Barry and Fay (nee Yanover) Koffman (see **Gennis**).
    - Milton (d. 2015), married to Sarah (nee Fine, d. 2012), daughter of Leon and Rachel (nee **Feller**) Fine. Their children are:
        - Ingrid Shapiro, married to Samuel (d. 2006).
        - Marilyn **Kimmel**, married to Daniel, son of Arthur and Sarah (nee **Hanser**) **Kimmel**.
        - Wendy Green, married to Michael.
    - Sheldon (d. 2022), married to Sonia (nee Lazear), daughter of Samuel Lazear and Anna (later **Saslove**). Their daughter Myra is married to Sam Krane, son of Jack and Evelyn (nee Levi) Krane (see **Krantzberg**).

For links to other entries, see Baslaw, Bessin, Feller, Gennis, Hanser, Kimmel, Krantzberg, Petigorsky, Saslove.

Pictured is Mr. Abraham Shaffer at the wheel, Mr. Murray Baslaw on the running board, Mrs. Mary Shaffer in the back with Frances Ash, Beatrice Shaffer and Rita Ash. Irving Shaffer in scout uniform on the hood of the car and Harold Shaffer id beside Abraham in the front seat. November 2, 1917. (OJA 1-174).

Exterior view of The Ottawa Bargain Store, later A. Shaffer's Department Store. 147 Rideau Street, Ottawa, ca. 1912. (OJA 2-039)

SHERMAN

The Sherman family is descended from Laiviee Isaac Sherman (d. 1934), and Hasia (d. 1956). The original family name was Shusterman. Children of Laivee Isaac and Hasia were:

- Harry (d. 1995), married to Sylvia (d. 1980) Sherman. Children of Harry and Sylvia are:
  - Sol, married to Molly (nee **Schreiber**, d. 1997), daughter of Rev. Samuel and Leah (nee Schiff) **Schreiber**. Sol's second marriage was to Ina.
  - Louis (d. 2017), married to Barbara (nee **Roodman**). Barbara's second marriage was to Isaac Gutmajer (d. 2012). Lori, the daughter of Louis and Barbara, was married to Peter **Greenberg**, son of Irving and Evelyn (nee Feldman) **Greenberg** (see **Pollock**).
  - Jack, married to Beatrice (nee **Shinder**), daughter of Harry and Sylvia (nee Glazer) **Shinder**. Bea's second marriage is to Murray Garceau, and Jack's second marriage was to Julie (nee Moran, d. 2018). Children of Jack and Beatrice are:
    - Ian, married to Randi (nee Goldstein), daughter of Stanley and Joyce (nee Druckman) Goldstein. Stanley later married Norma (nee MacLeod). Randi's sister Cathy **Kerzner** was married to Avrum **Kerzner**, son of Isaac and Bernice (nee **Greenberg**) **Kerzner**. Randi's brother Allan is married to Stephanie (nee Greenspan). Stephanie's aunt Leah Miller is married to Ken Miller.
    - Karen Custoreri, married to Paul.
    - Andrea Bentolila, married to Joe.
- Freda Lipson (d. 2001), married to Samuel Lipson (d. 1977). Mac Lipson (d. 1999), son of Freda and Samuel was a reporter for the CKOY radio station.
- Malca Bookman (d. 1966), married to Ben Bookman (d. 1972). Malca and Ben were first cousins. Ben's mother was Ethel Kilinovsky, who was the mother of Meyer Kilinovsky from her first marriage (see **Saslove** family B.) Ben's half brother was Jacob Bookman (see **Weinstein**). Malca and Ben's children were:
  - Max Bookman (d. 1967), married to Celia (nee Sherman, d. 2009). Their daughter Rebecca is married to Sam **Halpern** son of Charles and Katie (nee **Skulsky**) **Halpern**.
  - Ethel Hartman (d. 2005), married to Syd (d. 2000).
  - Leon, married to Doris (nee Cowan).
- Gittel Zelnick (d. 1973), married to Israel (d. 1960).
- Rochel Postel.
- Max.
- Philip.

For connections to other entries see Greenberg, Halpern, Kerzner, Pollock, Roodman, Saslove, Schreiber, Shinder, Skulsky, Weinstein.

Mr. Harry Sherman with his delivery truck, ca. 1955, a sketch of Sherman's Confectionery as it would have appeared in the late 1930s, and a photograph of the building where Harry Sherman's second shop was located on Bronson Avenue. (Sketch and second shop photo by C. MacDonald.)

SHINDER

The Shinder family descends from Isaac (d. 1957), and Ethel (d. 1924) Shinder. Their children were:

- Harry (d. 1981), married to Sylvia (nee Glazer, d. 1988). Sylvia was a distant cousin of the **Bodnoff** / Ginsberg family. Children of Harry and Sylvia are:
  - Ethel Malek, married to David. Their granddaughter Arielle Goldberg (nee Kreisman), daughter of Irwin and Audrey (nee Malek) Kreisman, is married to Ryan, son of Ernie and Reva (nee **Potechin**) Goldberg.
  - Solomon, married to Zelaine (nee Speisman).
  - Bea Garceau, first married to Jack **Sherman**, son of Harry and Sylvia **Sherman**, then to Murray Garceau.
  - Lionel (d. 1993), married to Leslie (nee Yanover, d. 1998), daughter of Charles and Rose (d. 2001) Yanover.
- Malya Sandler (d. 1973), married to Issie (d. 1986). Their children were:
  - Ethel **Rivers** (d. 1975), married to Irving (d. 1997), son of Jacob and Leah (nee Keller) **Rivers**. Irving's second wife was Evelyn **Tradburks**, first married to Irwin **Tradburks**. Ellen, the daughter of Irving and Ethel, was

married to Howard Osterer (d. 2014), son of Joseph and Blanche (nee **Betcherman**) Osterer (see **Glustein**).

- ○ Mildred **Greenberg** (known as Minnie, d. 2014), married to Milton (known as Mutt, d. 1997), son of Morris and Bertha (nee **Gennis**) **Greenberg**.
- ○ Harry (d. 1985).

- Samuel (d. 1974), married to Annie (nee **Weiner**, d. 1968), daughter of Yehuda Leib and Sheva (nee Millstone) **Weiner**. Sam's second marriage was to Yetta (nee Weinman, d. 1981) **Landau**, who was originally married to my great uncle Sam **Landau**.

- Goldie Shabinsky (d. 1980), married to Maurice (d. 1987), son of Louis and Annie (nee **Taller**) Shabinsky. Their children are:
  - ○ Eileen **Landau**, married to Bob (d. 2004), son of my great uncle Sam and Yetta (nee Weinman) **Landau**. As noted above, Yetta **Landau** later married Eileen's uncle Samuel Shinder.
  - ○ Gloria Trainoff, married to Barry (d. 2020), son of Morris (d. 1983), and Esther (nee **Shore**, d. 1973) Trainoff. Morris Trainoff is a nephew of Yetta (nee Trainoff) **Viner**, married to Morris **Viner**. Sydney (d. 1992) Trainoff, son of Morris and Esther, was married to Susan (nee **Waserman**), daughter of Karl and Lillian (nee Brill) **Waserman**. Susan subsequently married Maury Kleinman.
  - ○ Solomon, married to Laya (nee **Greenberg**), daughter of Moses and Bessie (nee **Schecter**) **Greenberg**.

- Jack (d. 1946), married to Nellie (nee Pascar, d. 1968). Their children are:
  - ○ Gertrude Goldstein (d, 2002), married to Jack (d. 1988). Their children are:
    - ▪ Diane, originally married to Allan **Kathnelson**, son of Hiram and Lillian (nee Nadler) **Kathnelson**, and then to Allen Abramson.
    - ▪ Ernest, married to Ray (nee **Halpern**), daughter of Charles and Katie (nee **Skulsky**) **Halpern**.
  - ○ Ethyl Lightstone (d. 1991), married to Emanuel (d. 1999), son of Michael (d. 1976), and Leah (d. 1985) Lightstone. Michael's brother Samuel (d. 1960) was married to Libbie (d. 1963). Samuel and Libbie were the parents of Reuben (d. 2010), married to Rose (d. 1974); Moses (d. 1976); and Morton. Reuben's son Leslie Lightstone is married to Laya Crust, a native of Winnipeg whose mother was a sister to Margaret Rachlis (d. 2002), married to Jack Rachlis (d. 1992). Lorne Rachlis, the son of Jack and Margaret Rachlis, is married to Louise (nee Vinokur), daughter of Jack and Lillian (d. 2013) Vinokur.
  - ○ Israel (d. 2014), married to Jennie (nee **Greenberg**, d. 1991), daughter of Roger and Rose (ne Bezumny) **Greenberg**. Israel's second wife was Maureen Newton (nee **Gershon**, d. 2005, see **Lichtenstein**).
  - ○ Bernard, married to Adele (nee Abrahamson), daughter of Arnold and Bella (nee **Vechsler**) Abrahamson.

- Joseph (d. 1972), married to Sarah (d. 1985). Their children are:
  - ○ Cecil (d. 1997), married to Florence.
  - ○ Esther Neiss, married to Alvin.

For connections to other entries, see Betcherman, Bodnoff, Gennis, Greenberg (both families), Halpern, Kathnelson, Landau, Lichtenstein, Potechin, Rivers, Sherman, Shore, Skulsky, Taller, Tradburks, Vechsler, Viner, Waserman, Weiner.

Photo from Isaac Shinder's 85th birthday party:
Front row: L-R: Lionel Shinder, Linda Shinder, Eileen Shinder, Ernest Goldstein (directly behind), Jack Lightstone, Sylvia Shinder (directly behind), Janet Shinder, Dianne Goldstein, Gert Goldstein (directly behind) and Gloria Shabinsky. Second row: Harry Shinder, Nellie Shinder, Annie Shinder, Sam Shinder, Zaida Isaac Shinder, Roochel Shinder, Joe Shinder, Sarah Shinder, Ethel Rivers, and Jennie Shinder (with Jack on her lap). Third row: Goldie Shabinsky, Maurice Shabinsky, Manny Lightstone, Ethyl Lightstone, Israel Shinder, Harry Sandler, Eleanor Sandler (holding Pam), Ethel Malek, David Malek, Minnie Greenberg (holding Neil), Mutt Greenberg, Florie Shinder (holding Leslie), Cecil Shinder, Irving Rivers, Jack Goldstein, and Issie Sandler (holding Dianne). Fourth row: Louis Shinder, Myrna Shinder, Sol Shabinsky, Laya Shabinsky, Sol Shinder, Ethylene Shinder, Beatrice Shinder, Esther Shinder and Eileen Shabinsky. (OJA, unnumbered.)

Ottawa Talmud Torah Board's annual Chanukah party, December 18, 1979.

The party was held at the Jewish Community Centre on 151 Chapel St.
L-R: Rabbi Yaacov Kaploun (Director of education, Hillel Academy), Sol Shinder (Q.C., President of the Ottawa Vaad Ha'Ir), Dr. Hal Willis (Director of education, Ottawa Board of Education) and Dr. Charles Freedman (President of the Ottawa Talmud Torah Board). (OJA 6-214)

SHORE

The Shore family is descended from Moses (d. 1940) and Sarah Freda (d. 1941). Their children included:

- Mary Sinder (d. 1985), married to David. Their daughter Sonya **Bodnoff** (d. 2010) was married to Morley (d. 1990), son of Irving Benjamin and Ann (nee Rastovsky) **Bodnoff**.
- Charles (d. 1953), married to Anna (nee **Betcherman**, d. 1980), daughter of Fischel and Brocha **Betcherman**. Their children were:
  o David (d. 2020), married to Debi (nee Weisbord). Their son Mark was married to Andrea (nee **Saslove**), daughter of Ralph and Sylvia (nee **Weiner**) **Saslove**.
  o Mendel (d. 2017), married to Anita (nee Steinberg) daughter of Hymie and Rebecca (nee Baker) Steinberg (see **Glustein**).
  o Evelyn Rotenberg (d. 2016).
  o Faye Fogel (d. 1986), married to Harold (d. 1993).
- Joseph (d. 1954), married to Sarah (nee Dubinsky, d. 1987), daughter of Benjamin and Libby (nee **Pollock**) Dubinsky. Their children were:
  o Rosalie.
  o Manuel (d. 1985), married to Libby (d. 2006).
  o Peter (d. 1996).
  o Gordon (d. 1999), married to Goldie (d. 1998).
- Harry (d. 1942).

- Jack (d. 1942), married to Ann (nee Horwitz, d. 1983).
- Max (d 1979), married to Lillian.
- Rose Pleet (d. 1971), daughter of Leo and Rachel **Pleet**, married to Abraham (d. 1960).
- Esther Trainoff (d. 1973), married to Morris (d. 1983). Their children are:
    - Barry (d. 2020), married to Gloria (nee Shabinsky, see **Shinder**) Trainoff.
    - Sydney (d. 1992), married to Susan (nee **Waserman**), daughter of Karl and Lilian Waserman.
- Ida Lieff (d. 1944), married to Meyer (d. 1974), son of Moses and Bertha **Lieff**.

For connections to other entries, see Betcherman, Bodnoff, Glustein, Lieff, Pleet Pollock, Saslove, Shinder, Waserman, Weiner.

Shore's Dairy ca. 1935 which was located at 24 Byward Market Square.
The gentleman out front is a Mr. Dave Sinder. (OJA 2-023)

L-R: Joe Shore, Harry Shore, Charles Shore, Max Shore, Jack Shore, Henry Shore circa 1915. (OJA 1-946-01)

David and Mendel Shore (twins) in the Canadian Navy during World War II (photo courtesy of Suzi Shore-Sauve).

SHULMAN

The Shulman family descends from Max (d. 1969), and Rose (d. 1964) Shulman. Their children were:

- Ettie **Kimmel** (d. 1988), married to Phillip (d. 1979), son of Jacob Leib and Elka (nee Guz) **Kimmel**. Their children are:
    - Milton, married to Joyce (nee **Saslove**), daughter of Morris and Edythe (nee **Taller**) **Saslove**.
    - Stanley, married to Carol **Sadinsky** Spiro (d. 2010), daughter of Joseph and Molly (nee **Craft**) **Sadinsky**.
- Joseph (d. 1973) married to Fay (nee Muskovitch, d. 2011), the owners of Shulman's Fruit on the Byward Market. Their son Barry is married to Lynne (nee **Kronick**), daughter of David and Daphne (nee Newton) **Kronick**. Their daughter Nadine (d. 2015) was married to her first cousin Brian Mordfield, son of Fay's sister.
- Maurice (d. 1959).
- Jack (d. 1996).

Harry Shulman (d. 1955), Max's brother, was married to Lily (nee Jaffe) d. 1953). Their daughter Etta **Karp** (d. 2020) was married to Ben (d. 1991), son of Max and Dora Kapinsky. Ben and Etta's son Richard is married to Joy (nee **Roodman**), daughter of Herman and Zelda (nee **Dworkin**) **Roodman**.

For connections to other entries, see Craft, Dworkin, Karp, Kimmel, Kronick, Roodman, Sadinsky, Saslove, Taller.

SILVER

The Silver family is descended from Benjamin (d. 1939), and Rachel Bluma (nee Szeroszewsky, d. 1940). Their children were:

- Hershel (d. 1963), married to Odas (nee Szeroszewsky, d. 1993). Their children are:
    - Menachem Mendel.
    - Louis (Label, d. 2022), married to Leona (nee **Viner**, d. 2022), daughter of Cecil and Freda (nee **Skulsky**) **Viner**.
    - Aaron (d. 2011), married to Goldie (nee Caplan).
    - Esther Leah, married to Shlomo Zerach Saalkind.
    - Dora Mann, married to Reuvain Mann (d. 2014).
    - Joe.
    - Reuven, married to Ruth (nee Chinn).
- Isaac, married to Feige (nee Szeroszewsky, sister of Odas – i.e. two brothers married two sisters, and both sisters are relatives of their mother-in-law as well – i.e. the Silver and Szeroszewsky families married into each other multiple times).
- Libbie Cohen (d. 1962), married to Lyon (Aryeh Leib, d. 1974). Their children were:

- o Mayer (d. 1995), married to Yospa, nee Szeroszewsky, a cousin of Odas and Feige, d. 1991). Their daughter Dorothy is married to Rabbi Nisson Wolpin, a third cousin of my mother-in-law Sara (nee Aberbach) Rachlin (see **Cohen**).
- o Leah Mindel Goldstein, married to Mose.
- o Eliezer.
- o Reiny Zbar, married to Mischa Zbar. Mischa Zbar served as a kosher butcher in Ottawa for many decades before moving to Israel. Their son David Zbar, married to Naomi, was killed in action on the Golan Heights in 1974. Their son Benjamin was also involved in the Kosher butcher business in Ottawa, eventually merging with Joe Lichtenstein to form United Kosher. Benjamin also served as an assistant Chazzan at Beth Shalom. Benjamin's daughter Rachael Rosenberg is married to David, the son of Harry (d. 2016) and Faigel (d. 2011) Rosenberg, a prominent economist, originally from Ottawa.
- o Rachel Schall, married to Issie.
- o Menucha Nitkin, married to Joseph.
- o Mordechai.
- o Esther **Steinberg** (d. 2016), married to Moses Wolfe (d. 2011), son of Louis (d. 1983), and Leah (nee Sanders) **Steinberg**.
- • Eliezer (d. 1910), married to Rachel Tova (nee Yellin).

Odas Silver's father Mayer Sher (Szeroszewsky) had a sister Anna Aronson (d. 1951) married to Mordechai Aronson (d. 1952). Mordechai and Anna's children were:
- • Bernard (d. 1989).
- • Jack (d. 1967).
- • Fanny (d. 1990).
- • Isadore (d. 1985).
- • Harry (d. 1985), married to Esther (nee Raport) daughter of Michael (d. 1949), and Elizabeth (nee **Sugarman**), and sister of Helen **Greenberg**, married to Louis, son of Roger and Rose (nee Bezumny) **Greenberg**; and Esther Slonemsky (d. 1987), married to Cecil. Harry and Esther's son Lester Aronson (d. 2020) was married to Myra (nee **Slack**), daughter of Louis and Stella (nee Gilbert) **Slack**.

Rachel Bluma Silver had a brother Yosef Szeroszewsky, whose granddaughter Frieda Pernikoff (nee Schecter) was married to Aaron Pernikoff. Aaron's brother Rabbi Mayer Pernikoff (d. 1997) was married to Sophie (nee **Glustein**), daughter of Jacob and Rachel (nee Brissman) **Glustein**, and sister of Shirley Cement, who was married to Rabbi Yechiel Cement.

For connections to other entries, see Cohen, Glustein, Greenberg, Skulsky, Slack, Steinberg, Sugarman, Viner.

SKULSKY

The Skulsky family descends from Menachem Mendel and Chaya Skulsky. Their children were:

- Samuel, married to Jenny (nee **Glustein**, d. 1970), daughter of Harry and Sarah (nee Belinke) **Glustein**. Their daughter Rebecca was married to Zawel Goldberg. Zawel and Rebecca's son Samuel is married to Sheryl (nee Newman), daughter of Laz Newman (see **Fine**).
- Freda **Viner** (d. 1973), married to Cecil (d. 1933), son of Joseph and Gittel (nee Silverman) **Viner**. Their children were:
  o Arthur (d. 1997), married to Sonia (nee Goldman, d. 2003), daughter of Walter and Malka Goldman. Their daughter Gladys **Greenberg** is married to John, son of Samuel and Bessie (nee **Murray**) **Greenberg**.
  o Gordon (d. 2010) married to Shirley (nee Fredlender).
  o Milton (d. 2013) married to Terry.
  o Sylvia Altschuler (d. 1976), married to Saul. Their daughter Diane **Goldfield** (d. 1997), was married to Morley (d. 2016), son of Charles and Eva **Goldfield**.
  o Leona **Silver** (d. 2022), married to Label, son of Hershel and Odes (nee Szeroszewsky) **Silver**.
  o Millicent Schaenfield (d. 2015), married to David (d. 1995).
  o Dora Schaenfield (d. 2006), married to Samuel (d. 2006). Samuel and David were brothers (two brothers married two sisters). Their son David is married to Rona (nee Hersh), daughter of Saul and Ettie (nee **Waserman**) Hersh.
  o Betty Gold.
  o David **Viner** (d. 1998).
  o Joseph **Viner** (d. 2001).
- Solomon (Sholowm, d. 1942). His children were:
  o Katie **Halpern** (d. 1999), married to Charles (d. 1959), son of Herman and Rae **Halpern**. Their daughter Ray Goldstein is married to Ernest, son of Jack and Gertrude (nee **Shinder**) Goldstein.
  o Moses (Chuck, d. 2008).
  o Nathan (d. 2002).
  o Annie Phillippson, married to Arnold.
  o Ida Wiseman (d. 1995).
  o Betty Wax (d. 2002), married to Harry.

For connections to other entries, see Fine, Glustein, Goldfield, Greenberg, Halpern, Murray, Shinder, Silver, Viner, Waserman.

SLACK

The Slack family is descended from Harry (d. 1950), and Dora (nee Gunnerotsky d. 1979). The original surname was Schlak. Dora's brother Levi is married to Rachel. Levi and Rachel Gunnerotsky's son is Sol Gunner, married to Estelle (nee **Schecter**), daughter of Sydney and Lena (nee **Petigorsky**) **Schecter**. Children of Harry and Dora were:

- Moses (d. 1975), married to Charlotte (nee **Kerzner**, d. 2000), daughter Itzik Mayer and Pessia (nee Neistein) Kerzner.
- Louis (d. 1977), married to Stella (nee Gilbert, d. 1995), daughter of Maurice and Betsy (nee Brown) Gilbert. Myra Aronson, the daughter of Louis and Stella, was

married to Lester (d. 2020), son of Harry and Esther (nee Raport) Aronson (see **Silver**).

- William (d. 1976), married to Clara (nee Balsky, d. 2001), daughter of Morris and Gittel Balsky.
- Benjamin Slack.
- Samuel (d. 2001), married to Sylvia (known as Sue, d. 2012). Their daughter Sharon **Appotive** is married to David, son of Joseph and Bas Sheva (nee Parnass) **Appotive**. Their daughter Joy Mender is married to Seymour Mender.
- Pesach (d. 1928).

Dora's parents were Yitzchak and Nechama (nee Schlak) Gunnerotsky. Nechama was a sister to Harry Slack. Thus Dora was Harry's niece. Another sister of Harry Slack and Nechama Gunnerotsky was Dora Shenkman (nee Schlak, d. 1953), married to Max (d. 1941). Children of Max and Dora Shenkman were Benjamin, Samuel, Harold (d. 1998), and Abraham (d. 1926). Max Shenkman's brother was Wolf (d. 1950), married to Mary (d. 1958).

For connections to other entries, see Appotive, Kerzner, Petigorsky, Schecter, Silver.

Story hour at the Jewish Community Centre Library. 1960's. Librarian Teme Levine hands out books to Stella Slack while Harry Kotlarsky and others look at 78 rpm recordings of music. (OJA 19-044)

SLONEMSKY (SLONE)

See Coplan.

SLOVER

The Slover family descends from Abraham Chaim (d. 1921), and Malca (d. 1935). Their children were:

- Bertha **Taylor** (d. 1971), married to Samuel (d. 1943). Children of Samuel and Bertha are:
  - Charles (known as Chick), married to Rose (nee **Kardash**), daughter of Abraham and Tzipora (nee Rosenthal) **Kardash**.
  - Irving (d. 2012), married to Ethel (nee **Greenberg**, d. 2009), daughter of Samuel and Bessie (nee **Murray**) **Greenberg**. Their son Brent is married to Risa, the daughter of Harry and Esther (nee **Betcherman**) **Froman**.
  - Malca **Polowin**, married to Chuck (d. 2021), son of Benjamin and Bessie **Polowin**.
  -
- Eva **Fine** (d. 1977), the second wife of Harry **Fine** (also known as Hyman, d. 1988).
- Ephraim (also known as Frank, d. 1933), married to Jenny. Children of Ephraim and Jenny were:
  - Lawrence (d. 2004) married to Mona (nee **Cohen** d. 2005), daughter of Sam and Fanny (nee Hoichberg) **Cohen**.
  - Sidney (d. in action, 1943).
  - Arnold (d. 1990).
- Gertrude Gertler, married to Hyman (Note: this is a different Hyman Gertler than the former cantor of Beth Shalom in the 1960s and early 1970s. Cantor Hyman Gertler is noted under **Pollock**).
- Sarah Finkelstein (d. 1934), married to Henry (d. 1946). Their children were:
  - Laura **Rubin**, (d. 1984) married to Harold (d. 1971), son of Jacob Moses and Zishcha (nee **Coplan**) **Rubin**.
  - Muriel Levine (d. 1990), married to Isaac (Ike, d. 1994).
  - Helen Webber-Ziderman.
  - Esther Cooper (d. 1984).

David Slover (d. 1977), married to Belle (nee **Flesher**, d. 1991), daughter of Joseph and Rachel (nee Pont) **Flesher**, was a nephew of Abraham Chaim Slover. Children of David and Belle are:

- Norman, married to Sandra (nee Levine). Sandra's brother Ellis is married to Teri Levine (nee **Leikin**), daughter of Julius and Ruth **Leikin**.
- Morley.
- Beverley.

For connections to other entries, see Betcherman, Cohen, Coplan, Fine, Flesher, Froman, Greenberg, Kardish, Leikin, Murray, Polowin, Rubin, Taylor.

SMITH

The Smith family descends from Louis (d. 1967) and Annie (nee Glazer, d. 1953) Smith. The original family name was Sendzul. Children of Louis and Annie are:

- Morris (d 1987), married to Fay (nee **Flesher**, d. 2002), daughter of Israel and Eta **Flesher**.
- Molly Narwa (d. 2011), married to Moshe (d. 1982).
- Nathan (d. 2006), married to Lorenza. He gave his name to Nate's Delicatessen.
- Cecil (d. 1995), married to Edna (nee Cohen, d. 1988).
- Solomon (d. 1966), married to Lily (nee Cohen, d. 1964).
- Jack (d. 2009), married to Inez (nee Brown, d. 1975), and then to Linda (nee Rosen). Jack Smith was a well-known kosher caterer and restaurateur in Ottawa. Jack and Inez' children are:
  - Leiba **Krantzberg**, who was married to Robert, son of Julius and Claire (nee Singerman) **Krantzberg**.
  - Anna Silverman, who was married to Ivan Silverman, sister of Noreen Boslov and Audrey Levy (see **Gosewich**).
  - David, who carries on the kosher catering business in Ottawa.
  - Moishe, who was the first non-US citizen to serve as president of B'nai B'rith International, a position he held from 2006-2011.
  - Leslie, married to Maureen. Their son Aaron is married to Erin (nee Osterer), son of Howard and Ellen (nee **Rivers**) Osterer (see **Glustein**).
  - Karla Morrison, married to Joe.
  - Leah.
  - Eileen Ingram, married to Doug.
  - Nathan, married to Cindy.
  - Mark, married to Sharon.
- Freda (d. 2014).
- Hyman, married to Erika.
- David (d. 2020), married to Darlene.
- Isidore (known as Scotty, d. 2009), married to Isabel (d. 2021).
- Samuel (d. 1974).
- Fanny.
- Lily (d. 1969), married to Sydney Boslov (see **Gosewich**)

Louis Smith's mother Yocheved (nee Zarenda) had a sister Hanna Greenspon, married to Marcus. Hanna and Marcus' daughter Ida Borts (d. 1948) was married to Abraham (d. 1968), son of Samuel Pesach (d. 1915), and Asna (d. 1927) Borts. Their children were:

- Shirley Klempner (d. 1995), married to Harold.
- Sidney (d. 1980), married to Myrtle (d. 2011).
- Cecil (d. 1991), married to Annette.
- Irvine (d. 1986) married to Bertha (nee Lang, d. 2002), son of David (d. 1966) and Clara (d. 1962). Their son Howard was married to Sandra (nee **Waserman**), daughter of Paul and Nessie **Waserman**.
- Clarence (d. 1969).

For a different Smith family, descendants of Bernard (d. 1953) and Rebecca (nee Rhinestein, d. 1940), see Betcherman.

For connections to other entries, see Flesher, Glustein, Gosewich, Krantzberg, Rivers, Waserman.

Jack Smith with some of his children at his 50th birthday party.

Photo by Andre Sima, Ottawa, January 14, 1982.
L-R: Nathan, Ivan and Anna (Smith) Silverman, Karla, Jack, Lieba (Krantzberg), Leslie and Maureen with their children Misha and Aaron, Mark, Moishe and Patty (Flesher). The party took place at Machzikei Hadas Congregation. (OJA 1-586)

SMOLKIN

The Smolkin family is descended from Abraham (d. 1933), and Sima (nee Levine) Smolkin. Abraham's second wife was Eva Lapidus Smolkin (nee Kravetz, d. 1932), who was first married to Max Lapidus. The Smolkin family spread through Ottawa, Montreal, as well as several smaller towns including Cornwall, Almonte, Carp, and Smiths Falls.

Max and Eva Lapidus were the parents of Dora Kriger (d. 1986), married to Jacob (d. 1965). Dora and Jacob Kriger were the parents of:
- Akiva (d. 2011), married first to Shirley (nee Movshovitz, d. 1972), and then to Shirley (nee **Glustein**) Kline, who was first married to Phillip Kline.
- Maynard (d. 2016).

The children of Abraham and Sima Smolkin were:

- Max (d. 1969), whose three wives were Annie (nee Maskolinsky, d. 1925), Celia (nee Bernstein), Sarah (nee Ancelovitz), who was originally married to Harry Cohen, (d. 1946).
- Esther Hoffman, married to Paul Hoffman.
- Charles, married to Rae (nee Epstein).
- Ida Finkelstein (d. 1973), married to Jacob (d. 1980), son of Bernard (d. 1930) and Bertha (nee Barret, d. 1963). Jacob Finkelstein's siblings were Isadore (d. 1950), Leah (d. 1993), Rebecca (d. 1966), Tilly, Esther, Harold, Henry. Children of Ida and Jacob Finkelstein were:
  - Sybil Goodman (d. 1998), married to Isadore (d. 2000).
  - Anne Abugov (d. 1998), married to Alex. Alex and Anne were part of the Cornwall community.
- John (d. 1955), married to Anna (nee Ginsburg, d. 1959). Their children were:
  - Maxwell (d. 2010 at the age of 102), married to Pearl (nee Wiseman d. 2004), daughter of Abraham and Malca (nee Vineburg) Wiseman, and sister of Judith Ain (d. 2000) married to Kenneth (d. 1970). Max and Pearl's son David Smolkin is married to Tova.
  - Benjamin (d. 2002), married to Shirley (nee Sabbath). Their children are:
    - Michael (d. 1950).
    - Howard, married to Patricia (d. 1991). Their daughter Nicole Shapiro is married to Michael, son of Jack and Carol-Sue (nee **Swedlove**) Shapiro.
  - Etta Bart, married first to Harvey Shapiro, and then to Stuart Bart.
  - Moses (d. 1971), married to Bess (nee Friedman, d. 1988). Their son is Paul. Bess's sister was Ida **Ellenberg Vechsler**, married to Abraham **Ellenberg** and then Richard **Vexler (Vechsler)**
  - Sally Bellan, married to Alex.
  - Samuel (d. 2003), married to Therese (nee Menard, d. 2010).
  - Robert (d. 2002), married to Pauline (nee Katchen, d. 1989).
  - Rose **Levitan** (d. 1990), married to Archie (d. 1960), son of Morris and Rachel **Levitan**. Their children are:
    - John (d. 2006), married to Lynn (nee Davis), daughter of Barry (d. 2013) and Selma (nee Davidson) Davis.
    - Richard, married to Patty (nee Armitage), and was married to Polly (nee Baker), daughter of Harry (d.1985) and Elsie (nee Goldenberg. d. 2006) Baker (see **Pleet**). Richard and Polly's daughter, Lenora **Zelikovitz**, is married to Evan, son of Leon and Zelda **Zelikovitz**.
    - Susan Goldstein, married to Myron.
    - Marcia Gur-Arie married to Yehuda.
- Becky **Dworkin**-Boro, married to Myer **Dworkin**, and then to Jack Boro.
- Anne Haymer, married to Louis.

- Bernard married to Goldie (nee Blumkin).
- Gittel Ginsburg (d. 1949) married to Isser (d. 1947). Isser was the brother of Anne Smolkin, married to Gittel's brother John (i.e. a brother and a sister married a sister and a brother). Children of Isser and Gittel were:
  - Mervin (d. 2006), married to Evelyn (nee **Pollock**), daughter of Abraham and Esther **Pollock**, who were cousins with the Ottawa **Pollock** family.
  - Emma (d. 1955).
  - Max (d. 1998), married to Mary (d. 2011).
  - Martin (d. 2008), married to Theadora (d. 2007). Their daughter Janet **Cohen** is married to Eric, son of Morris and Mina (nee **Dover**) **Cohen**.
- Leah.

For connections to other entries, see Cohen, Dover, Dworkin, Ellenberg, Glustein, Levitan, Pollock, Pleet, Swedlove, Vechsler, Zelikovitz.

SOLOWAY

See Greenberg.

Zelda Soloway and nursing students at Jewish General Hospital, 1953.
(OJA 1-936-24)

Hyman Soloway   Maurice Wright

(https://solowaywright.com/the-firm/)

STEINBERG

Steinberg is a common name, and there is more than one Steinberg family, or Steinberg individuals in Ottawa. This entry will deal with one family that has several interconnections. This Steinberg family descends from Yaakov. The original family name was Sternberg. Yaakov had many children, three whom resided in Ottawa. The Ottawa-based families included:

- Louis (d. 1983), married to Leah (nee Sanders, d. 1964), daughter of Chaim Nuta and Annie (nee Toft) Chandross. Their children were:
  - Claire Kevanstein (d. 2011), married to Abraham (d. 1989), son of Henry (d. 1953) and Miriam (d. 1953) Kevanstein. Abraham was the brother of Louis Kevanstein (d. 2006), married to Rachel (d. 2003).
  - Moses (d. 2011), married to Esther (d. 2016, nee Cohen), daughter of Lyon (d. 1974), and Libbie (nee **Silver**, d. 1962) Cohen.
  - Abraham Joseph (d. 1979), married to Tsyvia (nee Rabinovitch).
  - Bennet (d. 1977), married to Mary (nee Weinman, d. 2003), daughter of Herschel and Tsippe Weinman, and sister of Ethel Brill Benoway (d. 2004). Ethel's first husband was Joseph Brill (d. 1942), and second husband was Morris Benoway (d. 1977). Joseph and Ethel's daughter is Sally **Levitan**, married to Elliott **Levitan**, son of Maurice and Fanny Levitan.
  - Jack (d. 2012), married to Joyce (nee Litwin, d. 2002). Their children are:
    - Michael, married to Francine (nee Budevich), and then to Bonnie (nee Maloney).
    - Ellie **Greenberg**, married to Max **Greenberg**, son of Ben and Ida (nee **Kardish**), **Greenberg**. Ellie's first husband was Stephen Muenz.

- Anne.
- Leah Findlay, married to Richard.
  o Israel Victor (d. 2007), married to Shirley (nee Cohen).
- Max (d. 1959), married to Annie (d. 1955). Their son Jack (d. 1996), married to Libby (Lily, nee Gandelman, d. 1997), daughter of Abe and Molka (see **Gandall**).
- Usher Sternberg (d. 1956), married to Fannie (D. 1958). Their son Ralph (d. 1997), was married to Anne (nee Ginsburg, d. 2006). Ralph and Anne's son Bill (d. 1983) was married to Roslyn (nee **Waserman**). Ralph and Anne's daughter Laya Jacobsen is married to Ted.

For connections to other entries, see Gandall, Greenberg, Kardish, Levitan, Silver, Waserman.

SUGARMAN

The Sugarman family descends from Eliezer and Florence Sugarman. Their children were:

- Harry (d. 1928), married to Esther (nee Rappaport, d. 1909). Their children were:
  o Mary Rabin (d. 1941), married to Abraham (d. 1929).
  o Elizabeth Raport (d. 1923), married to Michael (d. 1949). Their children were:
    - Edith Slonemsky (d. 1987), married to Cecil.
    - Irene Pearlman (d. 1995), married to Saul (d. 1956).
    - Samuel (d. 1968).
    - Lillian (d. 2003).
    - Helen **Greenberg** (d. 1979), married to Louis (d. 1974), son of Roger and Rose (nee Bezumny) **Greenberg**.
    - Esther Aronson (d. 1984), married to Harry, (d. 1985) son of Mordechai and Anna (nee Szeroszewsky) Aronson (see **Silver**). Harry and Esther's son Lester Aronson is married to Myra (nee **Slack**), daughter of Louis and Stella (nee Gilbert) **Slack**.
  o Hyman (d. 1960), married to Jessie (nee Phillips, d. 1964). Their children were:
    - Philip (d. 1991), married to Gusta (nee Seidler, d. 1994), daughter of Norman and Bertha Seidler, and sister of Selma Coopersmith, married to Saul, son of Benjamin and Naomi (nee **Lithwick**) Coopersmith. Their daughter Brenda **Saslove** is married to Harold, son of Abraham and Anne (nee **Taller**) **Saslove**. Joan (nee Schwartzfeld) Robern, married to Michael Robern, is a cousin of the Seidler family. Michael's parents were Haskel (d. 2000), and Maxine (nee Chetwynd, d. 1990) Robern. Joan Robern is also a cousin of members of the Winnipeg based Malkin family. Another member of the Malkin family, Aaron Malkin (d. 2016) was married to Dina (nee Gordon, d. 2016), daughter of Jacob d. 1996) and Sarah (d. 1988) Gordon. Jacob Gordon was a beloved teacher, who taught Bar Mitzvah lessons to several generations of Ottawans. Joan's sister

Teresa (Terry) Schwartzfeld (d. 2009), was married to Stephen Cotsman.

- Laurence (d. 1991), married first to Shirley (nee **Polowin**, d. 1984), daughter of Jacob and Dina (nee Gordon) **Polowin**, and then to Barbara (nee **Molot**), daughter of Abram and Edith **Molot**.
- Elie (d. 1927), married to Sarah (d. 1922). Their children were:
  ○ Susan Katz (d. 1971), married to Samuel (d. 1962). Their children were:
    - Bertram (d. 1973), married to Marilyn (nee Becker).
    - Esther Robinson, married to Irving.
    - Arnold, married to Rita (nee Shane).
    - Sidney, married to Dorothy (nee Sangster).
    - Miriam **Weiner** (d. 2013), married to Louis (d. 2011), son of Israel and Anne **Weiner**.
    - Edward.
  ○ Anna Lerman (d. 1955), married to Charles.
  ○ Lillian Evenchick (d. 1979), married to Meyer (d. 1969). Their children were:
    - Shirley Lacome (d. 2010), married to Bernard (d. 2014).
    - Abbey (Avrom, d. 2008), married first to Lillian, (nee Berlin, d. 2014) and then to Suzanne Beaulieu.
- Israel (d. 1946), married to Elizabeth (d. 1956), daughter of Israel's brother Abraham Joseph and Charlotte Sugarman. Note, this is an uncle/niece marriage, uncommon but perfectly permitted according to Jewish law. Their daughter Florence Mazur (d. 1935), was married to Bill.
- Abraham Joseph (d. 1935), married to Charlotte (d. 1940). Their children were:
  ○ Annie Baxt (d. 1968), married to Hyman (d. 1941)
  ○ Bessie, married to Louis (d. 1969).
  ○ Esther Diamond (d. 1961), married to Maurice.
  ○ Hattie (d. 1971).
  ○ Rebecca (d. 1971).
  ○ Elizabeth (d. 1956), married to her uncle Israel Sugarman (d. 1946).
- Elizabeth Rapaport.

For connections to other entries, see Greenberg, Lithwick, Molot, Polowin, Saslove, Silver, Slack, Taller, Weiner.

SWEDLOVE

The Swedlove family is descended from Herschel (d. about 1920) and Rebecca (nee Weiss) Swedlove. The original surname was Swerdlow. Their children were:

- Morris (d. 1996), married to Annie (nee Poulin, d. 1980).
- Esther Rossman (d. 1978), married to Louis. Their children were:
  ○ Dr. Jacob Rossman (d. 1958). Dr. Rossman was married to Frances (d. 2015), who then remarried Mortimer English (d. 1996), son of Bennett (d. 1941), and Sarah (d. 1939) English, and brother of Dr. Alexander (d. 1964), Corrine (d. 1986), and Stephen (d. 1973). Dr. Rossman lived in Ottawa, but the rest of the siblings lived in Port Colborne and Fort Erie.
  ○ David (d. 1972).

- o Ben, married to Sarah (nee Ginsberg).
- o Alec (d. 2008), married to Anne (nee Fishman, d. 2010).
- Selig, married to Rachel (nee Achbar, d. 1988). Their children were:
  - o Freda **Lithwick** (d. 2013), married to Hyman (d. 1990), son of Max and Dora (nee Ness) **Lithwick**.
  - o Casey (d. 2006), married to Bess (nee Jack, d. 2015). Their children are:
    - Carol-Sue Shapiro (d. 2020), married to Jack, son of Abraham and Nelly (nee **Hanser**) Shapiro. Jack and Carol-Sue's son Michael is married to Nicole (nee **Smolkin**), daughter of Howard and Patricia **Smolkin**.
    - Alan (d. 2003).
  - o Harold (d. 1966), married to Ruth (nee Koh, d. 1996).
- Samuel (d. 1973), married to Fanny (nee **Cohen**, d. 1949), daughter of Charles and Sheina (nee Margolies) **Cohen**. Their children were:
  - o Joseph (d. 1989), married to Irene (nee Aisenberg, d. 2009), daughter of Harry and Ente (nee **Lithwick**) Aisenberg.
  - o Tillie Paulin, married to Arthur.
  - o Philip (d. 1993), married to Deborah (nee **Polowin**, d. 1993), daughter of Jacob and Dina (nee Gordon) **Polowin**.
- Rose Achbar (d. 1981), married first to Morris Mendelson, and then to Arie Louis Achbar (d. 1987). Their children are:
  - o Benjamin (son of Morris Mendelson and Rose – took on name Achbar, d. 2018)., married to Marjorie, daughter of Frank and Annie Sinclair (see **Flesher**). Ben and Rose's son Stanley is married to Cynthia, daughter of Bill and Frances (nee **Kizell**) Waiser.
  - o Zelda **Freedman** (daughter of Arie Louis and Rose), married to Lawrence (d. 1996), son of Michael and Anna **Freedman**.
  - o Dr. Helen Cooper (daughter of Arie Louis and Rose).
- Dora Halperin (d. 1970), married to Joseph (d. 1961). This family lived in St. Catharines. Their grandson David Halperin, son of Saul and Girda (nee Tyber), is married to Ruth (nee **Lichtenstein**), son of Joseph and Jean (nee Newton) **Lichtenstein**.

For connection to other entries, see Cohen, Flesher, Freedman, Hanser, Kizell, Lichtenstein, Lithwick, Polowin, Smolkin.

TANNER

See Gershon.

TALLER

The Taller family descends from Motel (Mordechai) Taller and Annie (nee Sadawoi / Sadavoy). The original surname was Tallfskey. The two branches of the family known in Ottawa descend from Motel and Annie's two sons Nathan and Maier, with one of the sons of Nathan married a daughter of Maier.

Nathan Taller branch

This branch stems from Nathan (d. 1929), married to Nuchama (nee Sadavoy – note the multiple connections to the Sadavoy family). Their children were:

- Jacob (d. 1953), married to his first cousin Ethel (d. 1963), daughter of Nathan's brother Maier and his wife Anna. Their children were:
  - Edythe **Saslove** (d. 1964), married to Morris (d. 1980), son of Jacob and Hanna (nee Brodsky) **Saslove**. After Edythe's death, Morris married Anna Lazear (nee Kentrowitz), the mother of his son-in-law Phil Lazear. Children of Morris and Edythe are:
    - Marion Shapiro (d. 2003), married to Al (d. 2004).
    - Norma Lazear, married to Philip, son of Samuel (d. 1959), and the aforementioned Anna (d. 2002).
    - Joyce Kimmel, married to Milton, son of Philip and Ettie (nee **Shulman**) **Kimmel**.
    - June Kurland, married to Jerry.
  - Moses (d. 1978).
  - Fae Kwechansky (d. 1967) married to Louis (d. 1981).
  - Elizabeth **Roodman** (d. 1997), married to Jacob (d. 1996), son of Moshe and Basheva (nee Camen) **Roodman**.
  - Samuel (d. 1991), married to Anne (nee Silver, d. 2006), daughter of Zalman and Rachel Silver. Their children are:
    - Enid **Gould**, married to Jeff, son of Victor and Rachel (nee **Bodnoff**) **Gould**.
    - Marilyn **Waserman**, was married to Phillip, son of Ernest and Sadie (nee Emanuel) **Waserman**.
    - Rhoda Simbrow, married to Jeffrey.
  - Eva Wortman (d. 1984), married to Ben (d. 1975).
  - Anne **Saslove** (d. 2007), married to Abraham son of Jacob and Hanna (nee Brodsky) **Saslove**, and brother of Morris, who was married to Anne's sister Edythe (two **Saslove** brothers married two Taller **sisters**). Their son Stephen is married to Brenda (nee **Sugarman**), daughter of Phillip and Gusta (nee Seidler) **Sugarman**.
  - Norman (d. 1998), married to Stella (nee Ysorsky, d. 1991). Stella's brother was Maurice Young (d. 2014), married to Evelyn (d. 2014). Evelyn was the sister of Cissie Greenberg (d. 2001), married to Jack (d. 2001). Children of Norman and Stella are:
    - Leslie (d. 2007), was married to Zena (nee Balinsky), and then to Susan (nee Villeneuve).
    - Rosalind Silverman.
    - Norean Harris, married to Jimmy Harris.
  - Morton (d. 2010), married to Sally (nee Landau), daughter of Mayer (d. 1973), and Rose (d. 1979) Landau (not related to my Landau family). Their daughter Lynda Wakter, married to Alex, currently serves as the executive director of the Jewish National Fund for Ottawa and Atlantic Canada.
  - Archie (d. 1997), married to Lillian (nee Pepper, d. 2005). Their son Joel (d. 2017) was married to Gaye (nee Kaiman), daughter of Sol and Sylvia (nee **Cherm**) Kaiman.
- Jenny.

- Rebecca Witten, married to Nathan.
- Rachel Sobcov (d. 1968), married to Isaac (d. 1932). The Sobcov café at Hillel Lodge is named in honor of this family. Their children were:
  - Sam (d. 1978), was married to Ann (nee **Kronick**, d. 1970), daughter of Selig and Raisyl **Kronick**.
  - Jacob (d. 1989), married to Cecile (d. 1987).
  - Michael (d. 1950) married to Dora (d. 1987).
  - Ralph (d. 1999).
  - Norman (d. 1992).
  - Jessie (d. 1993).
- Frances Greenberg, married to Samuel. Their daughter Jessie (d. 1945) was married to Frank **Wexler**, brother of Charles **Wexler**, who was married to Pearl (nee **Goldfield**).

Maier Taller branch:

This branch stems from Maier (d. 1929), married to Anna (nee Borotnick, d. 1932). Their children were:

- Ethel Taller (d. 1963), married to her first cousin Jacob (d. 1953), the son of Maier's brother Nathan and his wife Nuchama. See above for full family details.
- Annie Shabinsky (d. 1952), married to Louis (d. 1972). Their children were:
  - Maurice (d. 1987), married to Goldie (nee **Shinder**, d. 1980), daughter of Isaac and Ethel **Shinder**. Their children are:
    - Eileen **Landau**, married to Bob (d. 2004), son of my great uncle Sam and Yetta (nee Weinman) **Landau**.
    - Gloria Trainoff, married to Barry (d.2020).
    - Solomon, married to Laya (nee **Greenberg**), daughter of Moses and Bessie (nee **Schecter**) **Greenberg**.
  - Bennie (d. 1994), married to Alice (nee Bergman, d. 1964). Mindi Hartman, married to Irwin, is a niece of Alice. Children of Bennie and Alice are:
    - Marvin (d. 2021), married to Rhoda (nee Sonken), daughter of Saul and Edith (nee **Molot**) Sonken.
    - Michael.
    - Phyllis Levitt, married to Milton.
  - Reuben Shaver (surname changed from Shabinsky, d. 1960), married to Esther (nee **Lieff** d. 1979), daughter of Leon and Minnie (nee Doctor) **Lieff**. Their son Michael (d. 2011) was married to Sandra (nee Nadelle), daughter of Harry (d. 1957) and Minnie (nee Zelick, d. 1983) Nadelle, and sister of Ontario Court Judge Jack Nadelle, married to Diane; and Frances (d. 1978).
  - Sarah Dobrinsky (d. 2000), married to Ben (d. 2010).
  - Abraham Shabinsky (d. 1924 as a baby).
  - Samuel (d. 2003), married to Ann (nee Turner, d. 1998).
- Eva Taller (d. 1963), married to Hyman (d. 1960). Hyman's original surname was Jordan, but took on his wife's surname. Their children were:
  - Jack (d. 1989), married to Pearl (nee Cohen, d. 2006), daughter of Jacob (d. 1950) and Bessie (nee Butovsky, d. 1977) Cohen, and sister of Sarah

(nee Cohen) **Cantor**, wife of Benes **Cantor**; and Maxwell Cohen. Bessie's brother was Jacob Butovsky (d. 1967), married to Anna (d. 1976).

- o Kalmon (d. 1928).
- o Max (d. 1976), married to Sally.
- o Samuel (d. 1997), married to Bessie (nee **Cantor**, d. 2010), daughter of Hyman and Ida (nee Mincoff) **Cantor**, sister of Benes Cantor (note the double connection to the **Cantor** family in this Taller branch). Their children are:
  - ▪ Mendy was married to Ruth (nee **Kerzner**, d. 1996), and currently married to Lori (nee **Fine**), daughter of Reuben and Phyllis (nee Ross) **Fine**.
  - ▪ Herbie married to Vivian (nee Gelman), daughter of Ben and Rebecca (nee **Schecter**) Gelman.
  - ▪ Carolyn Katz, married to Sid.
- • Bella Bernstein, married to Wolfe.
- • Morris (d. 1964), married to Anne (nee **Kronick**, d. 2001), daughter of Jacob and Toba **Kronick**. Their son Myles (d. 2019) was married to Roslyn (nee Weidman), daughter of Harry (d. 1983) and Rae (d. 1983) Weidman.

For connections to other entries, see Bodnoff, Cantor, Cherm, Fine, Goldfield, Gould, Greenberg, Kerzner, Kimmel, Kronick, Landau, Lieff, Molot, Roodman, Saslove, Schecter, Shinder, Shulman, Sugarman, Waserman.

Fae and Marion beside the Taller mattress factory, on the Bayview side, circa late 1930s. (Source: David Kwechansky)

TAYLOR

The Taylor family is descended from Yitzchak Taylor. His children were:

- Samuel (d. 1943), married to Bertha (nee **Slover**, d. 1971), daughter of Abraham Chaim and Malca Slover. Children of Samuel and Bertha are:
  - Charles (known as Chick), married to Rose (nee **Kardash**, d. 2012), daughter of Abraham and Tzipora (nee Rosenthal) **Kardash**.
  - Irving (d. 2012), married to Ethel (nee **Greenberg**, d. 2009), daughter of Samuel and Bessie (nee **Murray**) **Greenberg**. Their son Brent is married to Risa, the daughter of Harry and Esther (nee **Betcherman**) **Froman**.
  - Malca **Polowin**, married to Chuck, son of Benjamin and Bessie **Polowin**.
- Albert (d. 1961), married to Pitzi (also known as Fanny, nee **Pollock**, d. 1983), daughter of Pinchas and Rivka (nee **Gencher**) **Pollock**. Their children are:
  - Gerald (d. 2010), married to Barbara.
  - Sheldon, married to Cynthia, and then to Corrinne (nee Rothman).
  - Samuel (d. 1945 as an infant).

For connections to other entries, see Betcherman, Froman, Gencher, Greenberg, Kardish, Murray, Pollock, Polowin, Slover.

Summer at Cooper cottage in Britannia, 1942. l-r: Henry Finkelstein, Laura Rubin, Bertha Taylor, Sam Taylor, Harry Fine, Eva Fine, Rose Cooper, 2nd Row: Joe Cooper, Rose. (OJA 1-309)

TORONTOW

The Torontow family stems from Abraham Raphael (Ralph, d. 1923), and Ethel Rhoda (nee Solomon, d. 1937). Abraham Raphael was the son of Joseph and Dora Torontow. Their children were:

- Joseph (d. 1984), married to Dora (nee Laitman, d. 1972). Their children are:
  - Fay Kapinsky (also called Fanny, d. 1997), married to Napoleon (Nap, d. 2000), son of Max and Dora Kapinsky (see **Karp**). Their children are:
    - Sheldon, married to Sandy.
    - Mina **Max** (d. 1998), married to Leonard, son of Sol and Lillian (nee Abrams) **Max**. Their daughter Melanie **Polowin** is married to Michael, son of David and Betty (nee Cowan) **Polowin**.
  - Saul (d. 1974), married to Eve (nee **Baylin**, d. 2006), daughter of Max and Rose **Baylin**, and later married to Izzie **Flesher**.
  - Sarah Rubin (d. 1990), married to Joshua.
  - Norman (d.2020), married to Stella (nee **Gandall,** d. 2020), daughter of Hyman and Celia (nee Schnider) **Gandall**. Norman Torontow was a co-owner of the Thelen-Torontow Lighting Centre.
- Samuel (d. 1966), married to Annie (nee Grossman, d. 1978). Their children were:
  - Isobel Firestone (d. 2002), married to O. J. (Jack) Firestone, a well-known art collector.
  - Edith Koffman (d. 2006), married to Harry (d. 2006), son of Sam and Pearl (nee **Gennis**) Koffman.
- Saul (d. 1948), married to Doris (nee Cohen, d. 1994), daughter of Sam and Ida (nee Berezin) Cohen (see **Ages**). Their daughter Rhoda **Bodnoff** (d. 2020) was married to Ronald (d. 1981), son of Irving Benjamin and Ann (nee Rastovsky) **Bodnoff**.
- Harry (d. 2008 at the age of 105), first married to Sarah (nee **Gottdank**, d. 1958), daughter of David and Rachel (nee Nitupski) **Gottdank**; and then to Sarah (nee Lazarus, d. 2001). Children of Harry and Sarah (**Gottdank**) are:
  - David, married to Dorothy (nee **Agulnik**), daughter of Harry and Sonia **Agulnik**.
  - Abraham Raphael (Ray), who was married to Ruth (nee Addelman), daughter of Percy (d. 2003) and Ethel (d. 1990) Addelman. Percy's sister Fanny Freedman was married to William Freedman (see **Krantzberg**). Ruth's second husband is Uri Tal, who served as the director of the gym and the Jewish community center and physical education teacher at Hillel Academy during the 1970s.
- Ann **Dover** (d. 1999), married to David (d. 1986), son of John and Minnie (nee Cohen) **Dover**. Their children are:
  - Myra Evans.
  - Jay (d. 2017), married to Betty. Their son John is married to Cheryl (nee Zides) son of Milton and Lorraine (nee Levine) Zides (see **Glustein**).
- Sarah **Saslove** (d. 1964), married to Adolph Isidore (d. 1942), son of Yisrael and Anna (nee Malchulsky) **Saslove**. Their children are:
  - Edward (killed in action in 1945).

- o Ralph, married to Sylvia (nee **Weiner**, d. 2006), daughter of Israel and Anne **Weiner**. Their daughter Andrea was married to Mark **Shore**, son of David and Debi **Shore**.
  - o Martin, married to Anna Ruth (Ricki, nee Hart, d. 2016).
- Louis (d. 1962), married to Miriam (d. 1956). Their children are:
  - o Cyril (d. 2009), married to Norma (nee Hetherington).
  - o Sylvia Monson, married to William (d. 1975).
  - o Dody Adler (d. 1996) married to Ned (d. 1980).
  - o Ann **Betcherman**, married to Samuel (d. 1984), son of Isaac **Betcherman**.
- Moses (d. 1960), married to Anne (nee Witton, d. 1952). Their children are:
  - o Edward (d. 1992), married to Pearl (nee Tanzer, d. 2013). Their children are:
    - Brenda Saxe, married to David. Their daughter Allison was married to Gary **Goldfield**, son of Morley and Diane (nee Altschuler) **Goldfield**.
    - Barbara Katz-Rosenthal, married to Joel.
    - Murray.
  - o Jean Naemark (d. 2014), married to Maxwell (d. 1999).
  - o Solomon (d. 1923).
  - o Leah (d. 2007).
  - o Ralph (d. 2002), married to Eleanor.
  - o Henry (Hank. d. 1976), married to Beatrice.
- Jack (d. 1955).
- Michael (d. 1945).

For connections to other entries, see Ages, Agulnik, Baylin, Betcherman, Bodnoff, Dover, Flesher, Gandall, Gennis, Glustein, Goldfield, Gottdank, Karp, Krantzberg, Max, Polowin, Saslove, Shore, Weiner.

The Torontow family's Passover Seder in the early 1920s.

On the left side of the table we have L-R: Cy, Dody, Frances, Edith, Sylvia, Sally, Harry, Ann Dover, Dave Dover, Ann, Sam, Miriam, Louis, Mike, Jack, Saul, Normie (Baby), Joe. Right side L-R: Henry, Eddy, Isabelle, Saul (Red), Jay, Jean (Naemark), Chenya (Ann), Moe, and Dora. (OJA 1-1211)

Group photograph at a Torontow family reunion, September, 1949.

Photograph taken at the Chateau Laurier Hotel, Ottawa.
L-R standing: Harry Torontow, Moe Torontow, Sam Torontow, Louis Torontow, Jack Torontow, Joseph Torontow, and David Dover, Sitting: Sarah Torontow Saslove, Sarah (Gottdank), Anne, Ann, Miriam (Ferguson), Sheila, Dora, Ann Dover (Torontow).
(OJA 1-591-018)

TRADBURKS

The Tradburks family is descended from Osias (d. 1952), and Machla (Minnie, d. 1965). Their children were:

- Gertrude **Mirsky** (d. 1967), married to Lazarus (d. 2007), son of Harris and Ida Cayla (nee Cohen) **Mirsky**). Lazarus married Sibyl (nee Moscovitch, d. 2006) after Gertude's death. Children of Gertrude and Lazarus are:
  - Kenneth, married to Linda (nee Cohen), daughter of Lefty and Jenny (nee **Kardish**) Cohen.
  - Cayla **Baylin**, married to Michael (d. 2015), son of Sam and Carolyn (nee Progosh) **Baylin**.
- Melvin (d. 1989).

- Irwin (d. 1974), married to Evelyn (nee Goldberg), daughter of Samuel and Rose (nee **Max**) Goldberg. After Irwin's death, Evelyn married Irving **Rivers**, son of Jacob and Leah (nee Keller) **Rivers**. Children of Irwin and Evelyn are:
    - Rabbi Reuven Tradburks, married to Joyce. Rabbi Tradburks served as the rabbi of Kehillat Shaarei Torah of Toronto for many years before moving to Israel. He currently serves as director of the Israel office of the Rabbinical Council of America.
    - Susan Diamond, married to Dr. Aubie Diamond, who serves as a mohel in Toronto.
    - Joanne Kalman.
- Benjamin (d. 1976), married to Mollie (nee Roberts. D. 2007). Their daughter Anna Lee Chiprout is married to Danny Chiprout.
- Lewis (d. 1969).
- Beck Koffman (d. 1999), married to Jack (d. 1981), son of Sam and Pearl (nee **Gennis**) Koffman.
- Sara Wallack (d. 1965), married to Samuel (d. 1965).

For connections to other entries, see Baylin, Gennis, Max, Mirsky, Rivers.

Rabbi Reuven Tradburks
(https://www.torahinmotion.org/users/rabbi-reuven-tradburks)

VECHSLER (VEXLER)

The Vechsler family is descended from Moses and Adela (nee Bercovic, d. 1934) Vechsler. Children of Moses and Adela were:

- Rose Ross (d. 1966), married to Charles (d. 1962). This branch lived in the United States.
- Myers Jack (d. 1974), married to Winifred (nee Coates).
- Richard Vexler (d. 1969), married to Rose Ann (nee Progosh, d. 1939). Rose Ann was a sister of Louis Progosh (see **Baylin**). Richard and Rose's son Myer (d. 2008), was married to Marion (nee **Ellenberg**), daughter of Moses and Rachel Leah **Ellenberg**. Richard's second wife was Ida (nee Friedman, d. 2009), whose first

husband was Abraham **Ellenberg** (d. 1933), and whose sister was Bess **Smolkin**, married to Moses.

- Harry (d. 1949), married to Rae (nee Wolofsky, d. 1989). Their son Ted (d. 2007) was the father of Howard Mintz, married to Sharron, daughter of Irving and Lois (nee Tinkoff) Mintz. Irving Mintz was a first cousin of my father Issie **Landau**, and a brother of Jim Mintz, married to Molly (nee Singerman, see **Diener** and **Pleet** for further connections of the Mintz family).
- Bella Abrahamson, married to Arnold (d. 1960), son of Lewis (d. 1947), and Annie (d. 1941) Abrahamson. Their children are:
  - Adele **Shinder**, married to Bernard, son of Jack and Nellie (nee Pascar) **Shinder**.
  - Ann **Dover**, married to Mark, son of Robert and Sasa (nee **Max**) **Dover**.
- Jack.

The Wexler family (see Phil Kline under Glustein and Goldfield entries) is a different family from the Vexler family.

For connections to other entries, see Baylin, Diener, Dover, Ellenberg, Landau, Max, Pleet, Shinder, Smolkin.

VICTOR

The Victor family is descended from Aizik Victor, and his two wives Chava Berman and Rozil (nee Gordon).

Children of Aizik and Chava were:

- Bessie Gower (d. 1952), married to Louis (d. 1957). Original surname was Gewertz.
- Rose Staller (d. 1944), married to Abraham. They remained in Europe.
- Tillie **Hanser** (d. 1963), married to Daniel (d. 1926). See **Hanser** for a full description of this family, with connections to the **Kimmel**, **Lesh**, **Lithwick**, **Shaffer**, **Rivers**, **Swedlove**, and **Smolkin** families.
- Leiba Vekhter, married to Sheina (nee Breslav). They remained in Europe.

Son of Aizik and Rozil was:

- Harry (d. 1948), married to Dora (nee Friedman, d. 1982). Their children were:
  - Herbert (d. 1998), married to Ruth (nee Eskin, d. 2021). Ruth's sister was Mary Goldberg (d. 2009), married to George (d. 1985). George and Mary Goldberg were the parents of Ronald, married to Marilyn, and Beverly Gershkovitch, married to Irving.
  - Ruth (d. 1997).
  - Samuel (d. 1977), married to Bertha (nee Wail, d. 2003). Their daughter Sandy was married to Howard Freed, son of George and Bess (nee **Craft**) Freed. Sandy later married Richard Merrill.

- Gertrude **Feller** (d. 1999), married to Henry (Hank, d. 2001), son of William and Eva (nee Rosen) **Feller**. Their son Robert is married to Bernice (nee **Lieff**), daughter of Samuel and Libby (nee **Kardish**).
- Bess Faigan, married to Allan.

Stephen Victor (see Rivers); and Dr. Max Vechter, married to Helen (d. 2013) are not related to this Victor family.

For connections to other entries see Craft, Feller, Hanser, Kimmel, Lesh, Lieff, Lithwick, Rivers Shaffer, Smolkin, Swedlove.

VINER

The Viner family is descended from Joseph (d. 1916) and Gittel (nee Silverman, d. 1938) Viner. The family originates from Zhitomir, Ukraine, and their original name was Vinerman. Joseph's parents were David (d. 1914), and Sarah Vinerman. Joseph's siblings included Labe **Weiner**, married to Sheva; Gitel **Lachovitz** (d. 1942), married to Max (d. 1950); and Fruma Esther Leffell (d. 1942), married to Jonah (d. 1956).   Children of Joseph and Gittel children were:

- Cecil (d. 1938), married to Freda (nee **Skulsky**, d. 1973), daughter of Menachem Mendel and Chaya **Skulsky**. Their children were:
  - Arthur (d. 1997), married to Sonia (nee Goldman, d. 2003), daughter of Walter and Malka Goldman. Their daughter Gladys **Greenberg** is married to John, son of Samuel and Bessie (nee **Murray**) **Greenberg**.
  - Gordon (d. 2010) married to Shirley (nee Fredlender).
  - Milton (d. 2013) married to Terry.
  - Sylvia Altschuler (d. 1976), married to Saul. Their daughter Diane **Goldfield** (d. 1997), was married to Morley (d. 2016), son of Charles and Eva **Goldfield**.
  - Leona **Silver**, married to Label, son of Hershel and Odes (nee Szeroszewsky) **Silver**
  - Millicent Schaenfield (d. 2015), married to David (d. 1995).
  - Dora Schaenfield (d. 2006), married to Samuel (d. 2006). Samuel and David were brothers (two brothers married two sisters). Samuel and Dora's son David is married to Rona (nee Hersh), daughter of Saul and Ettie (nee **Waserman**) Hersh.
  - Betty Gold.
  - David (d. 1998).
  - Joseph (d. 2001).
- Morris (d. 1966), married to Yetta (nee Trainoff, d. 1958). Yetta was the sister of Zisa Trainoff, father of Morris Trainoff (see **Shinder**).
- Sarah **Appotive** (d. 1972), married to Abraham (d. 1962). See **Appotive** for details of connections to **Macy** and **Slack** families.
- Harry (d. 1970), married to Ida (nee Cherun, d. 1924), and then to Edith (d. 1981). Ida Cherun was a sister of Alexander Cherun, married to Edith (nee Goldman, see **Feller**).
- Tillie **Cherm** (d. 1975), married to Harry (d. 1969). See **Cherm** for details of connections to **Fine**, **Taller**, and **Waserman** families.

- Malca Segal (d. 1971), married to Hymie (d. 1953).
- Milton (d. 1918), married to Eva (d. 1957). Their children were:
  - Esther **Cantor** (d. 2000), married to Bunim (d. 1974), son of Hyman and Ida **Cantor**.
  - Joseph (d. 1985), married to Ettie (nee Silver, d. 2005).
- Anne **Wasserman** (d. 1997), married to Israel (d. 1976).
- Irving (d. 1981), married to Clara (nee **Halpern**, d. 1987), daughter of Herman and Dina **Halpern**. Their children were:
  - Joseph (d. 2014), was married to Ruth (nee **Macy**), daughter of Sam and Freda (nee Kishinofsky) **Macy**. Their daughter Susan is married to Gilad Vered, son of Zeev and Sara Vered (see Soloway branch of **Greenberg** family). Their son Gary is married to Debra (nee Sadowsy) daughter of Moses and Belle (nee Robitaille) Sadowski (see **Pollock**)
  - Herbert (d. 1998).
  - Deena (nee Hyman, d. 1979), married to Louis (d. 1987), son of Solomon (d. 1932), and Rachel (d. 1941) Hyman.

The Leffell family was based in Montreal. Fruma Esther Leffell's great-granddaughter, Jennifer (nee Eklove) Niedzviecki, is married to Orie Niedzviecki, son of Nina.

For connections to other entries see Cantor, Cherm, Feller, Fine, Goldfield, Greenberg, Halpern, Lachovitz, Macy, Murray, Pollock, Shinder, Silver, Skulsky, Slack, Taller, Waserman, Weiner.

WASERMAN

The Waserman family descends from Harry (d. 1974), and Anna (nee Gruvick) Waserman. Their children are:

- Karl (d. 2002), married to Lillian (nee Brill, d. 1983). Their daughter Susan was married to Sydney Trainoff (d. 1992, see **Shinder**), daughter of Morris and Esther (nee **Shore**), Trainoff, and then to Maury Kleinman.
- Ettie Hersh, married to Saul (d. 2003). Their children are:
  - Barry, married to Brenda.
  - Rona Schaenfield, daughter of Samuel and Dora (nee **Viner**) Schaenfield.
- Nathan, married to Edna (nee Tuckman, d. 1978), daughter Benjamin and Rachel (nee **Marcovitch**) Tuckman. After Edna's death, Nathan married Phyllis.
- Paul (d. 1985), married to Nessie (d. 2005). Their children are:
  - Sandra Morrissette, married to Robert. Sandra was formerly married to Howard Borts, son of Irvine and Bertha (nee Lang) Borts (see **Smith**).
  - Mona Kotler, married to Gordon.
- Hyman (d. 1972), married to Dora (nee **Cherm**, d. 2003), daughter of Harry and Tillie (nee **Viner**) **Cherm**.
- Ernest (d. 2003), married to Sadie (nee Halpern, d. 2005). Sadie's sister was Rebecca Lobel (see **Lesh**). Children of Ernest and Sadie are:
  - Roslyn, married to Bill Sternberg (d. 1983), son of Ralph (d. 1997) and Anne (nee Ginsburg, d. 2006) Sternberg (see **Steinberg**). Ralph and Anne's daughter is Laya Jacobsen, married to Ted.

- o Philip, was married to Marilyn (nee **Taller**), daughter of Samuel and Anne (nee **Silver**) **Taller**.
- o Julia Shapero, married to Howard, son of Irving and Sadie (nee **Bodnoff**) Shapero.

For connections to other entries, see Bodnoff, Cherm, Lesh, Marcovitch, Shinder, Shore, Smith, Steinberg, Taller, Viner.

WEINER

The Weiner family descends from Labe and Sheva (nee Millstone) Weiner. Labe's parents were David and Sarah Vinerman (see **Viner**). Labe is the brother of Joseph Viner and Gittel **Lachovitz**. Children of Labe and Sheva were:

- Annie **Shinder** (d. 1968), married to Samuel (d. 1974). Sam's second marriage was to Yetta (nee Weinman, d. 1981), who was first married to my great uncle Sam **Landau**.
- Harry (d. 1950), married to Toby (nee **Bodnoff**, d. 1990), daughter of Abraham David and Annie (nee Ginsberg) **Bodnoff**. Their children were:
  - o Luella (d. 1987).
  - o Dorothy (d. 2014).
  - o Sheila Schinman (d. 2010), married to Saul Schinman. Sheila and Saul moved from Ottawa to New Jersey in the early 1970s.
- Edward (d. 1980), married to Eva (d. 1951). Their children were:
  - o Lawrence (d. 2008), married to Bess (nee **Kardash**, d. 2007), daughter of Percy and Libby **Kardash**.
  - o Leo (d. 1999), married to Shirley (nee Fox, d. 2008).
- Hyman (d. 1975), married to Ida (d. 1976).
- Israel (Isadore, d. 1963), married to Anne (d. 1952). Israel's second wife was Bertha. Children of Israel and Anne were:
  - o Louis (d. 2011), married to Miriam (nee Katz, d. 2013), daughter of Samuel and Susan (nee **Sugarman**) Katz.
  - o Paul (d. 2015), married to Eleanor (nee Oster, d. 2013).
  - o Sylvia **Saslove** (d. 2006), married to Ralph, son of Adolph and Sarah (nee **Torontow**) **Saslove**. Their daughter Andrea was married to Mark **Shore**, son of David and Debi **Shore**.
- Pearl Gold (d. 1951), married to Joseph.
- Golda **Goldmaker** (d. 1945), married to Zeidel (d. 1970).
- Bluma Nathanson, married to Samuel (d. 1976), son of Nusin (d. 1944), and Gitel (d. 1935) Nathanson. Samuel's brother was Harry Nathanson (d. 1970), married to Anne (d. 1979). Harry and Anne's daughter Bertha (Tootsie) Greenberg (d. 2018) was married to Arnold (d. 2017), son of Charles and Bertha (nee Leibovitch, d. 1995) Greenberg. Children of Samuel and Bluma were:
  - o Louis (d. 1988), married to Edith (d. 2007).
  - o Sylvia Bronsther (d. 2015), married to Bertram (d. 2010).

For connections to other entries, see   Bodnoff, Goldmaker, Kardish, Lachovitz, Landau, Saslove, Shinder, Shore, Sugarman, Torontow, Viner.

WEINSTEIN

The children of Joseph (d. 1961), and Sonia (d. 1969) Weinstein are:

- Percy (d. 2003), married to Mildred (nee Bookman, d. 2022), daughter of Jacob and Bertha (nee **Gorelick**) Bookman. Jacob Bookman was a half brother of Ben Bookman (see **Sherman**). Percy and Mildred's daughter Daphne is married to Stanley Arron, and their son Lawrence is married to Sharon (nee Nadolny), the daughter of Herb and Dorothy Nadolny.
- Max (d. 2022), married to Cynthia (nee Barook).
- Sarah Resnick (d. 2021), married to Dr. Morris Resnick (d. 1995). Note that this Sarah and Morris Resnick are different than the Sarah and Moe Resnick of the Goldmaker family.
- Yetta Arron (d. 2012), married to Lawrence (Larry, d. 2008), son of Isidore (d. 1953), and Jennie (d. 1968) Arron. Their son Jeff was married to Sharon (nee Koffman, d. 1993), daughter of Barry and Fay (nee Yanover) Koffman (see **Gennis**).

Other children of Isidore and Jennie Arron are Louis (d. 1998), married to Anne (d. 1982); Jack (d. 2002), married to Sylvia (nee Lewis, d. 2001); Dorothy Nadolny (d. 2023), married to Herb (d. 2005). Herb Nadolny was the son of Max (d. 1979), and Ida (d. 1972) Nadolny, and the brother of Samuel (d. 1998), married to Rachel (d. 2005). Herb and Dorothy's son Lawrence is married to Sharon (nee Weinstein) – i.e. Yetta and Lawrence Arron are the aunt and uncle of both Lawrence and Sharon. Stanley Arron (d. 2019), the son of Louis and Anne Arron, was married to Daphne, daughter of percy and mildred Weinstein (again, a niece of Yetta and Lawrence); and was formerly married to Carole (nee Saxe), daughter or David and Frances (nee **Torontow**) Saxe. Carole is currently married to Norman Zagerman (see **Krantzberg**).

For connections to other families, see Gennis, Gorelick, Krantzberg, Sherman, Torontow.

Grade 6 class at Hillel Academy – 1964.Included are Brian Beck, Mark Zaret, Rena Kalin and Claire Sporn. Standing is Lawrence Weinstein. (OJA 6-104)

Flight Lieutenant Jack Arron (third from the right) standing with other crew members of "Trichinopoly" airplane in flight gear, 1943. (OJA 1-843-02)

WEISS

Weiss is a common surname, and not all people with the Weiss surname in Ottawa are necessarily related. The wise family described here descends from Barney (d. 1951), and Henrietta (d. 1967. Their children were:

- Inez **Zelikovitz** (d. 2013), married to Joseph (d. 1998), son of Morris and Sarah (nee **Cohen**) **Zelikovitz**.
- Pauline Hochberg (d. 2019), married to Hyman (d. 1985), son of Nathan (d. 1933), and Yetta (d. 1977) Hochberg. Nathan and Yetta were also the parents of Abraham (d. 2005), married to Bernice (d. 2009). Linda **Kerzner**, daughter of Abe and Bernice Hochberg, is married to Steven **Kerzner**, son of Sydney and Ethel (nee Kott) **Kerzner**. Linda **Kerzner** serves as chair of the Ottawa Jewish Federation. Hy Hochberg served as head of the Ottawa Vaad Ha'Ir for many years.
- Bea Dubinsky, married to Abraham (d. 2003), son of Benjamin and Libby (nee **Pollock**) Dubinsky.
- Lillian Miller.
- Tessie **Zelikovitz**, married to Max (d. 2009), son of Joshua and Minnie **Zelikovitz**. Their daughter Margo **Kardish** is married to David, son of Israel and Eva (nee Feldberg) **Kardish**. Note that by marriage, Tessie is the aunt of her sister Inez (i.e. two Weiss sisters married a **Zelikovitz** uncle and nephew).

For connections to other entries see Cohen, Kardish, Kerzner, Pollock, Zelikovitz.

L-R: The Capital Hotel and Weiss' Delicatessen at 212 Rideau St, Barney Weiss sitting in front of the deli, Beatrice Weiss (one of Barney's and Henrietta's five daughters) sitting in a booth in the deli, and Henrietta and Barney standing in front of the hotel.
(OJA 1-1195, 1-1191,1-1194, 1-1192)

Mothers and daughters on a fun trip to the grounds of the Parliament buildings! The first three ladies are unknown, but the next two ladies are Inez (Weiss) Zelikovitz and her mother, Henrietta. ca. 1940's. (OJA)

Hy Hochberg and Lora Fonberg Shapiro. Summer 1939. (OJA)

WOLINSKY

See Bessin, Petegorsky, Shaffer.

ZAGERMAN

See Krantzberg, Sadinsky.

ZELIKOVITZ

The Zelikovitz family is descended from Joshua (d. 1932), and Minnie (d. 1947) Zelikovitz. Their children were:

- Morris (d. 1968), married to Sarah (nee **Cohen**, d. 1966), daughter of Samuel and Mesha Pia **Cohen**. Their children were:
  o Bella Randall married to Mitchell.
  o Abraham, married to Mollie (nee Fine, d. 1998.) Their children are:
    ▪ Leon, married to Zelda (nee Borshy). Their children are Evan, married to Lenora (nee **Levitan**), daughter of Richard and Polly (nee Baker) **Levitan**; Martin; Karen Isaacson (d. 2016), married to Benjamin.
    ▪ Pia Guralnick, married to Mel.
    ▪ Rita.
  o Israel (Butch), married to Laura (nee Nadler, d. 2015).
  o Joseph (d. 1998), married to Inez (nee **Weiss**, d. 2013), daughter of Barney and Henrietta Weiss. Joe Zelikovitz played halfback and flying wing for the Ottawa Rough Riders from 1935-1938.
  o William (d. 1997), married to Lillian (nee Waisberg, d. 1982).
  o Hannah Miller, married to Saul.
- Solomon (d. 1990), married to Sonia (d. 1980). Their children were:
  o Dora Ulrich (d. 2012), married to Harold (d. 2006).
  o Fay **Loeb** (d. 2017), married to Jules (d. 2008), son of Moses and Rose Loeb.
  o Joseph (d. 1994)
- Nathan (d. 1975) married to Sarah (nee **Kronick**, d. 1987), daughter of Selig and Raisyl Rivka **Kronick**. Their children are:
  o Marlene Burack.
  o Judith Schneiderman (d. 2018), married to Lawrence.
- David (d. 1991), married to Rebecca (d. 1991). Their children are:
  o Sheila Mandel, married to Harold.
  o Susan Green, married to Ronald (d. 2016), son of Nathan (d. 1986), and Bertha (nee Cherun, d. 1992) Green. Bertha Green was the sister of Alex Cherun and Ida **Viner**.
  o Rabbi Chaim (Harold), married to Yetta (nee Weiss). Rabbi Zelikovitz was a co-founder of Yeshiva Mercaz Hatorah of Belle Harbor.
- Max (d. 2009), married to Tessie (nee **Weiss**), daughter of Barney and Henrietta **Weiss**, and sister of her niece by marriage Inez Zelikovitz. Their children are:
  o Jess, married to Wendy.
  o Enid Bultz.

- o Margo **Kardish**, married to David, son of Israel and Eva (nee Feldberg) **Kardish**.

For connections to other entries, see Cohen, Kardish, Kronick, Levitan, Loeb, Viner, Weiss.

Joe Zelikovitz (Aka: Zeli, Aka: The Flying Hebrew) - 1914-1998 (OJA 1-578-02)

Brittania Beach in the early 1940s. Joe and Inez Zelikovitz on the right. (OJA)

List of Cross References of Ottawa Jewish Families

The first table lists each of the 108 entries of the book, showing all surnames mentioned in that entry that have their own entries (this information is also included at the bottom of each entry), as well as a separate column for all non-entry surnames mentioned within that entry. The second table lists all the 950 surnames entered in the book (these do not include surnames only mentioned in photo captions), showing the entries in which that name is mentioned. If one does not find one's family of interest within the entries themselves, one should consult the second cross-reference table. By studying the entries as well as the two cross-reference tables, one can get a picture of the complex web of connectedness of Ottawa based Jewish families.

A row in these two tables does not guarantee that there is a relationship between all names mentioned. In some cases, unrelated families share the same surname. This is frequent with common names such as Cohen and Greenberg. These will be listed in the same row of the table, and no connection is guaranteed.

A listed surname in the second table does not guarantee that it is of an Ottawa family. There are cases where a surname from outside of Ottawa was used to link together two Ottawa families. There are also surnames which represent former Ottawans who left the city, or the maiden names of those who married into a family from Ottawa. All, however, represent some connection to Ottawa, and the vast majority do represent families who lived in Ottawa at one point or another.

Index of Entries, with Links to Other Entries and List of Surnames Mentioned

Entry	Other surname listed, who have their own entries	Other surnames listed, which do not have their own entries
Aaron	Feinstein, Gennis, Marcovitch, Murray, Rivers	Breatross, Flatt, Steinman, Strolovitch, Wolfe
Ages	Baylin, Bodnoff, Coplan, Gandall, Gershon, Kardish, Kronick, Pollock, Rivers, Torontow, Waserman, Weiner	Abramowitz, Appel, Bahar, Berezin, Cohen Dembe, Dubrofsky, Feldberg, Fried Ginsberg, Goldberg, Gross, Held, Kushin, Meirovich, Pearl, Rackow, Rafal, Shiller, Solomon, Tarantour, Victor
Agulnik	Diener, Gottdank, Kardish, Torontow	Brozovsky, Glass, Kronick (Chwojnik), Lome, Luterman, Mendelson, Ostroff, Rawicka, Reznitzky, Rishall,
Appotive	Landau, Macy Slack, Viner	Beckenstein, Brottman, Feldblum, Katz, Parnass, Silverman, Tuchman
Baslaw	Goldfield, Saslove, Shaffer	Boguslovski, Finn, Harris, Yarofsky
Baylin	Bodnoff, Dworkin, Flesher, Gandall, Kardish, Mirsky, Torontow, Tradburks	Allice, Alper, Amor, Aranov, Progosh, Reiter, Satlin, Schnider, Silverman, Smyth, Soltanoff, Steinberg
Bessin	Baslaw, Diener, Freedman, Goldfield, Goldmaker, Petigorsky, Schecter, Schreiber, Shaffer	Borenstein, Chodikoff, Diena, Hochman, Kapeller, Kurtz, Lang, Levinoff, Sacher, Sibeth, Tenenbaum, Zelcovin
Betcherman	Florence, Froman, Glustein, Gould, Greenberg, Molot, Pullan, Rivers, Saslove, Shore, Smith, Taylor, Torontow	Abrahams, Addelman, Fein, Fogel, Kaplan, Michelson, Osterer, Rhinestein, Rosenstein, Rotenberg, Sandler, Smith, Sonken, Steinberg, Weisbord
Bilsky	Feller, Halpern, Mirsky	Alexandor, Bronfman, Fine, Freiman, Goldstein, Hirschhorn, Jacobs, London, Luxenberg, Markson, Rosenfeld, Roston, Schragge, Steinkopf
Bodnoff	Ages, Baylin, Coplan, Craft, Feller, Gandall, Gennis, Gould, Greenberg, Kardish, Kronick,	Allice, Arnoni, Aronovitch Benwick, Berezin, Blacker, Blair, Chezin, Dembe, Dubrofsky, Feldberg, Fisch,

	Pollock, Shore, Taller, Torontow, Waserman, Weiner	Fisher, Ginsberg, Gross, Kuttas, Leckman, Marcus, Mayberger, Meirovich, Midlin, Mintz, Putterman, Rastovsky, Richman, Rosen, Rosenberg, Schachnow, Schinman, Schnider, Shapero, Sheft, Shiller, Simon, Sinder, Spielberg, Steinberg, Swedko, Teitelbaum, Zbar
Bordelay	Gennis, Gorelick, Kardish, Lieff	Greenberg, Koffman, Levine, Steinberg
Cantor	Kerzner, Krantzberg, Kronick, Leikin, Max, Mosion, Rivers, Schecter, Taller, Viner	Ben-Dat, Brodie, Butovsky, Cohen, Farber, Feig, Gelman, Katz, Keller, Kott, Pivnick, Zagerman, Zellick
Cherm	Fine, Reichstein, Taller, Viner, Waserman	Huniu, Kaiman, Kimmel, Orlik, Schwey, Spector
Cohen	Betcherman, Bodnoff, Cantor, Diener, Dover, Fine, Florence, Gould, Halpern, Krantzberg, Landau Leikin, Levitan, Lithwick, Pollock, Polowin, Silver, Slover, Smolkin, Swedlove, Zelikovitz	Aber, Aberback, Abtan, Addelman, Aisenberg, Bauer, Benwick, Bilsky, Bordan, Bronfman, Bronstein, Bulka, Cantor, Cape, Cherney, Cornblat, Davy / Davidowicz, Deitcher, Dobkin, Drazin, Dunsky, Eckstein, Ehrenkranz, Eisenstadt, Emerson, Epstein, Fagin, Fasman, Feig, Ferrucci, Fine, Fink, Freedman, Friendly, Ginsburg, Godel, Golden, Gordon, Gosewich, Grafstein, Gursky, Hart, Hochberg, Jakobovitz, Karon, Kardish, Keeb, Lecker, Lemonik, Liverant, Malomet, Margolies, Moldaver, Montagnes, Morell, Morin, Ontell, Paulin, Petrushka Plaskow, Putterman, Rabinovitch, Rachlin, Rapaport, Rasminsky, Richler, Riven, Rosen, Rosenfield, Rotenberg, Sacksner, Saslove, Segalowitz, Shnay, Silbinger, Silverman, Slavin, Slipacoff, Smith, Snyder, Speyer, Teitelbaum, Weiss, Wiehl, Wigdor, Wolpin, Woolfson, Yeres, Zinman

Coplan	Bodnoff, Florence, Gould, Kardish, Kizell, Kronick, Levitan, Mosion, Pullan, Rubin, Slover	Abelson, Blachov, Cooper, Gertsman, Goldstick, Gorelick, Horwitz, Pameth, Ruben, Slone, Slonemsky
Craft	Bodnoff, Kardish, Sadinsky, Mosion, Victor	Allice, Berkovitch, Freed, Freedlander, Michelin, Richman, Ritter, Swedko, Udashkin
Diener	Agulnik, Bessin, Cohen, Greenberg, Landau, Pleet, Schreiber, Weiner	Borenstein, Ehrenkranz, Friberg, Friedberg, Kurtz, Lang, Luterman, Mintz, Padolsky, Sacher, Silbert, Singerman, Tenebaum
Dover	Cohen, Dworkin, Flesher, Glustein, Kizell, Koffman, Landau, Mirsky, Molot, Polowin Rivers, Saslove, Smolkin, Torontow, Tradburks, Vechsler	Abrahamson, Dolansky, Evans, Feinberg, Fireman, Ginsburg, Goldberg, Goldstein, Goodman, Hollander, Horowitz, Hollander, Joseph, Loeb, Lecker, Lerner, Levine, Levinson, Max, Nathanson, Ritt, Saipe, Sourkes, Spector, Steinberg, Ulpian, Waiser, Zabitsky, Zides,
Dworkin	Baylin, Dover, Ellenberg, Karp, Petegorsky, Roodman, Shulman, Smolkin, Vechsler, Viner.	Azmier, Banks, Boro, Brill, Fertig, Fonberg, Freedman, Goldman, Levine, Minkoff, Progosh, Saipe, Schwartz, Silver, Sogman
Ellenberg	Dworkin, Marcovitch, Flesher, Freedman, Glustein Vechsler	Chodikoff, Danoff, Davis, Dutnoff, Engel, Greenberg, Labovitch, Progosh, Segall, Yankoo
Feinstein	Aaron, Murray	Dickstein, Flatt, Gossack, Kavanat, Levitin, Moskovic, Steinman
Feller	Bilsky, Bodnoff, Kardish, Kimmel, Kronick, Leikin, Lieff, Lithwick, Mirsky, Shaffer, Victor, Viner	Bercovici, Caplan, Cherun, Fine, Fript, Finerman, Goldman, Handel, Heimovitch, Kaufman, Lesonsky, Nathanson, Roston, Salzburg, Singer, Zittrer
Fine	Cantor, Cherm, Gorelick, Gosewich, Gould, Levinson, Levitan, Loeb, Palmer, Pollock, Polowin, Slover, Taller, Viner	Altman, Berger, Gertler, Goldenberg, Hymes, Kooperstock, Newman, Orlik, Ross, Shabsove, Smurlick, Zaret
Flesher	Baylin, Ellenberg, Gershon, Hanser, Kerzner, Kimmel, Kizell, Levitan, Lesh, Petigorsky,	Achbar, Breakstone, Cantor, Carlofsky, Hassan, Hecht, Labovitch, LaBreton, Lavitt, Lorwill, Mendelson, Pont,

	Sadinsky, Slover, Smith, Swedlove, Torontow	Rosenberg, Sinclair, Tanner, Waiser, Weiner
Florence	Betcherman, Cohen, Coplan, Kizell, Lieff	Addelman, Brownstein, Doctor, Fliegelman, Kroch, Pullan, Ruben, Schapira, Schoen, Shapiro
Freedman	Ellenberg, Greenberg, Lithwick, Loeb, Petigorsky, Schreiber, Swedlove	Achbar, Chodikoff, Glickman, Goldstein, Koreen, Phillips, Prizant, Rasminsky, Rotenberg, Schiff, Smith, Wolinsky
Froman	Betcherman, Greenberg, Krantzberg, Marcovitch, Taylor	Cobrin, Cowan, Haimovici, Ross, Sadinsky, Weiss, Zagerman
Gandall	Bodnoff, Landau, Mosion, Steinberg, Torontow	Gutteit, Mintz, Schnider
Gencher	Greenberg, Levitan, Pollock, Shabinsky, Shinder, Shreiber, Soloway, Taylor	Berezin, Engel, Gertler, Mortimer, Weiner
Gennis	Aaron, Bodnoff, Bordelay, Dover, Greenberg, Kardish, Levinson, Lieff, Marcovitch, Pleet, Saslove, Shaffer, Shinder Torontow, Tradburks, Weinstein	Arron, Bloom, Dragushan, Jacobson, Koffman, Peddlar, Rose, Rosen, Steinman, Strolovitch, Yanover, Zagon
Gershon	Ages, Flesher, Glustein, Lichtenstein, Reichstein, Rivers, Sadinsky, Shinder	Baker, Cohen, Goodman, Herszman, Newton, Tanner, Weinberg, Weiner, Wilko
Glustein / Glushtein	Baslaw, Betcherman, Dover, Dworkin, Ellenberg, Fine, Gershon, Goldfield, Kardish, Kizell, Petigorsky, Roodman, Shore, Silver, Skulsky, Smith	Aptowitzer, Belinke, Berliner, Brill, Brissman, Brown, Cement, Cowan, Danoff, Dear, Dubinsky, Dubrofsky, Dutnoff, Ehrenreich, Finkelman, Finkelstein, Fireman, Gladstone, Goldberg, Gross, Guttman, Haber, Halperin, Hoffman, Kline, Kriger, Lax, Lefton, Levine, Litwack, Monson, Movshovitz, Nemerovsky, Newman, Osterer, Perlman, Pernikoff, Rosenblatt, Rotenberg, Schecter, Setton, Silverman, Simon, Steinberg, Szeroszewsky, Warshavsky Wexler, Wolman, Yanofsky, Yosman, Zides

Goldfield	Baslaw, Bessin, Glustein, Goldmaker, Kizell, Pollock, Taller, Torontow, Viner	Altschuler, Budd, Budovitch, Cohen, Dunsky, Greenberg, Kline, Landis, Levinoff, Perlman, Rabinovitch, Rapp, Saxe, Shnay, Wexler, Zelcovin
Goldmaker	Bessin, Florence, Goldfield, Weiner	Bright, Dunsky, Goldberg, Hendin, Lang, Millstone, Rabinovitch, Resnick, Ross, Shnay
Gorelick	Bordelay, Fine, Horwitz, Pleet, Weinstein	Bookman, Greenberg, Levine, Newman, Satov, Zaretsky / Zaret
Gosewich	Fine, Greenberg, Kathnelson, Lithwick, Palmer, Saslove, Smith	Bosloy, Brewer, Caplan, Farber, Friendly, Gilboa, Hirschel, Kaplan, Levy, Markson, Newman, Pichosky, Rosenblum, Ross
Gottdank	Agulnik, Lieff, Mirsky, Palmer, Torontow	Nitupski
Gould	Bodnoff, Cohen, Coplan, Fine, Kronick, Palmer, Taller	Bergsiem, Ginsberg, Horowitz, Levine, Renaud, Smith, Smurlick
Greenberg	Betcherman, Bodnoff, Diener, Freedman, Froman, Gencher, Gennis, Glustein, Kardish, Kerzner, Landau, Levinson, Levitan, Macy, Murray, Pleet, Pollock, Saslove, Schreiber, Sherman, Shinder, Shore, Silver, Slack, Slover, Steinberg, Sugarman, Taylor, Viner	Adessky, Aronson, Ballon, Balsky, Bezumny, Boguslovsky Cohen, Dover, Druckman, Edelson, Freedman, Friberg, Gershon, Gilbert, Goldstein, Hodess, Iny, Kalir, Koffman, Koreen, Lesh, Litwin, Luterman, Mintz, Muroff, Nepomiazchy, Newton, Penso, Perlman, Raport, Rose, Rosman, Sanders, Sandler, Schecter, Schnell, Shabinsky, Shadlesky, Singerman, Soloway, Vered, Wiseberg, Zunder
Halpern	Ages, Bilsky, Cohen, Kardish, Macy, Sherman, Shinder, Skulsky, Viner	Abtan, Bahar, Bookman, Fagin, Fox, Freiman, Goldstein, Hirschhorn, Israel, Naginsky, Pilze, Silverman
Hanser / Hontsher	Kimmel, Kronick, Lesh, Lithwick, Rivers, Shaffer, Smolkin, Swedlove, Victor	Gantzer, Guz, Lang, Magidson, Rotman, Shapiro, Steinman, Zolov

Horwitz	Coplan, Gorelick, Weinstein	Arron, Borden, Chernove, Fenster, Goodman, Hertz, Levine, McClelland, Rodkin, Rosen, Slone, Zaret
Kardish / Kardash / Cardash	Ages, Agulnik, Bordelay, Feller, Gennis, Greenberg, Halpern, Kerzner, Lachovitz Lieff, Mirsky, Molot, Mosion, Murray, Rubin, Slover, Steinberg, Taylor, Tradburks, Victor, Weiner, Weiss, Zelikovitz	Baylin, Berezin, Bregman, Brozovsky, Caplan, Cohen, Copeland, Cratzbarg, Dubrofsky, Ellis, Feldberg, Gluzman, Goldberg, Jankielewitz, Kamil, Koffman, Krupnick, Lewis, Levitan, Levitz, Litwin, Mendelson, Muster, newman, Penso, Plotken, Saipe, Slonim, Steinberg, Udashkin, Wollock
Karp / Kapinsky	Dworkin, Marcovitch, Max, Polowin, Roodman, Sadinsky, Saslove, Shulman, Torontow	Abrams, Cowan, Jaffe, Keyfitz, Laitman, Simon
Kathnelson	Gosewich, Roodman, Shinder	Abramson, Goldstein, Kaplan, Markson Nadler
Kerzner / Kurzner	Cantor, Flesher, Greenberg, Kardish, Rubin, Sherman, Slack, Taller, Weiner, Weiss	Abelson, Abramowitz, Barg, Berman, Broitman, Cogan, Dain, Demb, Dickstein, Druckman, Goldstein, Hochberg, Hollander, Kott, Leibov, Lisak, Loomer, Meil, Neistein, Schecter, Schlessinger, Smith
Kimmel	Baslaw, Craft, Feller, Hanser, Lesh, Lithwick, Reichstein, Sadinsky, Saslove, Shaffer, Taller, Victor	Brodsky, Cherm, Chepovetsky, Guz, Magidson, Melamed, Rashevsky, Shulman, Spector, Spiro, Wiseman
Kizell	Coplan, Dover, Flesher, Florence, Glustein, Marcovitch, Rubin	Achbar, Beiles, Berman, Cowan, Dolansky, Feinberg, Horowitz, Kline, Litt, Litwack, Ruben, Saipe, Sinclair, Simon, Waiser
Krantzberg / Krane	Cantor, Cohen, Feller, Marcovitch, Mosion, Sadinsky, Shaffer, Skulsky, Torontow, Viner, Weinstein	Addelman, Arron, Berlin, Cherun, Cornblat, Epstein Finerman, Freedman, Froimovitch, Greenberg, Jewett, Kaplan, Krugel, Lazear, Levi, Millstein, Rosen, Ross,

		Saxe, Shmuter, Singerman, Tannenbaum, Tanzer, Vineberg, Zagerman
Kronick	Bodnoff, Coplan, Feller, Gould, Hanser, Kimmel, Leikin, Lichtenstein, Shulman, Taller, Zelikovitz	Abrahams, Blachov, Burack, Fine, Fonberg, Fript, Horlick, Newton, Rosenes, Samuels, Saverson, Shneiderman, Shulman, Sobcov, Weidman
Lachovitz / Lach	Kardish, Petigorsky, Potechin, Viner, Weiner	Bernstein, Bogomolny, Fertig, Kussner, Mendelson, Monheit, Monson, Nelson, Shentok, Steinberg, Strashin, Stulberg, Sugarman, Vorner
Landau	Appotive, Cohen, Diener, Dover, Gandall, Leikin, Macy, Murray, Pleet, Pollock, Rubin, Shinder, Taller, Vechsler, Viner, Weiner	Amsel, Biderman, Bindman, Brass, Calof, Davidow, Dermer, Ehrenkranz, Epstein, Friberg, Garber, Goldberg, Liff, Linowitz, Malkus, Menczer, Mintz, Morris, Mozersky, Parnass, Perlmutter, Pilcewicz, Posner, Rachlin, Rozenworcel, Sarwer-Foner, Schnider, Shabinsky, Sheinfeld, Shier, Silver, Singerman, Sosnovich, Swartzman, Tuchman, Tennenhouse, Weinman
Leikin / Leiken	Cantor, Cohen, Fine, Feller, Greenberg, Kronick, Landau, Loeb, Palmer, Slover	Altman, Angel, Applebaum, Bodovsky, Brandes, Farber, Fript, Harris, Hochberg, Katz, Kershman, Kessler, Merson, Newman, Rachlin, Rosenblatt, Spieler, Tavel, Wexler, Wormann, Yerenbourg
Lesh	Flesher, Hanser, Kimmel, Levitan, Reichstein, Saslove, Waserman	Cohen, Dachs, Futeral, Greenberg, Halpern, Hutt, Konick, Lobel, Ochas, Saltzbeurg, Slipacoff, Smith, Zin
Levinson	Cohen, Feller, Gennis, Greenberg, Landau, Macy, Mosion Saslove, Schecter	Ballon, Caplan, Craft, Cohen, Dover, Firestone, Friedgut, Fyman, Grossman, Hurtig, Hymes, Kishinofsky, Lichtenstein, Pasher Perlmutter, Simkin
Levitan	Fine, Flesher, Greenberg, Lesh, Molot, Pleet, Smolkin, Steinberg, Zelikovitz	Armitage, Baker, Benoway, Bezumny, Brill, Davidson, Davis, Goldenberg, Goldstein,

		Gur-Arie, Isacoff, Kahansky, Okumiansky, Rubin, Weinman
Lichtenstein	Gershon, Kronick, Landau, Mosion, Shinder, Swedlove	Biderman, Geller, Halperin, Harris, Levinson, Newton, Posner, Silver, Sosnovich
Lieff / Lifshitz	Bordelay, Feller, Florence, Gennis, Gottdank, Greenberg, Kardish, Palmer, Shore, Taller, Victor	Adessky, Barker, Bessner, Brovender, Cohen, Doctor, Ellis, Friedlan, Goldberg, Greenspoon, Grossman, Jacobs, Koffman, Lazarovitch, Narod, Resnick, Shabinsky, Shaver, Sobcuff, Soloway, Steinberg
Lithwick / Litvak	Cohen, Feller, Freedman, Glustein, Gosewich, Kimmel, Palmer, Reichstein, Saslove, Smolkin, Sugarman, Swedlove	Achbar, Ain, Aisenberg, Bahar, Blair, Bosloy, Chalefsky, Coopersmith, Esar, Farber, Fishbain, Glube, Golden, Goldsmith, Gottlieb, Green, Greenberg, Greenblatt, Guz, Klugsberg, Kriger, Kroll, Krupnick, Leibner, Lerner, Lesonsky, Magidson, Moscovitch, Movsovich, Ness, Pareno, Polsky, Rashevsky, Rosenberg, Schneiderman, Seidler, Silverstein, Tavel, Topol, Trachtenberg, Weiss, Witchel, Wolfe, Zittrer
Loeb	Cantor, Fine, Freedman, Leikin, Saslove, Taller, Zelikovitz	Brownstein, Glickman, Light, Radnoff, Shiller, Spieler
Macy / Mausberg	Appotive, Dover, Dworkin, Greenberg, Halpern, Levinson, Molot, Schecter, Viner	Katz, Kishinofsky, Parnass, Saipe, Soloway, Vered
Marcovitch / Marcus	Aaron, Ellenberg, Froman, Gennis, Karp, Kizell, Krantzberg, Saslove, Waserman	Beiles, Bleichner, Greenberg, Haimovici, Helfgot, Hershorn, Lazarus, Lifshitz, Ross, Samuels, Shaikin, Silver, Strolovitch, Tuckman, Weatherall, Yankoo, Zagerman
Max / Kavalsky	Cantor, Dover, Karp, Pollock, Polowin, Rivers, Torontow, Tradburks, Vechsler	Abrahamson, Abrams, Bromberg, Cowan, Feinberg, Goldberg, Gordon, Keller, Levencrown, Segal, Slone, Waiser, Wise
Mirsky	Baylin, Bilsky, Dover, Feller, Gottdank, Kardish, Tradburks	Cohen, Freiman, Goldstein, London, Pearlman, Perchanok, Martin, Moraff, Moscovitch,

		Progosh, Rabin, Rosenfeld, Seigal, Sklar, Vineberg
Molot	Betcherman, Dover, Dworkin, Gould, Kardish, Levitan, Macy, Polowin, Sugarman, Taller	Appel, Aronson, Bergman, Berman, Brill, Goldsmith, Gordon, Green, Gluck, Held, Isacoff, Kamerman, Kirshelblatt, Kishinofsky, Kleinplatz, Langstadt, Lewin, Morris, Myers, Piazza, Portnoy, Saipe, Schmelzer, Shabinsky, Smith, Sonken, Steinberg, Swetsky, Wolfson,
Mosion / Mason	Cantor, Coplan, Craft, Gandall, Kardish, Krantzberg, Lichtenstein, Rubin, Steinberg	Cohen, Gutteit, Harris, Lerner, Michelin, Newton, Udashkin, Zagerman
Murray	Aaron, Betcherman, Coplan, Dover, Froman, Kardish, Landau, Rubin, Shinder, Taylor, Viner	Atlas, Breatross Bromberg, Cratzbarg, Flatt, Gerson, Krupnick, Levinson, Liff, Morris, Prusky, Raskin, Reiman, Schlossberg, Selector Weinman, Wilner, Wolfe, Zunder
Palmer / Pomerantz	Gosewich, Gould, Greenberg, Leikin, Lieff, Lithwick, Pollock	Magidson, Phomin, Polsky, Ross, Rubin, Smith, Stotland, Tavel
Petigorsky / Petegorsky	Bessin, Dworkin, Flesher, Freedman, Glustein, Karp, Lachovitz, Polowin, Roodman, Shaffer, Shulman, Slack, Weiner	Cheigowsky, Chodikoff, Coan, Dutnoff, Fertig, Freedman, Geffen, Gunner / Gunnerotsky, Hochman, Nemerovsky, Pelcovits, Silver, Starker, Steinberg, Tennenbaum, Wolinsky, Yashinofsky / Jason
Pleet	Diener, Gennis, Gorelick, Greenberg, Levitan, Shore, Smolkin.	Baker, Bookman, Goldenberg, Goren, Gould, Kahn, Koffman, Kotlarsky, Oiring, Sadavoy, Schwartz, Singerman, Stein, Wolf, Zunder
Pollock	Ages, Bodnoff, Cohen, Fine, Gencher, Greenberg, Macy, Max, Polowin, Roodman, Sherman, Shore, Taylor, Viner, Weiss	Abramowitz, Abrams, Adelson, Azmier, Berezin, Budovich, Danoff, Dubinsky, Feldman, Gertler, Goldenberg, Gutmajer, Held, Hersenhorn, Holzman, Robitaille, Rothman, Sadowski, Saxe, Segalowitz, Soloway, Waiser, Zloten

Polowin	Cohen, Dover, Fine, Karp, Max, Molot, Petigorsky, Slover, Sugarman, Swedlove, Taylor	Abeles, Cheigowsky Cowan, Gordon, Grill, Hammer, Phillips, Schaffer, Shandler, Wise
Potechin	Kardish, Lachovitz, Petigorsky, Shinder, Taller	Bernstein, Frank, Galandauer, Goldberg, Gordon, Kreisman, Lurie, Malek, Morello, Perlove, Pludwinsky, Scher
Pullan	Betcherman, Coplan, Florence, Lieff	Brownstein, Doctor, Dorfman, Helner, Metrick, Pameth, Sachs, Saks, Wyneberg
Reichstein	Cherm, Gershon, Kimmel, Lesh, Lithwick	Glube, Gottlieb, Huniu, Spector, Tanner
Rivers / Riber	Aaron, Ages, Betcherman, Cantor, Gershon, Glustein, Hanser, Max, Shinder, Smith, Tradburks	Bernstein, Browns, Goldberg, Haberman, Kamen, Kaploun, Keller, Osterer, Sandler, Shapiro, Schacter, Steinman, Tate, Victor, Vital, Wallach
Roodman	Dworkin, Ellenberg, Glustein, Greenberg, Karp, Kathnelson, Landau, Petigorsky, Pollock, Sherman, Taller	Bar-Noy, Berezin, Brass, Camen, Cohen, Dutnoff, Feldman, Feldstein, Gaffen, Gutmajer, Lee, Shulman, Wolfe, Zimmerman
Rubin	Coplan, Kardish, Kizell, Mosion, Murray, Slover	Abelson, Brbomberg, Feldman, Finkelstein, Gellman, Gray, Kramil, Levy, Levitan, Liff, Lipman, Monson, Pameth, Rosen, Rosenblum, Saper, Schlossberg, Steinberg, Waterman
Sadinsky	Cantor, Craft, Flesher, Froman, Gershon, Karp, Kimmel, Krantzberg, Marcovitch, Mosion, Shulman, Weinstein	Arron, Bercovitch, Cohen, Cowan, Greenberg, Keyfitz, Michelin, Ross, Saxe, Spiro, Tanner, Zagerman
Saslove / Zaslovsky / Saslovsky	Ages, Baslaw, Dover, Fine, Gennis, Goldfield, Greenberg, Karp, Kimmel, Lesh, Lithwick, Loeb, Marcovitch, Schecter, Shaffer, Shore, Shulman, Sugarman, Taller, Torontow, Weiner	Ballon, Berezin, Caplan, Coblentz, Cohen, Davis, Edelson, Finn, Fried, Gelfand, Ginsberg, Goldsmith, Goodman, Haimovici, Hart, Hock, Kalin, Katznelson, Kentorowitz, Kilinovsky, Kurland, Lazear, Levinson, Lobel, Malchusky, Manheim, Radnoff, Radnoffsky, Sabbath, Saipe, Seidler, Shaikin, Shapiro, Slipacoff, Smurlick,

		Solomon, Tarantour, Volfzon, Weisman, Wolfe
Schecter	Bessin, Cantor, Gennis, Greenberg, Levinson, Macy, Petigorsky, Saslove, Slack, Taller	Ballon, Cheigowsky, Gelman, Gunner, Starker, Wolinsky
Schreiber	Bessin, Freedman, Greenberg, Sherman	Borenstein, Briskin, Diena, Freedman, Goldstein, Horshovski, Koreen, Kurtz, Lang, Prizant, Rotenberg, Sacher, Schiff, Smith, Tenenbaum
Shaffer	Baslaw, Bessin, Feller, Gennis, Hanser, Kimmel, Krantzberg, Petigorsky, Saslove	Fine, Finsten, Green, Katz. Koffman, Lazear, Shapiro, Wener, Wolinsky, Yanover, Yarofsky, Zagon
Sherman / Shusterman	Greenberg, Halpern Kerzner, Pollock, Roodman, Saslove, Schreiber, Shinder, Skulsky, Weinstein	Bentolila, Bookman, Custoreri, Druckman, Feldman, Garceau, Glazer, Goldstein, Greenspan, Gutmajer, Lipson MacLeod, Miller, Moran, Postel, Zelnick
Shinder	Betcherman, Bodnoff, Gennis, Greenberg (both families), Halpern, Kathnelson, Landau, Lichtenstein, Potechin, Rivers, Sherman, Shore, Skulsky, Taller, Tradburks, Vechsler, Viner, Waserman, Weiner	Abrahamson, Abramson, Bezumny, Brill, Crust, Garceau, Gershon,, Ginsberg, Glazer, Goldberg, Goldstein, Keller, Kleinman, Kreisman, Lightstone, Malek, Millstone, Neiss, Newton, Osterer, Pascar, Rachlis, Sandler, Schecter, Shabinsky, Speisman, Trainoff, Vinokur, Weinman, Yanover
Shore	Betcherman, Bodnoff, Glustein, Lieff, Pleet, Pollock, Saslove, Shinder, Waserman, Weiner	Baker, Brill, Dubinsky, Fogel, Horwitz, Rastovsky, Rotenberg, Shabinsky, Sinder, Steinberg, Trainoff, Weisbord
Shulman	Craft, Dworkin, Karp, Kimmel, Kronick, Roodman, Sadinsky, Saslove, Taller	Guz, Jaffe, Mordfield, Muskovitch, Newton, Spiro
Silver	Cohen, Glustein, Greenberg, Skulsky, Slack, Steinberg, Sugarman, Viner	Aberback, Aronson, Bezumny, Brissman, Caplan, Cement, Chinn, Gilbert, Mann, Nitkin, Pernikoff, Rachlin, Raport, Rosenberg, Saalkind, Sanders, Schall, Schecter, Slonemsky, Szeroszewsky, Wolpin, Yellin, Zbar

Skulsky	Fine, Glustein, Goldfield, Greenberg, Halpern, Murray, Shinder, Silver, Viner, Waserman	Altschuler, Belinke, Fredlender, Gold, Goldberg, Goldman, Goldstein, Hersh, Newman, Phillippson, Schaenfield, Silverman, Szeroszewsky, Wax, Wiseman
Slack	Appotive, Kerzner, Petigorsky, Schecter, Silver	Aronson, Balsky, Brown, Gilbert, Mender, Neistein, Parnass, Raport, Shenkman
Slover	Becherman, Cohen, Coplan, Fine, Flesher, Froman, Greenberg, Kardish, Leikin, Murray, Polowin, Rubin, Taylor.	Cooper, Gertler, Hochberg, Levine, Pont, Rosenthal, Webber-Ziderman
Smith / Sendzul	Flesher, Glustein Gosewich, Krantzberg, Rivers, Waserman	Borts, Bosloy, Brown, Cohen, Glazer, Greenspon, Ingram, Klempner, Lang, Levy, Morrison, Narwa, Osterer, Rosen, Singerman, Zarenda
Smolkin	Cohen, Dover, Dworkin, Ellenberg, Glustein, Levitan, Pollock, Pleet, Swedlove, Vechsler, Zelikovitz	Abugov, Ancelovitz, Armitage, Baker, Barret, Bart, Bellan, Blumkin, Boro, Davidson, Davis, Epstein, Finkelstein, Friedman, Ginsburg, Goldenberg, Goldstein, Goodman, Gur-Arie, Haymer, Hoffman, Katchen, Kline, Kravetz, Kriger, Lapidus, Lapidus, Maskolinsky, Menard, Movshovitz, Sabbath, Shapiro, Vineburg, Wiseman
Steinberg	Gandall, Greenberg, Kardish, Levitan, Silver, Waserman	Benoway, Brill, Budevich, Chandross, Cohen, Findlay, Ginsburg, Jacobsen, Kevanstein, Litwin, Maloney, Muenz, Rabinovitch, Sanders, Sternberg, Weinman
Sugarman	Greenberg, Lithwick, Molot, Polowin, Saslove, Silver, Slack, Taller, Weiner	Aronson, Baxt, Beaulieu, Becker, Berlin, Bezumny, Chetwynd, Coopersmith, Cotsman, Diamond, Evenchick, Gilbert, Gordon, Katz, Lacome, Lerman, Malkin, Mazur, Pearlman, Phillips, Rabin, Raport / Rappaport, Robern, Robinson, Sangster, Schwartzfeld, Seidler, Shane, Slonemsky, Szeroszewsky

Swedlove	Cohen, Flesher, Freedman, Hanser, Kizell, Lichteinstein, Lithwick, Polowin, Smolkin	Achbar, Aisenberg, Baker, Cohen, Cooper, English, Freedman, Ginsberg, Gordon, Halperin, Jack, Koh, Margolies, Mendelson, Newton, Paulin, Poulin, Rossman, Shapiro, Sinclair, Tyber, Waiser, Weiss
Taller	Bodnoff, Cantor, Cherm, Fine, Goldfield, Gould, Greenberg, Kerzner, Kimmel, Kronick, Landau, Lieff, Molot, Roodman, Saslove, Schecter, Shinder, Shulman, Sugarman, Waserman	Balinsky, Bergman, Bernstein, Borotnick, Butovsky, Camen, Cohen, Dobrinsky, Doctor, Gelman, Harris, Hartman, Jordan, Kaiman, Katz, Kentorowitz, Kwechansky, Kurland, Lazear, Levitt, Mincoff, Nadelle, Pepper, Ross, Sadavoy, Seidler, Shabinsky, Shapiro, Shaver, Silver, Silverman, Simbrow, Sobcov, Trainoff, Turner, Villeneuve, Wakter, Weidman, Weinman, Wexler, Witten, Wortman,Young, Ysorsky, Zelick
Taylor	Betcherman, Froman, Gencher, Greenberg, Kardish, Murray, Pollock, Polowin, Slover	Rosenthal, Rothman
Torontow	Ages, Agulnik, Baylin, Betcherman, Bodnoff, Dover, Flesher, Gandall, Gennis, Glustein, Goldfield, Gottdank, Karp, Krantzberg, Max, Polowin, Saslove, Shore, Weiner	Abrams, Addelman, Adler, Altschuler, Berezin, Cohen, Cowan, Evans, Firestone, Freedman, Hart, Heatherington, Katz, Koffman, Laitman, Levine, Malchulsky, Monson, Naemark, Nitupski, Rastovsky, Rubin, Saxe, Schneider, Solomon, Tanzer, Witten, Zides
Tradburk	Baylin, Gennis, Max, Mirsky, Rivers	Chiprout, Cohen, Diamond, Goldberg, Kalman, Keller, Koffman, Moscovitch, Progosh, Wallack
Vechsler / Vexler	Baylin, Diener, Dover, Dworkin, Ellenberg, Landau, Max, Pleet, Shinder, Smolkin	Abrahamson, Bercovic, Coates, Friedman, Mintz, Pascar, Progosh, Ross, Singerman, Tinkoff, Wolofsky
Victor	Craft, Feller, Hanser, Kimmel, Lesh, Lieff, Lithwick, Rivers, Shaffer, Smolkin, Swedlove	Berman, Breslav, Cohen, Eskin, Faigan, Freed, Friedman, Gershkovitch, Goldberg, Gordon, Gower, Merrill, Rosen, Staller, Wail

Viner / Vinerman	Cantor, Cherm, Feller, Fine, Goldfield, Greenberg, Halpern, Lachovitz, Macy, Murray, Pollock, Shinder, Silver, Slack, Skulsky, Taller, Waserman, Weiner	Altschuler, Cherun, Ecklove, Fredlender, Gold, Goldman, Hersh, Hyman, Kishinofsky, Leffell, Niedzviecki, Robitaille, Sadowski, Schaenfield, Segal, Silverman, Soloway, Szeroszewsky, Trainoff, Vered
Waserman	Bodnoff, Cherm, Lesh, Marcovitch, Shinder, Shore, Smith, Steinberg, Taller, Viner	Borts, Brill, Ginsburg, Gruvick, Halpern, Hersh, Jacobsen, Kleinman, Kotler, Lang, Lobel, Morrissette, Schaenfield, Shapero, Silver, Sternberg, Trainoff, Tuckman
Weiner	Bodnoff, Goldmaker, Kardish, Lachovitz, Landau, Saslove, Shinder, Shore, Sugarman, Torontow, Viner	Bronsther, Fox, Greenberg, Katz, Leibovitch, Millstone, Nathanson, Oster, Schinman, Weinman
Weinstein	Gennis, Gorelick, Krantzberg, Sherman, Torontow	Arron, Barook, Koffman, Lewis, Nadolny, Resnick, Saxe, Yanover, Zagerman
Weiss	Cohen, Kardish, Kerzner, Pollock, Zelikovitz	Dubinsky, Feldberg, Hochberg, Kott
Zelikovitz	Cohen, Kardish, Kronick, Levitan, Loeb, Viner, Weiss	Baker, Borshy, Burack, Cherun, Green, Guralnick, Mandel, Nadler, Randall, Schneiderman, Ulrich, Waisberg

Index of Surnames, Linked to Entries

Surname	Mentioned in Entry
Aaron	Feinstein, Gennis, Marcovitch, Murray, Rivers
Abeles	Polowin
Abelson	Coplan, Rubin
Aber	Cohen
Aberback	Cohen, Silver
Abrahams	Betcherman
Abrahamson	Dover, Max, Shinder, Vechsler
Abramowitz	Ages, Kerzner, Pollock
Abrams	Karp, Max, Pollock, Torontow
Abramson	Kathnelson, Shinder
Abtan	Cohen, Halpern
Abugov	Smolkin
Achbar	Flesher, Freedman, Kizell, Lithwick, Swedlove
Addelman	Betcherman, Florence, Krantzberg, Torontow
Adelson	Pollock
Adessky	Greenberg, Lieff
Adler	Torontow
Ages	Bodnoff, Gershon, Halpern, Kardish, Pollock, Rivers, Saslove, Torontow
Agulnik	Diener, Kardish, Torontow
Ain	Lithwick
Aisenberg	Cohen, Lithwick, Swedlove
Alexandor	Bilsky
Allice	Baylin, Bodnoff, Craft
Alper	Baylin
Altman	Fine, Leikin
Altschuler	Goldfield, Skulsky, Torontow, Viner
Amor	Baylin
Amsel	Landau
Ancelovitz	Smolkin
Angel	Leikin
Appel	Ages, Gershon, Molot
Applebaum	Leikin
Appotive	Macy, Landau, Slack
Aptowitzer	Glustein
Aranov	Baylin
Armitage	Levitan, Smolkin
Arnoni	Bodnoff
Aronovitch	Bodnoff
Aronson	Greenberg, Molot, Silver, Slack, Sugarman
Arron	Gennis, Gorelick, Horwitz, Krantzberg, Sadinsky, Weinstein
Azmier	Dworkin, Pollock

Bahar	Ages, Halpern, Lithwick
Baker	Gershon, Glustein, Levitan, Pleet, Shore, Smolkin, Swedlove, Zelikovitz
Balinsky	Taller
Ballon	Greenberg, Levinson, Saslove, Schecter
Balsky	Greenberg, Slack
Banks	Dworkin
Barg	Kerzner
Barker	Lieff
Bar-Noy	Roodman
Barook	Weinstein
Barret	Smolkin
Bart	Smolkin
Baslaw	Bessin, Glustein, Goldfield, Kimmel, Saslove, Shaffer
Bauer	Cohen
Baxt	Sugarman
Baylin	Ages, Bodnoff, Flesher, Gandall, Kardish, Mirsky, Torontow, Tradburks, Vechsler
Beaulieu	Sugarman
Beckenstein	Appotive
Becker	Sugarman
Beiles	Kizell, Marcovitch
Belinke	Glustein, Skulsky
Bellan	Smolkin
Ben-Dat	Cantor
Benoway	Levitan, Steinberg
Bentolila	Sherman
Benwick	Bodnoff, Cohen
Bercovic	Vechsler
Bercovici	Feller
Bercovitch	Sadinsky
Bergman	Molot, Taller
Berezin	Ages, Bodnoff, Gencher, Kardish, Pollock, Roodman, Saslove, Torontow
Berger	Fine
Bergsiem	Gould
Berkovitch	Craft
Berlin	Krantzberg, Sugarman
Berliner	Glustein
Berman	Kerzner, Kizell, Molot, Victor
Bernstein	Lachovitz, Potechin, Rivers, Taller
Bessin	Diener, Goldfield, Goldmaker, Petigorsky, Schecter, Schreiber, Shaffer
Bessner	Lieff
Betcherman	Cohen, Florence, Froman, Glustein, Greenberg, Molot, Murray, Pullan, Rivers, Shinder, Shore, Slover, Smith, Taylor, Torontow
Bezumny	Greenberg, Levitan, Shinder, Silver, Sugarman

Biderman	Landau, Lichtenstein
Bilsky	Cohen, Halpern, Mirsky
Bindman	Landau
Blachov	Coplan, Kronick
Blacker	Bodnoff
Blair	Bodnoff, Lithwick
Bleichman	Marcovitch
Bloom	Gennis
Blumkin	Smolkin
Bodnoff	Ages, Baylin, Cohen, Coplan, Craft, Feller, Gandall, Gennis, Gould, Greenberg, Kronick, Pollock, Shinder, Shore, Steinberg, Taller, Torontow, Waserman, Weiner
Bodovsky	Leikin
Bogomolny	Lachovitz
Boguslovski / Boguslovsky	Baslaw, Greenberg
Bookman	Gorelick, Halpern, Pleet, Sherman
Bordan	Cohen
Bordelay	Gennis, Gorelick, Kardish, Lieff
Borden	Horwitz
Borenstein	Bessin, Diener, Schreiber
Boro	Dworkin, Smolkin
Borotnick	Taller
Borshy	Zelikovitz
Borts	Smith, Waserman
Bosloy	Gosewich, Lithwick, Smith
Brandes	Leikin
Brass	Landau, Roodman
Breakstone	Flesher
Breatross	Aaron, Feinstein, Murray
Bregman	Kardish
Breslav	Victor
Brewer	Gosewich
Bright	Goldmaker
Brill	Dworkin, Glustein, Levitan, Molot, Steinberg, Shinder, Shore, Waserman
Briskin	Schreiber
Brissman	Glustein, Silver
Brodie	Cantor
Brodsky	Kimmel
Broitman	Kerzner
Bromberg	Max, Murray, Rubin
Bronfman	Bilsky, Cohen
Bronstein	Cohen
Bronsther	Weiner
Brottman	Appotive
Brovender	Lieff
Brown	Fine, Glustein, Slack, Smith

Browns	Rivers
Brownstein	Florence, Loeb, Pullan
Brozovsky	Agulnik, Kardish
Budevich	Steinberg
Budd / Budovitch	Goldfield, Pollock
Bulka	Cohen
Burnstine	Levinson
Butovsky	Cantor, Taller
Burack	Kronick, Zelikovitz
Calof	Landau
Camen	Roodman, Taller
Cantor	Cohen, Fine, Flesher, Kerzner, Krantzberg, Leikin, Loeb, Max, Mosion, Rivers, Sadinsky, Schecter, Taller, Viner
Cape	Cohen
Caplan	Feller, Gosewich, Kardish, Levinson, Saslove, Silver
Carlofsky	Flesher
Cement	Glustein, Silver
Chalefsky	Lithwick
Chandross	Steinberg
Cheigowsky	Petigorsky, Polowin, Schecter
Chepovetsky	Kimmel
Cherm	Fine, Kimmel, Reichstein, Taller, Viner, Waserman
Cherney	Cohen
Chernove	Horwitz
Cherun	Feller, Krantzberg, Viner, Zelikovitz
Chetwynd	Sugarman
Chezin	Bodnoff
Chinn	Silver
Chiprout	Tradburks
Chodikoff	Bessin, Ellenberg, Freedman, Petigorsky
Coan	Petigorsky
Coates	Vechsler
Coblentz	Greenberg, Saslove
Cobrin	Froman
Cogan	Kerzner
Cohen	Ages, Bodnoff, Cantor, Deitcher, Diener, Dover, Drazin, Florence, Gershon, Goldfield, Gottdank, Gould, Greenberg, Halpern, Kardish, Krantzberg, Landau, Leikin, Lesh, Levinson, Lieff, Lithwick, Mirsky, Mosion, Pollock, Polowin, Roodman, Sadinsky, Saslove, Silver, Slover, Smith, Smolkin, Steinberg, Swedlove, Taller, Torontow, Tradburks, Victor, Weiss, Zelikovitz
Cooper	Coplan, Slover, Swedlove
Coopersmith	Lithwick, Sugarman
Copeland	Kardish
Coplan	Ages, Bodnoff, Florence, Gould, Horwitz, Kizell, Kronick, Mosion, Murray, Pullan, Rubin, Slover
Cornblat	Cohen, Krantzberg

Cotsman	Sugarman
Cowan	Froman, Glustein, Karp, Kizell, Max, Polowin, Sadinsky, Torontow
Craft	Bodnoff, Kimmel, Mosion, Sadinsky, Shulman, Victor
Cratzbarg	Kardish, Murray
Crust	Shinder
Custoreri	Sherman
Dachs	Lesh
Dain	Kerzner
Davidow	Landau
Davidson	Levitan, Smolkin
Davis	Ellenberg, Levitan, Saslove, Smolkin
Davy / Davidowicz	Cohen
Dear	Glustein
Deitcher	Cohen
Demb	Kerzner
Dembe	Ages, Bodnoff
Dermer	Landau
Diamond	Sugarman, Tradburks
Dickstein	Feinstein, Kerzner
Diena	Bessin, Schreiber
Diener	Agulnik, Bessin, Cohen, Diener, Greenberg, Landau, Schreiber, Vechsler
Dobkin	Cohen
Dobrinsky	Taller
Doctor	Florence, Lieff, Pullan, Taller
Dolansky	Dover, Kizell
Dorfman	Pullan
Dover	Cohen, Gennis, Glustein, Greenberg, Kizell, Landau, Levinson, Macy, Mirsky, Molot, Murray, Polowin, Saslove, Shinder, Smolkin, Torontow, Vechsler
Dragushan	Gennis
Drazin	Cohen
Druckman	Greenberg, Kerzner, Sherman
Dubinsky	Glustein, Pollock, Shore, Weiss
Dubrofsky	Ages, Bodnoff, Glustein, Kardish
Dunsky	Cohen, Goldfield, Goldmaker
Dutnoff / Danoff	Glustein, Petigorsky, Pollock, Roodman
Dworkin	Karp, Macy, Molot, Petigorsky, Roodman, Shulman, Smolkin
Ecklove	Viner
Eckstein	Cohen
Edelson	Greenberg, Saslove
Ehrenkranz	Cohen, Diener, Landau
Ehrenreich	Glustein
Eisenstadt	Cohen
Ellenberg	Flesher, Freedman, Glustein, Marcovitch, Roodman, Smolkin, Vechsler
Ellis	Kardish, Lieff

Emerson	Cohen
Engel	Ellenberg, Gencher
English	Swedlove
Epstein	Cohen, Krantzberg, Landau, Leikin, Smolkin
Esar	Lithwick
Eskin	Victor
Evans	Dover, Torontow
Evenchick	Sugarman
Fagin	Cohen, Halpern
Faigan	Victor
Farber	Cantor, Gosewich, Leikin, Lithwick
Fasman	Cohen
Feig	Cantor, Cohen
Fein	Betcherman
Feinberg	Dover, Kizell, Max
Feinsten	Aaron
Feldberg	Ages, Bodnoff, Kardish, Weiss
Feldblum	Appotive
Feldman	Pollock, Roodman, Rubin, Sherman
Feldstein	Roodman
Feller	Bodnoff, Bilsky, Kardish, Kimmel, Krantzberg, Kronick, Leikin, Levinson, Lieff, Lithwick, Mirsky, Shaffer, Victor, Viner
Fenster	Horwitz
Fertig	Dworkin, Lachovitz, Petigorsky
Ferrucci	Cohen
Findlay	Steinberg
Fine	Bilsky, Cherm, Cohen, Feller, Glustein, Gorelick, Gosewich, Gould, Kimmel, Kronick, Leikin, Levitan, Loeb, Palmer, Pollock, Polowin, Saslove, Shaffer, Skulsky, Slover, Taller, Viner
Finerman	Feller, Krantzberg
Fink	Cohen
Finkelman	Glustein
Finkelstein	Glustein, Rubin, Smolkin
Finn	Baslaw, Saslove
Finsten	Shaffer
Fireman	Dover, Glustein
Firestone	Levinson, Torontow
Fishbain	Lithwick
Fisher	Bodnoff
Flatt	Aaron, Feinstein, Murray
Flesher	Baylin, Dover, Ellenberg, Gershon, Kerzner, Lesh, Levitan, Petigorsky, Sadinsky, Slover, Smith, Swedlove, Torontow
Fliegelman	Florence
Florence	Betcherman, Coplan, Goldmaker, Kizell, Lieff, Pullan
Freedman	Cohen, Greenberg, Krantzberg, Schreiber, Swedlove
Fogel	Betcherman, Shore
Fonberg	Dworkin, Kronick

Fox	Ages, Halpern, Weiner
Frank	Potechin
Freiman	Bilsky, Halpern, Mirsky
Fredlender	Skulsky, Viner
Freed / Freedlander	Craft, Victor
Freedman / Ben-Choreen	Bessin, Dworkin, Ellenberg, Lithwick, Loeb, Petigorsky, Schreiber, Swedlove, Torontow
Fried	Ages, Saslove
Friedberg	Diener
Friedlan	Lieff
Friedman	Smolkin, Victor
Freiman	Bilsky
Friberg	Diener, Greenberg, Landau
Friedgut	Levinson
Friendly	Gosewich
Friedman	Smolkin, Vechsler
Fript	Feller, Kronick, Leikin
Froimovitch	Krantzberg
Froman	Betcherman, Greenberg, Krantzberg, Marcovitch, Murray, Sadinsky, Slover, Taylor
Futeral	Lesh
Fyman	Levinson
Gaffen	Roodman
Galandauer	Potechin
Gandall	Ages, Baylin, Bodnoff, Landau, Mosion, Steinberg, Torontow
Gantzer	Hanser
Garber	Landau
Garceau	Sherman, Shinder
Geffen	Petigorsky
Gelfand	Saslove
Geller	Lichtenstein
Gellman	Rubin
Gelman	Cantor, Schecter, Taller
Gencher	Greenberg, Pollock, Taylor
Gennis	Aaron, Bodnoff, Gorelick, Greenberg, Kardish, Levinson, Lieff, Marcovitch, Pleet, Saslove, Shaffer, Shinder, Torontow, Tradburks, Weinstein
Gershkovitch	Victor
Gershon	Ages, Flesher, Glustein, Greenberg, Lichtenstein, Reichstein, Rivers, Sadinsky, Shinder
Gerson	Murray
Gertler	Fine, Gencher, Pollock, Slover
Gertsman	Coplan
Gilbert	Greenberg, Silver, Slack, Sugarman
Gilboa	Gosewich
Giller	Goldmaker
Ginsberg	Ages, Bodnoff, Gould, Saslove, Shinder, Swedlove
Ginsburg	Cohen, Dover, Smolkin, Steinberg, Waserman

Gladstone	Glustein
Glass	Agulnik
Glazer	Sherman, Shinder, Smith
Glickman	Freedman, Loeb
Gluck	Molot
Glube	Lithwick, Reichstein
Glustein / Glushtein	Betcherman, Dover, Ellenberg, Gershon, Goldfield, Greenberg, Kizell, Lichtenstein, Lithwick, Petigorsky, Rivers, Roodman, Shore, Silver, Skulsky, Smith, Smolkin, Torontow
Gluzman	Kardish
Gold	Skulsky, Viner
Goldberg	Ages, Dover, Glustein, Goldmaker, Kardish, Landau, Lichtenstein, Lieff, Max, Potechin, Rivers, Shinder, Skulsky, Tradburks, Victor
Golden	Bodnoff, Cohen, Lithwick
Goldenberg	Fine, Levitan, Pleet, Pollock, Smolkin
Goldfield	Baslaw, Bessin, Glustein, Goldmaker, Saslove, Skulsky, Taller, Torontow, Viner
Goldmaker	Bessin, Goldfield, Weiner
Goldman	Dworkin, Feller, Skulsky, Viner
Goldsmith	Molot, Saslove
Goldstein	Bilsky, Dover, Freedman, Greenberg, Halpern, Kathnelson, Kerzner, Levitan, Mirsky, Schreiber, Sherman, Shinder, Smolkin, Skulsky
Goldstick	Coplan
Goodman	Dover, Gershon, Horwitz, Saslove, Smolkin
Gordon	Cohen, Max, Molot, Pleet, Polowin, Potechin, Sugarman, Swedlove, Victor
Gorelick	Bordelay, Coplan, Fine, Horwitz, Kardish, Pleet, Weinstein
Gosewich / Gosewitz / Gosevitz	Cohen, Fine, Kathnelson, Lithwick, Palmer, Smith
Gossack	Feinstein
Gottdank	Agulnik, Lieff, Mirsky, Torontow
Gottlieb	Lithwick, Reichstein
Gould	Betcherman, Bodnoff, Coplan, Fine, Kronick, Molot, Palmer, Pleet, Taller
Gower	Victor
Grafstein	Cohen
Gray	Rubin
Green	Lithwick, Molot, Shaffer, Zelikovitz
Greenberg	Betcherman, Bodnoff, Diener, Ellenberg, Freedman, Froman, Gencher, Gennis, Goldfield, Gorelick, Gosewich, Kardish, Kerzner, Krantzberg, Leikin, Lesh, Levinson, Levitan, Lieff, Lithwick, Macy, Marcovitch, Palmer, Pleet, Roodman, Sadinsky, Saslove, Schecter, Schreiber, Sherman, Shinder, Silver, Slover, Skulsky, Steinberg, Sugarman, Taller, Taylor, Viner, Weiner
Greenblatt	Lithwick

Greenspan	Sherman
Greenspon	Smith
Greenspoon	Lieff
Grill	Polowin
Gross	Ages, Bodnoff, Glustein
Grossman	Levinson, Lieff
Gruvick	Waserman
Gunner / Gunnerotsky	Petigorsky, Schecter, Slack
Guralnick	Zelikovitz
Gursky	Cohen
Gur-Arie	Levitan, Smolkin
Gutmajer	Pollock, Roodman, Sherman
Gutteit	Gandall, Mosion
Guttman	Glustein
Guz	Hanser, Kimmel, Lithwick, Shulman
Haber	Glustein
Haberman	Rivers
Haimovici	Froman, Marcovitch, Saslove
Halperin	Lichtenstein, Swedlove
Halpern	Bilsky, Cohen, Kardish, Lesh, Macy, Sherman, Shinder, Skulsky, Viner, Waserman
Hammer	Polowin
Handel	Feller
Hanser / Hontsher	Flesher, Kimmel, Kronick, Lesh, Rivers, Shaffer, Swedlove, Victor
Harris	Baslaw, Leikin, Lichtenstein, Mosion, Taller
Hart	Cohen, Saslove, Torontow
Hartman	Taller
Hassan	Flesher
Haymer	Smolkin
Heatherington	Torontow
Hecht	Flesher
Held	Ages, Molot, Pollock
Heimovitch	Feller
Helfgot	Marcovitch
Helner	Pullan
Hendin	Goldmaker
Herman	Dover
Hersenhorn	Pollock
Hersh	Skulsky, Viner, Waserman
Hershorn	Marcovitch
Herszman	Gershon
Hertz	Horwitz
Hirschel	Gosewich
Hirschhorn	Bilsky, Halpern
Hochberg	Cohen, Kerzner, Leikin, Slover, Weiss
Hochman	Bessin, Petigorsky

Hock	Saslove
Hodess	Greenberg
Hoffman	Glustein, Smolkin
Hollander	Dover, Kerzner
Holzman	Pollock
Horlick	Kronick
Horwitz	Coplan, Shore
Horowitz	Dover, Gould, Kizell
Horshovski	Schreiber
Huniu	Cherm, Reichstein
Hurtig	Levinson
Hutt	Lesh
Hyman	Viner
Hymes	Fine, Levinson
Ingram	Smith
Isacoff	Levitan, Molot
Israel	Halpern
Jack	Swedlove
Jacobs	Bilsky, Lieff
Jacobsen	Steinberg, Waserman
Jacobson	Gennis
Jaffe	Karp, Shulman
Jakobovitz	Cohen
Jankielewitz	Kardish
Jewett	Krantzberg
Jordan	Taller
Joseph	Dover
Kahansky	Levitan
Kahn	Pleet
Kaiman	Cherm, Taller
Kalin	Saslove
Kalir	Greenberg
Kalman	Tradburks
Kamerman	Molot
Kamil	Kardish
Kapeller	Bessin
Kaplan	Betcherman, Gosewich, Kathnelson, Krantzberg
Kaploun	Rivers
Kardish / Kardash / Cardash	Ages, Agulnik, Baylin, Bodnoff, Cohen, Coplan, Craft, Feller, Gennis, Glustein, Gorelick, Greenberg, Hapnern, Kerzner, Lachovitz, Lieff, Mirsky, Mosion, Murray, Potechin, Rubin, Slover, Steinberg, Taylor, Weiner, Weiss, Zelikovitz
Karon	Cohen
Karp/Kapinsky	Craft, Marcovitch, Max, Petigorsky, Polowin, Roodman, Sadinsky, Saslove, Shulman
Katchen	Smolkin
Kathnelson	Gosewich, Roodman, Shinder

Katz	Appotive, Cantor, Leikin, Macy, Shaffer, Sugarman, Taller, Torontow, Weiner
Katznelson	Saslove
Kaufman	Feller
Kavanat	Feinstein
Keeb	Cohen
Keller	Cantor, Max, Rivers, Shinder, Tradburks
Kamen	Rivers
Kentorowitz	Saslove, Taller
Kershman	Leikin
Kerzner	Cantor, Flesher, Greenberg, Kardish, Sherman, Slack, Taller, Weiss
Kessler	Leikin
Keyfitz	Karp, Sadinsky
Kevanstein	Steinberg
Kilinovsky	Saslove
Kimmel	Cherm, Craft, Feller, Flesher, Gershon, Hanser, Kronick, Lesh, Lithwick, Sadinsky, Saslove, Shaffer, Shulman, Taller, Victor
Kirshenblatt	Molot
Kishinofsky	Levinson, Macy, Molot, Viner
Kizell	Coplan, Dover, Florence, Glustein, Goldfield, Marcovitch, Rubin, Swedlove
Kleinman	Shinder, Waserman
Kleinplatz	Molot
Klempner	Smith
Kline	Glustein, Goldfield, Kizell, Smolkin
Klugsberg	Lithwick
Koffman	Dover, Gennis, Greenberg, Kardish, Lieff, Pleet, Shaffer, Torontow, Tradburks, Weinstein
Koh	Swedlove
Konick	Lesh
Kooperstock	Fine
Koreen	Freedman, Greenberg, Schreiber
Kotlarsky	Pleet
Kotler	Waserman
Kott	Cantor, Kerzner, Weiss
Kramil	Rubin
Krantzberg / Krane	Marcovitch, Mosion, Sadinsky, Shaffer, Smith, Torontow, Weinstein
Kravetz	Smolkin
Kreisman	Potechin, Shinder
Kriger	Glustein, Lithwick, Smolkin
Kroch	Florence
Kroll	Lithwick
Kronick	Ages, Agulnik, Bodnoff, Cantor, Coplan, Feller, Gould, Leikin, Lichtenstein, Shulman, Taller, Zelikovitz
Krugel	Krantzberg

Krupnick	Kardish, Lithwick, Murray
Kurland	Saslove, Taller
Kurtz	Bessin, Diener, Schreiber
Kushin	Ages
Kussner	Lachovitz
Kuttas	Bodnoff
Kwechansky	Taller
Labovitch	Ellenberg, Flesher
LaBreton	Flesher
Lachovitz	Kardish, Petigorsky, Potechin, Viner, Weiner
Lacome	Sugarman
Laitman	Karp, Torontow
Landau	Appotive, Cohen, Diener, Dover, Gandall, Greenberg, Leikin, Levinson, Lichtenstein, Murray, Roodman, Shinder, Taller, Weiner, Vechsler
Landis	Goldfield
Lang	Bessin, Diener, Goldmaker, Hanser, Schreiber, Smith, Waserman
Langstadt	Molot
Lapidus	Smolkin
Lavitt	Flesher
Lax	Glustein
Lazarovitch	Lieff
Lazarus	Marcovitch
Lazear	Krantzberg, Saslove, Shaffer, Taller
Lecker	Cohen, Dover
Leckman	Bodnoff
Lee	Roodman
Leffell	Viner, Landau
Lefton	Glustein
Leibner	Lithwick
Leibov	Kerzner
Leibovitch	Weiner
Leikin / Leiken	Cantor, Cohen, Feller, Kronick, Landau, Loeb, Palmer, Slover
Lemonik	Cohen, Florence
Lerman	Dover, Sugarman
Lerner	Lithwick, Mosion
Lesh	Flesher, Greenberg, Hanser, Kimmel, Levitan, Reichstein, Saslove, Victor, Waserman
Lesonsky	Lithwick
Levencrown	Max
Levi	Krantzberg
Levine	Dover, Dworkin, Horwitz, Glustein, Gorelick, Gould, Slover, Smolkin, Torontow
Levinoff	Bessin, Goldfield
Levinson	Dover, Fine, Gennis, Greenberg, Macy, Murray, Saslove, Schecter

Levitan	Cohen, Fine, Flesher, Gencher, Greenberg, Kardish, Lesh, Molot, Pleet, Rubin, Smolkin, Steinberg, Zelikovitz
Levitin	Feinstein
Levitt	Taller
Levitz	Kardish
Levy	Gosewich, Rubin, Smith
Lewin	Molot
Lewis	Kardish, Weinstein
Lichtenstein	Gershon, Landau, Shinder, Swedlove
Lieff / Lifshitz	Feller, Florence, Gottdank, Kardish, Palmer, Pullan, Shore, Taller, Victor
Liff	Landau, Murray, Rubin
Lifshitz	Marcovitch
Light	Loeb
Lightstone	Shinder
Linowitz	Landau
Lipman	Rubin
Lipson	Sherman
Lisak	Kerzner
Lithwick	Gosewich, Freedman, Hanser, Kimmel, Palmer, Reichstein, Saslove, Sugarman, Swedlove, Victor
Litt	Kizell
Litwack	Glustein, Kizell
Litwin	Greenberg, Kardish, Steinberg
Liverant	Cohen
Lobel	Lesh, Saslove, Waserman
Loeb	Dover, Fine, Freedman, Leikin, Saslove, Zelikovitz
Lome	Agulnik
London	Bilsky, Halpern, Mirsky
Loomer	Kerzner
Lorwill	Flesher
Lurie	Potechin
Luterman	Agulnik, Diener, Greenberg
Luxenberg	Bilsky
MacLeod	Sherman
Macy	Appotive, Greenberg, Halpern, Landau, Levinson, Molot, Pollock, Schecter, Viner
Magidson	Hanser, Kimmel, Lithwick, Palmer
Malchusky	Saslove, Torontow
Malek	Potechin, Shinder
Malkin	Sugarman
Malkus	Landau
Malomet	Cohen
Maloney	Steinberg
Mandel	Zelikovitz
Manheim	Saslove
Mann	Silver

Marcovitch / Marcus	Aaron, Bodnoff, Ellenberg, Froman, Gennis, Karp, Kizell, Krantzberg, Sadinsky, Saslove, Waserman
Margolies	Cohen, Swedlove
Markson	Bilsky, Gosewich, Kathnelson
Martin	Mirsky
Maskolinsky	Smolkin
Mausberg	Macy
Max / Kavalsky	Cantor, Dover, Karp, Pollock, Polowin, Rivers, Shinder, Torontow, Tradburks, Vechsler
Mayberger / May	Bodnoff
Mazur	Sugarman
McClelland	Horwitz
Meil	Kerzner
Meirovich	Ages, Bodnoff
Melamed	Kimmel
Menard	Smolkin
Menczer	Landau
Mendelson	Agulnik, Flesher, Kardish, Lachovitz, Swedlove
Mender	Slack
Merrill	Victor
Merson	Leikin
Metrick	Pullan
Michelin	Craft, Mosion, Sadinsky
Michelson	Betcherman
Midlin	Bodnoff
Miller	Sherman
Millstein	Krantzberg
Millstone	Goldmaker, Shinder, Weiner
Mincoff	Cantor, Taller
Minkoff	Dworkin
Mintz	Bodnoff, Diener, Gandall, Greenberg, Landau, Vechsler
Mirsky	Baylin, Bilsky, Dover, Feller, Gottdank, Kardish, Lieff, Tradburks
Moldaver	Cohen
Molot	Betcherman, Dover, Kardish, Levitan, Macy, Polowin, Sugarman, Taller
Monheit	Lachovitz
Monson	Glustein, Lachovitz, Rubin, Torontow
Montagnes	Cohen
Moraff	Mirsky
Moran	Sherman
Mordfield	Shulman
Morell	Cohen
Morello	Potechin
Morin	Cohen
Morris	Landau, Molot, Murray, Rubin
Morrissette	Waserman
Morrison	Smith

Mortimer	Gencher
Moscovitch	Lithwick, Mirsky, Tradburks
Mosion / Mason	Cantor, Coplan, Craft, Gandall, Kardish, Krantzberg, Levinson, Lichtenstein, Rubin, Sadinsky
Moskovic	Feinstein
Movshovitz	Glustein, Lithwick, Smolkin
Mozersky	Landau
Muenz	Steinberg
Muroff	Greenberg
Murray	Aaron, Feinstein, Greenberg, Kardish, Landau, Rubin, Skulsky, Slover, Taylor ,Viner
Muskovitch	Shulman
Muster	Kardish
Myers	Molot
Nadelle	Taller
Nadler	Kathnelson, Zelikovitz
Nadolny	Weinstein
Naemark	Torontow
Naginsky	Halpern
Narod	Lieff
Narwa	Smith
Nathanson	Dover, Feller, Weiner
Neiss	Shinder
Neistein	Kerzner, Slack
Nelson	Lachovitz
Nemerovsky	Glustein, Petigorsky
Nepomiazchy	Greenberg
Ness	Lithwick
Newman	Fine, Glustein, Gorelick, Gosewich, Kardish, Skulsky
Newton	Gershon, Greenberg, Kronick, Lichtenstein, Mosion, Shulman, Swedlove
Niedzviecki	Viner
Nitkin	Silver
Nitupski	Gottdank, Torontow
Ochas	Lesh
Oiring	Pleet
Okumiansky	Levitan
Ontell	Cohen, Florence
Orlik	Cherm, Fine
Oster	Weiner
Osterer	Betcherman, Glustein, Rivers, Shinder, Smith
Ostroff	Agulnik
Padolsky	Diener
Palmer	Fine, Gosewich, Gottdank, Gould, Leikin, Lieff, Lithwik
Pameth	Coplan, Pullan, Rubin
Pareno	Lithwick
Parnass	Appotive, Landau, Macy, Slack
Pascar	Shinder, Vechsler

Pasher	Levinson
Paulin	Cohen, Swedlove
Pearl	AGes
Pearlman	Bilsky, Mirsky, Sugarman
Peddlar	Gennis
Pelcovits	Petigorsky
Penso	Greenberg, Kardish
Pepper	Taller
Perchanok	Mirsky
Perlman	Glustein, Goldfield, Greenberg
Perlmutter	Landau, Levinson
Perlove	Potchin
Pernikoff	Glustein, Silver
Petigorsky	Bessin, Flesher, Freedman, Glustein, Lachovitz, Polowin, Potechin, Roodman, Schecter, Shaffer, Slack
Petruskha	Cohen
Phillippson	Skulsky
Phillips	Freedman Polowin, Schreiber, Sugarman
Phomin	Palmer
Piazza	Molot
Pichosky	Gosewich
Pilczewicz	Landau
Pilze	Halpern
Pivnick	Cantor
Plaskow	Cohen
Pleet	Diener, Gennis, Gorelick, Greenberg, Landau, Levitan, Shore, Smolkin, Vechsler
Plotken	Kardish
Pludwinsky	Potechin
Pollock	Ages, Bodnoff, Cohen, Fine, Gencher, Goldfield, Greenberg, Landau, Max, Palmer, Roodman, Shore, Smolkin, Taylor, Viner, Weiss
Polowin	Cohen, Dover, Fine, Karp, Max, Molot, Petigorsky, Pollock, Slover, Sugarman, Swedlove, Taylor, Torontow, Wise
Polsky	Lithwick, Palmer
Pont	Flesher, Slover
Portnoy	Molot
Posner	Landau, Lichtenstein
Postel	Sherman
Potechin	Kardish, Lachovitz, Shinder
Poulin	Swedlove
Prizant	Freedman, Schreiber
Progosh	Baylin, Dworkin, Ellenberg, Mirsky, Tradburks, Vechsler
Prusky	Murray
Pullan	Betcherman, Coplan, Florence
Putterman	Bodnoff, Cohen
Rabin	Bilsky, Mirsky, Sugarman
Rabinovitch	Cohen, Goldfield, Goldmaker, Steinberg

Rachlin	Cohen, Landau, Leikin, Silver
Rachlis	Shinder
Rackow	Ages
Radnoff	Loeb, Saslove
Radnoffsky	Saslove
Rafal	Ages
Randall	Zelikovitz
Rapaport	Cohen
Raport / Rappaport	Greenberg, Silver, Slack, Sugarman
Rapp	Goldfield
Rashevsky	Kimmel, Lithwik
Raskin	Murray
Rasminsky	Cohen, Freedman
Rastovsky	Bodnoff, Shore, Torontow
Rawicka	Agulnik
Reichstein	Kimmel, Lesh, Lithwick
Reiter	Baylin, Bodnoff
Reiman	Murray
Renaud	Gould
Resnick	Goldmaker, Lieff, Weinstein
Reznitzky	Agulnik
Rhinestein	Betcherman, Florence, Gould
Richler	Cohen
Richman	Bodnoff, Craft
Rishall	Agulnik
Ritt	Dover
Ritter	Craft
Riven	Cohen
Rivers	Ages, Aaron, Betcherman, Cantor, Dover, Gershon, Hanser, Max, Shinder, Smith, Tradburks, Victor
Robern	Sugarman
Robinson	Sugarman
Robitaille / Rabinovitch	Pollock, Viner
Rodkin	Horwitz
Roodman	Karp, Kathnelson, Glustein, Petigorsky, Pollock, Shulman, Sherman, Taller
Rose	Gennis, Greenberg
Rosen	Bodnoff, Cohen, Gennis, Horwitz, Krantzberg, Rubin, Smith, Victor
Rosenberg	Bodnoff, Flesher, Lithwick, Silver
Rosenblatt	Glustein, Leikin
Rosenblum	Gosewich, Rubin
Rosenes	Kronick
Rosenfeld	Mirsky
Rosenfield	Cohen
Rosenstein	Betcherman
Rosenthal	Slover, Taylor

Rosman	Greenberg
Ross	Fine, Froman, Goldmaker, Gosewich, Krantzberg, Marcovitch, Palmer, Sadinsky, Vechsler
Rossman	Swedlove
Roston	Bilsky, Feller
Rotenberg	Betcherman, Cohen, Freedman, Glustein, Schreiber, Shore
Rothman	Pollock, Taylor
Rotman	Hanser
Rozenworcel	Landau
Ruben	Coplan, Florence, Kizell
Rubin	Coplan, Kardish, Kerzner, Kizell, Landau, Levitan, Mosion, Murray, Palmer, Slover, Torontow
Saalkind	Silver
Sabbath	Saslove, Smolkin
Sacher	Bessin, Diener, Schreiber
Sachs	Pullan
Sacksner	Cohen
Sadavoy	Pleet, Taller
Sadinsky	Craft, Gershon, Flesher, Froman, Karp, Kimmel, Krantzberg, Shulman
Sadowski	Pollock, Viner
Saipe	Dover, Dworkin, Kardish, Kizell, Macy, Molot, Saslove
Saks	Pullan
Saltzberg	Lesh
Salzburg	Feller
Samuels	Kronick, Marcovitch
Sanders	Greenberg, Silver, Steinberg
Sandler	Betcherman, Greenberg, Rivers, Shinder
Sangster	Sugarman
Saper	Rubin
Sarwer-Foner	Landau
Saslove	Baslaw, Betcherman, Cohen, Dover, Fine, Gennis, Gosewich, Greenberg, Karp, Kimmel, Lesh, Levinson, Lithwick, Loeb, Marcovitch, Schecter, Shaffer, Sherman, Shulman, Shore, Sugarman, Taller, Torontow, Weiner
Satlin	Baylin
Satov	Gorelick
Saverson	Kronick
Saxe	Goldfield, Krantzberg, Pollock, Sadinsky, Torontow, Weinstein
Schachnow	Bodnoff
Schacter	Rivers
Schaenfield	Skulsky, Viner, Waserman
Schaffer	Polowin
Schall	Silver
Schapira	Florence
Schecter	Bessin, Cantor, Glustein, Greenberg, Kerzner, Levinson, Macy, Petigorsky, Saslove, Shinder, Silver, Slack, Taller
Scher	Potechin

Schiff	Freedman, Schreiber
Schinman	Bodnoff, Weiner
Schlessinger	Kerzner
Schlossberg	Murray, Rubin
Schmelzer	Molot
Schneiderman	Kronick, Lithwick, Zelikovitz
Schnell	Greenberg
Schnider	Baylin, Bodnoff, Gandall, Landau, Torontow
Schoen	Florence
Schragge	Bilsky
Schreiber	Bessin, Diener, Freedman, Sherman
Schwartz	Dworkin, Pleet
Schwartzfeld	Sugarman
Schwey	Cherm
Segal	Cantor, Max, Viner
Segall	Ellenberg
Segalowitz	Cohen, Pollock
Seidler	Lithwick, Saslove, Sugarman, Taller
Seigal	Mirsky
Selector	Murray
Setton	Glustein
Shabinsky	Gencher, Greenberg, Landau, Lieff, Molot, Shinder, Shore, Taller
Shabsove	Fine
Shadlesky	Greenberg
Shaffer	Baslaw, Bessin, Feller, Gennis, Hanser, Kimmel, Krantzberg, Petigorsky, Saslove, Victor
Shaikin	Marcovitch, Saslove
Shandler	Polowin
Shane	Sugarman
Shapero	Bodnoff, Waserman
Shapiro	Florence, Hanser, Rivers, Saslove, Shaffer, Smolkin, Swedlove, Taller
Shaver	Lieff, Taller
Sheinfeld	Landau
Sheft	Bodnoff
Shenkman	Slack
Shentok	Lachovitz
Sherman	Greenberg, Halpern, Kerzner, Pollock, Roodman, Schreiber, Shinder, Weinstein
Shier	Landau
Shiller	Ages, Bodnoff, Loeb
Shinder	Gencher, Gershon, Greenberg, Halpern, Kathnelson, Landau, Lichtenstein, Murray, Potechin, Rivers, Sherman, Shore, Skulsky, Taller, Vechsler, Viner, Waserman, Weiner
Shmuter	Krantzberg
Shnay	Cohen, Goldfield, Goldmaker

Shore	Betcherman, Bodnoff, Glustein, Greenberg, Lieff, Pleet, Pollock, Saslove, Torontow, Shinder, Weiner
Shreiber	Gencher
Shulman	Karp, Kimmel, Kronick, Petigorsky, Roodman, Sadinsky, Saslove, Taller
Shusterman	Sherman
Sibeth	Bessin
Silbert	Diener
Silbinger	Cohen
Silver	Cohen, Dworkin, Glustein, Greenberg, Landau, Lichtenstein, Marcovitch, Petigorsky, Skulsky, Slack, Steinberg, Sugarman, Taller, Viner, Waserman
Silverman	Appotive, Baylin, Cohen, Glustein, Halpern, Skulsky, Taller, Viner
Silverstein	Lithwick
Simkin	Levinson
Simbrow	Talller
Simon	Bodnoff, Glustein, Karp, Kizell
Sinclair	Flesher, Kizell, Swedlove
Sinder	Bodnoff, Shore
Singer	Feller
Singerman	Diener, Greenberg, Krantzberg, Landau, Pleet, Smith, Vechsler
Sklar	Mirsky
Skulsky	Glustein, Halpern, Krantzberg, Sherman, Shinder, Silver, Viner
Slack	Appotive, Greenberg, Kerzner, Petigorsky, Schecter, Silver, Sugarman, Viner
Slavin	Cohen
Slipacoff	Cohen, Fine, Lesh, Saslove
Slone	Coplan, Horwitz, Max
Slonemsky	Coplan, Silver, Sugarman
Slonim	Kardish
Slover	Coplan, Cohen, Fine, Flesher, Greenberg, Kardish, Leikin, Polowin, Rubin, Taylor
Smith	Betcherman, Fine, Flesher, Florence, Freedman, Gosewich, Gould, Kerzner, Lesh, Molot, Palmer, Schreiber, Waserman
Smolkin	Cohen, Dover, Hanser, Levitan, Lithwick, Pleet, Swedlove, Vechsler, Victor
Smurlick	Fine, Saslove
Smyth	Baylin
Snyder	Cohen
Sobcov	Kronick, Taller
Sobcuff	Lieff
Sogman	Dworkin
Solomon	Ages, Glustein, Saslove, Torontow
Soloway	Gencher, Greenberg, Macy, Pollock, Viner
Soltanoff	Baylin

Sonken	Betcherman, Molot
Sosnovich	Landau, Lichtenstein
Sourkes	Dover
Spector	Cherm, Dover, Kimmel, Reichstein
Speisman	Shinder
Speyer	Cohen
Spielberg	Bodnoff
Spieler	Leikin, Loeb
Spiro	Kimmel, Sadinsky, Shulman
Staller	Victor
Starker	Petigorsky, Schecter
Stein	Pleet
Steinberg	Baylin, Betcherman, Bodnoff, Dover, Gandall, Greenberg, Glustein, Kardish, Lachovitz, Levitan, Lieff, Molot, Mosion, Petigorsky, Rubin, Shore, Silver, Waserman
Steinkopf	Bilsky
Steinman	Aaron, Feinstein, Gennis, Hanser, Rivers
Stern	Molot
Sternberg	Steinberg, Waserman
Stotland	Palmer
Strashin	Lachovitz
Strolovitch	Aaron, Gennis, Marcovitch
Stulberg	Lachovitz
Sugarman	Greenberg, Lachovitz, Lithwick, Molot, Polowin, Saslove, Silver, Taller, Weiner
Swartzman	Landau
Swedko	Bodnoff, Craft
Swedlove	Cohen, Flesher, Freedman, Hanser, Lichtenstein ,Lithwick, Polowin, Smolkin, Victor
Swetsky	Molot
Szeroszewsky	Glustein, Silver, Skulsky, Sugarman, Viner
Taller	Bodnoff, Cantor, Cherm, Fine, Goldfield, Gould, Kerzner, Kimmel, Kronick, Landau, Lieff, Loeb, Molot, Potechin, Roodman, Saslove, Schecter, Shulman, Shinder, Sugarman, Viner, Waserman
Tanner	Flesher, Gershon, Reichstein, Sadinsky
Tannenbaum	Krantzberg
Tanzer	Krantzberg, Torontow
Tarantour	Ages, Saslove
Tate	Rivers
Tavel	Palmer, Leikin, Lithwick
Taylor	Betcherman, Froman, Gencher, Greenberg, Kardish, Murray, Pollock, Polowin, Slover
Teitelbaum	Bodnoff, Cohen
Tenebaum	Diener, Schreiber
Tennenbaum	Petigorsky
Tennenhouse	Landau
Tincoff	Vechsler

Topol	Lithwick
Torontow	Ages, Agulnik, Baylin, Betcherman, Bodnoff, Dover, Flesher, Gandall, Gennis, Goldfield, Gottdank, Karp, Krantzberg, Lieff, Max, Saslove, Weiner, Weinstein
Trachtenberg	Lithwick
Tradburks	Baylin, Dover, Kardish, Koffman, Max, Mirsky, Rivers, Shinder
Trainoff	Shinder, Taller, Viner, Waserman
Tuchman	Appotive, Landau
Tuckman	Marcovitch, Waserman
Turner	Taller
Tyber	Swedlove
Udashkin	Craft, Kardish, Mosion
Ulpian	Steinberg
Ulrich	Zelikovitz
Vered	Greenberg, Macy, Viner
Vechsler / Vexler	Dover, Ellenberg, Landau, Max, Smolkin, Shinder
Victor	Ages, Craft, Feller, Gershon, Hanser, Kardish, Kimmel, Lieff, Rivers
Villeneuve	Taller
Vineberg	Krantzberg
Vineburg	Smolkin
Viner	Appotive, Cantor, Cherm, Feller, Fine, Goldfield, Greenberg, Halpern, Krantzberg, Lachovitz, Landau, Macy, Murray, Pollock, Shinder, Silver, Skulsky, Waserman, Weiner, Zelikovitz
Vinokur	Shinder
Vital	Rivers
Volfson	Saslove
Vorner	Lachovitz
Wail	Victor
Waisberg	Zelikovitz
Waiser	Dover, Flesher, Kizell, Max, Pollock, Swedlove
Wakter	Taller
Wallach	Rivers
Wallack	Tradburks
Warshavsky	Glustein
Waserman	Ages, Bodnoff, Cherm, Lesh, Marcovitch, Shinder, Shore, Skulsky, Smith, Steinberg, Taller, Viner
Waterman	Rubin
Wax	Skulsky
Weatherall	Marcovitch
Webber-Zigerman	Slover
Weidman	Kronick, Taller
Weinberg	Gershon
Weiner	Ages, Bodnoff, Diener, Flesher, Gencher, Gershon, Goldmaker, Landau, Kardish, Kerzner, Lachovitz, Landau,

	Petigorsky, Saslove, Shinder, Shore, Sugarman, Torontow, Viner
Weinman	Landau, Levitan, Murray, Shinder, Steinberg, Taller, Weiner
Weinstein	Gennis, Gorelick, Horwitz, Krantzberg, Sadinsky, Sherman
Weisbord	Betcherman, Shore
Weiss	Cohen, Froman, Kardish, Kerzner, Lithwick, Pollock, Swedlove, Zelikovitz
Wener	Shaffer
Wexler	Glustein, Goldfield, Leikin, Taller
Wiehl	Cohen
Wigdor	Cohen
Wilko	Gershon, Glustein
Wilner	Murray
Wise	Max
Wiseberg	Greenberg
Wiseman	Kimmel, Saslove, Skulsky, Smolkin
Witchel	Lithwick
Witten	Taller, Torontow
Wolf	Pleet
Wolfe	Aaron, Lithwick, Murray, Roodman, Saslove
Wolfson	Molot
Wolinsky	Bessin, Freedman, Petigorsky, Schecter, Shaffer
Wollock	Kardish
Wolofsky	Vechsler
Wolman	Glustein
Woolfson	Cohen
Wolpin	Cohen, Silver
Wormann	Leikin
Wortman	Taller
Wyneberg	Pullan
Yankoo	Ellenberg, Marcovitch
Yanofsky	Glustein
Yanover	Gennis, Shaffer, Shinder, Weinstein
Yarofsky	Baslaw, Shaffer
Yashinofsky / Jason	Petigorsky
Yellin	Silver
Yerenbourg	Leikin
Yeres	Cohen
Yosman	Glustein
Young	Taller
Ysorsky	Taller
Zabitsky	Dover, Landau
Zagerman	Cantor, Froman, Krantzberg, Marcovitch, Mosion, Sadinsky, Weinstein
Zagon	Gennis, Shaffer
Zarenda	Smith
Zaretsky / Zaret	Fine, Gorelick, Horwitz
Zbar	Bodnoff, Silver

Zelcovin	Bessin, Goldfield
Zelick	Taller
Zelikovitz	Kardish, Kronick, Levitan, Loeb, Smolkin, Weiss
Zellick	Cantor
Zelnick	Sherman
Zides	Dover, Glustein, Torontow
Zimmerman	Roodman
Zinman	Cohen
Zinn	Lesh
Zittrer	Feller, Lithwick
Zloten	Pollock
Zolov	Hanser
Zunder	Greenberg, Murray, Pleet

Group Photos from the Ottawa Jewish Archives

The following photos, with a few exceptions from the Ottawa Jewish Archives Facebook group, could apply to several family groups. Therefore, I have placed them together here as a supplement, rather than attaching them to the description of any specific family. For the most part, I have taken the captions directly from the Facebook group. This collection of photos is arranged in chronological order.

Young People's League Purim Play, 1927. (OJA 4-053).

This photograph was taken at the "Institute" - a small building at the back of Adath Jeshurun Synagogue, a.k.a. the King (Edward) Street Shul, which served as a Jewish centre and youth facility.

Front row, L-R: Nat Wolfe, Dr. Sam Mirsky, Rabbi Nathan Kollin, Doris Cohen-Torontow, Cantor Joseph Rabin, Arnold Katz, and Harry (Harold) Goldman, Unknown;

Back row, L-R: Meyer Drazin, Sam Epstein, Harold Shenkman, Bert Katz, Harold Coplan, Martin K. Levinson, and William Braverman.

A banquet held on March 17th, 1935, celebrating Adath Jeshurun paying off of the synagogue mortgage. (OJA 5-071)

Included are: H. Sugarman, V. Sugarman, Sol Max, Lil Max, Mr. & Mrs. Max Senior, Mr. Robinson & Mrs. Aisenberg, Mr. & Mrs. A.J. Freiman, Anne & Dave Dover, Martin Ginsberg, Mr. & Mrs. Jacob Rivers, Mr. & Mrs. A. Lithwick, Esther Robinson, Mrs. G. Cohen, Mr. & Mrs. Goldfield, Mr. & Mrs. L. Greenberg, Rebecca Gabriel Cohen, and may more.

A costume party photo taken by Hy Gould in 1936. (OJA 1-720-017)

Included in the photograph are Lou Greenberg, Lawrence Freiman, Rose Gould, Audrey Freiman, Cecile Rossman, Henry Pass, Malca Pass, Marsha Caplan, Sam Caplan, Sol Max, Lil Max, Maury Rossman, Max Zelikovitz, Etta Caplan, Sylvia Smith, Sam Lepofsky, Martin Levinson, Yetta Pearlman, Lillian Gould, Pearl Lepofsky, Miriam Wershof, Esther Raport, and A. Aronson and none other than Betty Boop!

A group of junior B'nai B'rith members dressed in costumes for a "Women of the Bible" event – 1938. (OJA 4-006)

Standing L-R: Rossie (Greenberg) Rose, Esther (Pleet) Sadavoy, Ann (Dworkin) Silver, Isabel Colle, Mollie (Karon) Apel (Appel), Adeline (Sigler) Hyman - President of the District, Lora (Fonberg) Shapiro, Advisor Mrs. Sybil Isaacs, Anne (Silver) Taller, Yetta (Dworkin) Scheinine

Front: Freda (Lesh) Levitan, Claire (Pleet) Koffman.

The Smoke Bar Softball Team, ca. 1939. (OJA 3-012)

L-R Front row: Morley Goldfield, John Greenberg, Benny London. Back row: Martin Ginsberg, Bo Blancher, Norman Levine, Percy Addelman, Harry Kotlarsky, Jack Krantzberg, Jack Baylin and Bert Loeb.

Ladies graduating class of the Ottawa Hebrew Sunday School, standing on the front steps of Adath Jeshurun synagogue on King Edward street – 1942. (OJA 6-309)

Top row L-R: Ann Tarantour Lazear (class valedictorian), Ann Ain (Feldman), Lilly Cardash, Muriel Bodnoff, Rosaline Shoihet (Adelberg); Selma Tarantour.

Front row L-R: Mrs. Zivian (School Superintendent and Principal), Joy Edelson, Sarah Zaretsky, Sybil Goldfield, Jean Newton (Lichtenstein) and Rabbi Fasman.

Seamstresses of the Ottawa Hadassah-Wizo War Work group. These amazing women worked in part with the Red Cross to sew and create care packages to be sent overseas to soldiers – 1942. (OJA 4-475)

Front row L-R: Mrs. N. Edelstein, Mrs. J. Lithwack, Mrs. M. Shenkman, Mrs. A.M. Goldman, Mrs. J. Sobcuff, Mrs. S. Silver, Mrs. H. Berlin, Mrs. L. Rosenthal, Mrs. N. Witen, Mrs. Z. Rill, Mrs. J. Baker, Mrs. Tannenbaum.

Second row: Mrs. M.B. Corman, Miss Freda Florence, Mrs. H. Solway, Mrs. M.B. Abrams, Mrs. C. Dubinsky, Mrs. Frances Vineberg, Mrs. S. Brodie, Mrs. C. Tanner, Mrs. R. Edelstein, Mrs. Baker, Mrs. S. Goldberg, Mrs. H. Fine, Mrs. H. Sugerman, Mrs. L.S. Greenberg, Mrs. M. Kizell, Mrs. L. Coplan, Mrs. R. Heilingher, Mrs. L. Freiman.

Back row: Mrs. D. Dover, Mrs. J. Feldman, Mrs. H. Saxe, Mrs. H. Goldenberg, Mrs. R. Dover, Mrs. J. Snow, Mrs. J. Goldberg, Mrs. D. Wolochou, MRs. B. Litzback, Mrs. M. Greenberg, Mrs. M. Goldberg, Mrs. S. Lepofsky, Mrs. C. Slonemsky, Miss Helen Abelson.

Lawrence "Duke" Abelson
Flying Officer, d. 1943

Mark Abramson
Flying Officer

Joseph Ash
Flying Officer, d. 1942

Eli Baker
Flight Lieutenant

William Bloom
Aircraftman

Max Gennis
Flying Officer, d. 1943

Moe Cardash
Leading Aircraftman

Arnold Greenberg
Air Gunner

Mel Goldberg
Leading Aircraftman

William Kahansky
Flight Sergeant

Morrie Konick
Squadron Leader

Edward Saslove
Flying Officer, d. 1945

Abraham Schwartz
Pilot Office, d. 1943

Don Snipper
Flight Leiutenant

Jack Spevak
Pilot Officer, d. 1941

Phil Swedlove
Officer

Morton Taller
Corporal

Cyril Torontow
Wing Commander

Herbert Wolf
Flight Sergeant, d. 1941

Harry Zumar
Flight Lieutenant

A few of Ottawa's Jewish Servicemen who served in the Royal Canadian Air Force (RCAF) during the Second World War.

Ottawa Jewish service personnel in London, England during the Second World War - Sept, 1943. (OJA 9-001)

Top row L-R: M. Krantzberg, Allan Kapinsky, Dave Polowin.
Front row: Nathan Levitin, Phillip Cohen, Lottie Molot and Israel Hoffman.

Marty Cardash, Alfie Friedman, Marty Saslove, Leonard Max, Richard Palef, Morty Mayberger, with Melvin Schecter in the backround among other campers. c. Summer 1946-47.

B'nai B'rith Ottawa's Basketball Team - 1947 or 1948. (OJA 3-009)

Top Row L-R: Mervin Greenberg, Ralph Saslove, Mark Zunder, Elliot Levitan. Bottom Row: Norman Torontow, Eddie Saslove, Morley Goldfield, Israel Zunder, Herbert Gosewich, John Greenberg.

Pioneer Women Anne Pepper, Clara Levinson, Greta Baylin, Sylvia Shinder, and Alice Edelson assemble bedding for to be shipped along with other supplies as aid to Israel in 1948. (OJA 4-026)

Students are dressed up for a Purim Carnival at the Ottawa Talmud Torah in 1949.
(OJA 1-1229)

Seated we have: Bernice Greenberg, Judy Zelikovitz, Ethel Mickenberg, Estelle
Schecter Gunner, Beatrice (Bea) Greenberg, & Sid Kardash.
1st row standing: Ronnie (Ron) Goldberg, Mark Molot, Stanley Eisenberg, Gita Kizell,
Marlene Zelikovitz, Riva Schreiber, Sue Zelikovitz, Rochelle Shapiro, Roslyn Woolfson,
Tybie Drazin & Vickie Lithwick.
2nd row: Gerald Zaichuk, Joel Clenman, Unknown, Rochelle Pleet, Joan Eisenstadt,
Bunny Lazarus, Mel Schecter, unknown, Yudi Brozofsky, Herbie Beiles as Moses,
Norton Lithwick, cowboy Michael Molot, & an unknown. And at the very back: Mr.
Werner Bauer is the teacher in hat and leaning forward are Bernie Shinder & Billy
Altow.

R&A Cohen Furniture," Jewish Men's Softball League Champs – 1949. (OJA 3-276)

R & A was for Reuben and Andy and their store was located at Laurier and Bank St.

Top row L-R: Morley Goldfield, Ben Machen, Norman Torontow, Eddie Saslove and Joseph Osterer
Front row: Sol Sherman, Gerry Dover, Jack Sherman, Sid Addelman and Sidney Aisenberg.

The R&A Cohen Furniture Store team as the Jewish Boys Softball League champions of 1949.
(OJA 3-270)

Top row L-R: Jack Goldfield, Ed Saslove, Morley Goldfield, Ernie Potechin, Norman Torontow, and Ben Machen.
Centre row: Sol Sherman, Gerry Dover, Sidney "Rocky" Aisenberg, Matt Ages, Sid Addleman, and Srul Zunder.
Front row: Sam Koffman presenting a trophy to Joe Osterer as Izzy Shore (president of the league) looks on.

Chanukah at the Ottawa Talmud Torah circa 1950. (OJA 6-061)

From left to right in the first row are Harvey Mendelson, David Shoihet, Stanley Kimmel, Gerry Greenberg, Syd Trainoff.
Second row: Vicki Lithwick, Judy Zelikovitz, Audrey Silverman, Sheila Brozofsky and Dorothy Saslove. Fourth row: Sid Kardash, Jess Zelikovitz, Mel Shecter and Norman Beiles. Fifth row: Gerald Zeichick, Rabbi Emmanuel Lifschutz, David Zelikovitz, David Lifschutz, Rochelle Schapira, Hymie Klein, Mrs. Sarah Zelikovitz and Mrs. Ellen Lithwick.

From left: Bernie Putterman, Nathan Diener, unknown, Sam Zunder, Issie Landau (my father), Milton (Murph) Greenberg. This would be from the early 1950s. Bernie Putterman came to Ottawa from Poland with his mother in 1937, at the time when Jewish immigration into Canada was particularly restricted (it was the "None is Too Many" era). Bernie Putterman married Muriel (nee Bodnoff), and settled in Windsor. (Courtesy of Michael Landau, John Diener, Connie Putterman)

The installation banquet was held for newly elected officers of the Ottawa Hebrew Benefit Society at the 40th anniversary banquet, January 1953: Top row, second from left, my grandfather Jacob Landau; front second from right: Charlie Horwitz; top, second from right: Moe Slack. (OJA 4-065)

Ottawa Talmud Torah Afternoon School Graduating Class, June 9, 1953.

L-R:Top Row; David Shoihet, Larry Segal, Eddie Altman, Sidney Kardish, Stanley Sadinsky, Middle Row; Phyllis Brill, Shelley Brozofsky. Shirley (Podolsky) Arnoni, Joan (Eisenstadt) Sacksner, Diane (Slavin) Grafstein, Vicki Lithwick, Judy Zelikovitz, Seated; Joe Nadrich, Stanley Kimmel, Rabbi Simon Eckstein, Rabbi Kravetz, Mr Louis Achbar, Herbie Beiles, and Benji Zbar. (OJA-6-014)

Board and members of Adath Jeshurun Synagogue in Ottawa with Rabbi Dr. Belkin of Yeshivah University. L-R back row includes; H. Pleet, Max Dworkin and Sam Caplan. Middle row; Hy Hochberg, Hy Soloway, Saul Saslove, Mr. Alexandor, Louis Achbar, Sam Berger, Lawrence Freiman, Alex Betcherman, Tom Sachs, Hy Gould. Seated; Rabbi S. Burstein, Rabbi Kravetz, Rabbi Belkin, Rabbi Eckstein, Rabbi Mendel Lewittes, Rev. J. Rabin. (OJA 5-002)

A testimonial banquet for Reverend Joseph Rabin to mark the completion of his 25th year of service to the Adath Jeshurun Congregation, held on March 7, 1954.
L-R: Samuel Caplan, Isidore Stone, Reverend Rabin and Rabbi Simon L. Eckstein.
(OJA 1-750)

Rabbi Herzog, the Chief Rabbi of Israel arrives in Ottawa at the old railway station on Rideau Street, 1954. L-R: Hyman Bessin, Rabbi Sam Burstein, Rabbi Simon Eckstein, Rabbi Herzog, Lawrence Freiman, Abe Lieff, Rabbi Kravetz. Photographer: Marvin Flatt (OJA 6-024)

August 19th is World Photo Day and to celebrate here is an Ottawa Jewish Archives favorite - a photograph of campers playing in an old 1905 Ottawa Transport Commission (OTC) streetcar at Camp B'nai B'rith in Quyon, Quebec - 1954.

L-R: Unknown, Unknown, Paul Mirsky, John Molot (boy standing behind with dark hat), Richard Addleman (boy below), Jeff Gould (wearing conductor's hat), Raymond Fine, Bobby Smith, Ivan Silverman, Lawrence Greenberg and Neil Dworkin.
(OJA 4-102)

Dedication and official opening of the Library of the Jewish Community Centre,
April 17, 1955.(OJA 19-001)

Head table L-R: L-R: Rabbi Boruch Kravetz, Mordecai Kessler, Marion (Mrs Hyman) Bessin, Mildred (Mrs. Morris) Zagerman, Bernard Alexandor at the podium, Rabbi Simon L. Eckstein, Morris Zagerman, Rabbi S.M. Burstein, Lillian (Mrs. Hyman) Gould, and Hyman Gould.

Ladies from the 5th Annual Stardust Ball ca. 1955. (OJA 4-268)

Top row L-R: Diane Slavin, Audrey Silverman, Carol Zagerman, Reva Sherman, Unknown, Roslyn Waserman.
Middle row L-R: Unknown, Unknown, Rochelle Shapiro, Unknown, Nicki Cook, Unknown, Bess Kardash, Cally Gluzman, Tina Tarantour-Goldberg, Dorothy Kizell, Shelly Brozofsky, Chaperone - Unknown.
Bottom row L-R: Judy Zelikovitz, Phyllis Brill, Debbie Altow, Barbara Roodman, Roslyn Wilko, Unknown, Vicki Lithwick, Unknown, Pauline Gandall, Marcia Krantzberg.

L-R Front row: Sharon Ritter, Roz Magidson, Elissa Witten. Back row: Bev Slover, Sherry (last name unknown), Sheila Fagen, Judy Goldie, Judy Sigler, Myra Palmer. Summer 1959.

Beth Shalom's First Bat Mitzvah Class – 1960. (OJA 5-321)

Front row L-R: Sandra Globerman, Beth Roodman, Gail Gaffen, Cynthia Gora, Amber Mosion, Harriet Rose, Mavis Rose, Elizabeth Gertsman.

Middle row: Anna Cohen, Margo Robitaille, Janice Greenberg, Harienne Rosenes, Queenie Mickenberg, Francine Achbar, Cynthia Rivers, Nita Freedman, Annette Hurtig, Midgie Koffman, Brenda Torontow, Bernice Lieff.

Back row: Rabbi Simon Eckstein, Lana Waxman, Marlene Slack, Sue Soloway, Judy Molot, Anna Bilsky, Barbara Rosenes, Marcia Saipe, Rhoda Coopersmith, Carol Weiner, Beverly Allice, Yanda Waise, Ann Max, Roy Saipe.

Beth Shalom Synagogue costume party. (OJA 5-270)

L-R: Back row: Sam Caplan, Lou Weiner, Issy Shore, Irving Betcherman, Bert Loeb, Harold Pearl, David Fine, Dave Zelikovitz, Lou Achbar. Front row: Meyer Drazin, Musty Koffman, Norman Torontow.

Abraham Shaffer, Hy Bessin, Gilbert Greenberg, Sidney Lithwick, Dora Lithwick, Jacie Horwitz, and others with Ottawa's first female mayor Charlotte Witton at the sod turning ceremony for Hillel Lodge on Wurttemberg St., 1964. (OJA 4-446-07)

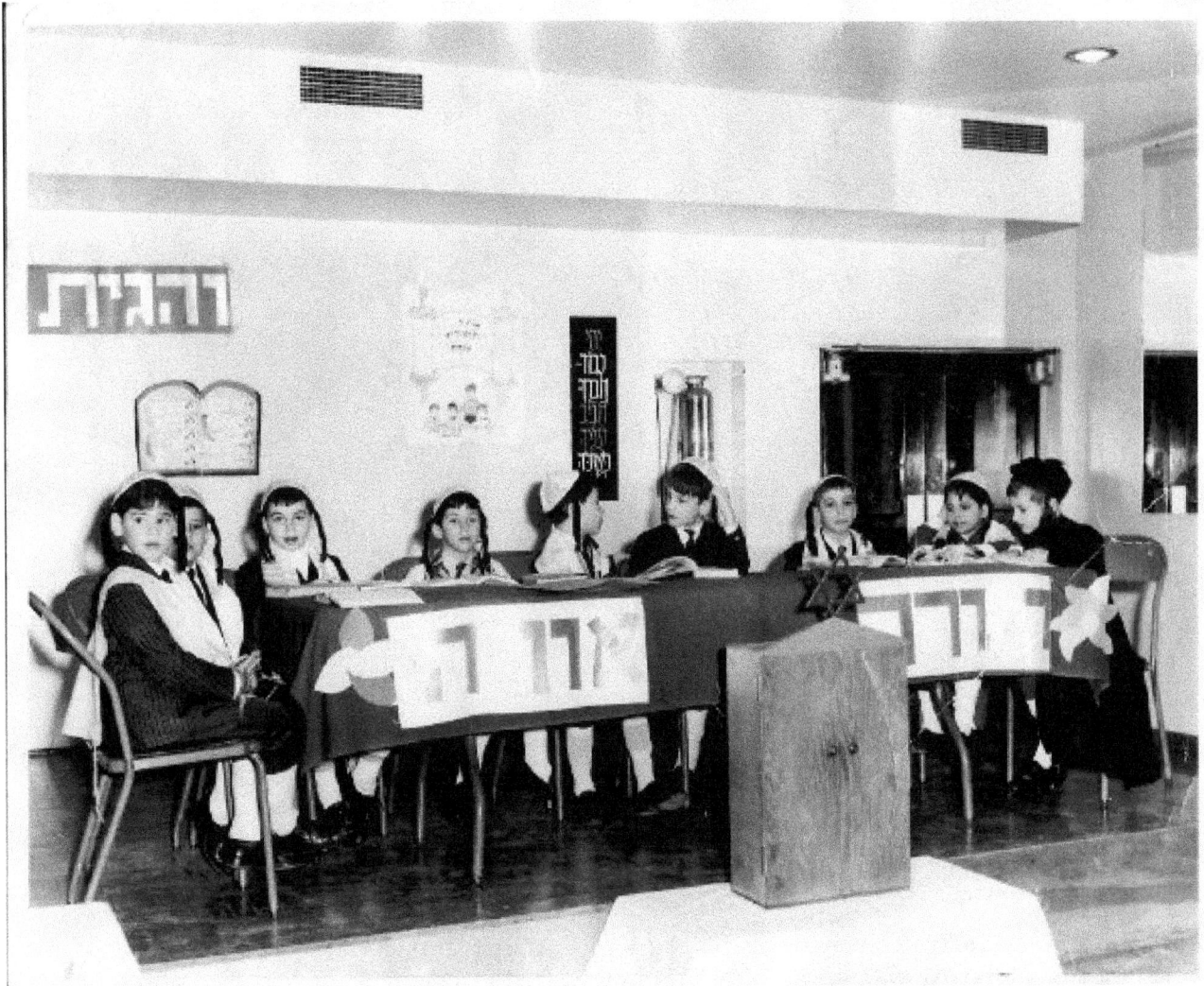

Hillel Academy Central Branch Chumash party, Grade 2, 1968: From left: Jeffrey Taylor, Kevin Cantor, Leonard Kahansky, Mark Toronto, Israel Gencher, Kevin Berman, Allan Malek, Mark Greenberg, Jerrold Landau. (from my private collection)

Testimonial dinner for Louis Rasminsky's retirement as Governor of the Bank of Canada took place. The dinner was held at the Jewish Community Centre (Feb 1973). (OJA 1-603-01)

Louis was the 3rd Governor of the Bank of Canada and served from 1961 - 1973. In fact his signature was on all paper money issued during that period (see photo below, lower right)

L-R: Seated; Abe Palmer, chairman (President of the Jewish Community Council of Ottawa), Lyla Rasminsky and Louis Rasminsky (C.C., C.B.E., L.L.D). Standing; Sol Kanee (President Canadian Jewish Congress), David Loeb (Officer of the Vaad), Hy Soloway (President of the Jewish Community Centre), Muriel Levine (Ladies Auxiliary Beth Shalom Congregation), Theodore P. Metrick (President Beth Shalom Congregation), Norman Zagerman (officer of the Vaad), Rabbi Jacob Cement, and Dr. Theodor Meron (Israeli Ambassador to Canada). (OJA 1-603-01)

Canadian currency signed by Governor of Bank of Canada Louis Rasminsky

A Visit to the Ottawa Jewish Cemetery

(Written by Jerrold Landau in 2006.)

As a native of Ottawa who moved to Toronto in 1980, I find that family visits to my hometown are always replete with nostalgia. Since the passing of my late father, Issie Landau, of blessed memory, in 1996, no visit to Ottawa is complete without a pilgrimage to the cemetery on Bank Street. The few moments that I spend in reflection over my father's grave, combined with the annual cycle of ritually prescribed yahrzeit and yizkor observances, do scant justice to 34 years of closeness, companionship and nurturing that marked my relationship with my father. Although my father's grave is the magnet that attracts me to the cemetery, the experience has grown to extend far beyond, and indeed fortifies my personal link to the history of the Ottawa community. Allow me to share with you my typical itinerary during my cemetery visit. I am sure that many others have similar stories to tell.

My first stop is the grave of my father in the newer, right-hand section of the cemetery, and the neighboring grave of my uncle Irving Shier. Both are double stones, which provide a stark and uncomfortable reminder of the inevitabilities of life. I move on with the silent prayer that it should be many years before the other side of those monuments is filled in. I then scan the surrounding area. Although that area is still sparsely populated, with each visit it seems that more and more spaces have been filled as the years go on.

I then walk a few sections over, to the older area of the Beth Shalom cemetery. As I stop by the graves of my grandparents, Jacob and Rose Landau, memories of my early childhood come to the fore. A mere five plots over, at the aisle, are the twin graves of my wife's paternal grandparents, Louis and Fanny Rachlin. I married Tzippy in Toronto some 12 years after leaving Ottawa – yet her father, Bernie, is an Ottawa native whose family connections go deep back into the early Jewish history of the city. There is no evidence that our grandparents knew each other. Yet by coincidence, or more likely by providence, they were laid to their eternal rest in uncannily close proximity.

As I wander around that section, many childhood memories dance before me. I stop by the graves of Werner and Becky Bauer, and read the flowery inscription on the grave of respected teacher. I am taken back to my grade 3 and 4 classroom at Hillel Academy. Mr. Bauer was in his prime then, and we always feared him as he would slide down the aisles in anger at any sign of misbehavior. Yet we always appreciated his sense of humor, his creative Purim costumes, and the fact that he came to school each day on his bicycle, which we affectionately dubbed the 'Bauermobile'. More importantly, we left his classes well-grounded in the basics of Chumash, Rashi, and Jewish law. Yes, truly a respected and beloved teacher.

I never fail to stop at the graves of Jacob and Sarah Gordon and read the epitaph of another revered teacher who tutored several generations of Ottawans for their Bar Mitzvahs. Thoughts go back to Bar Mitzvah classes, where Mr. Gordon would rap our knuckles with a pencil if we made an error, and gleefully exclaim, "Dats de von dere", with a twinkle in his eye when we got something right. In my present existence in Toronto, I frequently have opportunity to serve as a Baal Tefilla and Torah reader. On all such occasions, my thoughts never fail to hearken back to the source of it all, Mr. Gordon, or "Jake" as we lovingly referred to him. I recall a visit to Ottawa some years back, when I last saw Mr. Gordon. It was at the daily morning minyan at Beth Shalom, and he was well into his nineties at the time. I asked him how he was doing, and with the same twinkle in his eye, he quipped, "Still above the ground dere".

I notice the grave of Cantor Joseph Rabin, who was the mohel of both me and my father-in-law. There is Benes Cantor, who aside from being the father of my classmate Kevin, is remembered as the longtime parnas at Beth Shalom, who would proudly march up and down the aisles as he handed out the silver aliya cards. Irving Rivers is close by – and I recall how each Simchas Torah he efficiently handed out the Torahs for the hakafos. Just across the aisle is the grave of Ann Silver – whose office was just outside our kindergarten class. She calmly put up with the antics of us five-year-olds.

I then walk to the back of that section to visit the graves of Tzippy's great uncle and aunt, Sam and Eva Epstein. For the first few years of our marriage, a visit to Ottawa would be inconceivable without enjoying a glass of tea and a kichel at their Besserer Street apartment. Well into his 80s, Uncle Sam would proudly fix the siddurim and chumashim at all the Ottawa shuls.

As I cross over to the left side of the cemetery, I take a moment to reflect in front the Holocaust memorial monument. I think of the parents of some of my Hillel classmates who were Holocaust survivors: Nathan Diener, Haskel Robern, and may they live long, Joe Lichtenstein and David Moskovic. I think of those who I knew from my long association with the Machzikei Hadas shul: the parnas Harry Hecht, and may they live long – Mendel and Valerie Good. I think back to Bill Palmer, and how he used to wander the halls of the JCC haunted by demons of the Holocaust era.

I proceed to the Agudath Israel section of the cemetery. Although I was less familiar with that part of the community, the names are nevertheless recognizable. I pause for a moment at the graves of my great aunt and uncle, Sam and Yetta Landau. Uncle Shea, as he was known, passed away before I was born. Aunt Yetta then married into the Shinder family, as did their son Bob Landau – thereby cementing the inter-family relationships that are so common in the Ottawa community.

Next it is time for a rendezvous with my maternal family, as I visit the grave of my great-grandmother Sarah Goldberg. Her grave is always hard to find, as it is partly obscured by an overgrown evergreen bush. My mother, Edie, hails from Winnipeg, and has no roots in Ottawa. However, over a decade before she got married and moved to Ottawa, her paternal grandfather, Shmuel Leib Goldberg, served for a time in Ottawa as the shamash and melamed at the James Street Shul. Bubby Sarah died while they lived in Ottawa. Zeidy Shmuleib subsequently moved back to Winnipeg and lived into his nineties. Many of the elder generation of Ottawans who had connections with the James Street Shul have memories of my great-grandparents.

I then head over the oldest part of the cemetery, where numerous members of the earlier generations of Tzippy's family are buried. This part of the cemetery is arranged somewhat haphazardly, and I do not always find all of the graves. All four of Tzippy's paternal great-grandparents are buried there: Yehuda and Annie (nee Leikin) Rachlin, and Solomon and Sadie (nee Rosenfeld) Epstein. Even more remarkable, there are the graves of three great-great grandparents. There is the grave of Itta Cohen, the mother of Solomon Epstein, who died in 1925. The surname Cohen became Epstein in a typical story of a surname change in the Pale of Settlement to escape the Russian draft. Through this branch of the family, we are related to the extended Cohen family of Ottawa. Louis Rosenfeld died in 1904 at the age of 48. The monument is an old-style pillar, and the letters on the grave are hard to make out. His wife, Fruma Esther Rosenfeld, who died in 1944, is buried several rows back. She was the first Jewish midwife in Ottawa, and her wish was to be buried among the children. I look about, and indeed, there are many tiny gravestones of young children in the vicinity. I wonder to myself: "Does anyone remember them? Does anyone come to visit anymore?" Another silent prayer crosses my thoughts, "May we all be spared such tribulations."

Nearby are the graves of numerous of Tzippy's aunts, uncles, and cousins, too numerous to mention – descendants of the Cohens, Rosenfelds, and Rachlins. There is Aunt Faith Rachlin, who died a few years ago after living out her life in a residence for those with Downs Syndrome in Morrisburg. She was laid to rest near her parents. There is Great Uncle Sam Rachlin, who died at age 26 of blood poisoning after a shaving accident (or by some accounts, after suffering a wound while changing a flat tire – it depends which great uncle is asked). And there is Great-Great Uncle Kasriel Cohen, whose epitaph testifies to the fact that he taught Torah publicly throughout his long life.

My journey into the past has now ended, and it is time to jump back into the world of the living. I look at my watch, and almost an hour has past. My mother, Tzippy and the children are probably wondering what is keeping me. As I head back to my car, I traverse the front row of the cemetery, where many communal leaders are buried. I see graves which bear the names Zelikovitz, Leikin, and Betcherman, to name a few. I then drive home, and proceed with the rest of the child-oriented activities that mark our visits to Ottawa. Somehow, after the rendezvous with my past, near and far, the rest of the day seems a trifle mundane.

My oldest daughter, Rachel, ten years old, has asked me if she can come with me to visit Zeidy. In the future, I will surely take her along. In due course, Yisrael, Hadassa, and Eliezer will join me as well. Not only will they visit the grave of their Zeidy Issie, but they will also touch base with 4 great-grandparents, 5 great-great grandparents, and 3 great-great-great grandparents, spanning a century of Jewish life in Ottawa.

www.ingramcontent.com/pod-product-compliance
Lightning Source LLC
Chambersburg PA
CBHW050410110426
42812CB00006BA/1856